COMPILED BY THE HELPFUL '8'
EDITED BY SADIE LEVINE.

THE WAY TO A MAN'S HEART

Our most grateful thanks are due to:-
SALEK BENEDICT for the cover design.
GERED MANKOWITZ for his photographic work.
CHINACRAFT for the loan of their China and Cutlery used in the cover photograph.

MESSAGE FROM H. OSCAR JOSEPH, O.B.E.
(Chairman - Central British Fund for Jewish Relief and Rehabilitation).

In expressing my best wishes for the success of The Helpful 8's newest project, I want to take the opportunity of thanking them for the help which they have given and the substantial sums which they have raised in the course of their activities for Jewish refugees in many countries, and for deprived and sick Jewish children and old people in Eastern Europe, North Africa and elsewhere.

Through their efforts food, medical supplies, financial help and assistance in resettlement have been provided for those who, through no fault of their own, find themselves dependent on help or organisations like the C.B.F.

I should like to take this opportunity of wishing them continued success in their splendid work.

H. Oscar Joseph

Published in Great Britain by
VALLENTINE, MITCHELL & CO. LTD
Gainsborough House, Gainsborough Road,
London E11 1RS

First edition 1971
Second edition 1973
Third edition 1976
Reprinted 1976
Reprinted 1980

ISBN 0 85303 175 4

Printed in Great Britain by
Hartnoll Printers Limited, Bodmin, Cornwall.

Contents~

Dear Cooks,

Our dream has become a reality—the painstaking project is finished—now it is here for you to enjoy. We have tried with the help of our many friends to compile our favourite and also our most useful recipes. Some have been invented and others have been modified to fit into our Jewish Tradition. By purchasing a copy of "The Way To A Man's Heart" you are helping us to help others—in particular children who are less fortunate than our own.

We would like to thank:— Hazel Barrie, Elaine Lawrence, Sadie Levine, Bunny Rosalki, Vallentine Mitchell and all our friends for their help.

A special thank you goes to our "Hungry Husbands" who have tolerated us during the preparation of this book, but who, we hope will now benefit from our culinary experience.

In the hope that some of these recipes will become your "favourites" we wish you "Bon appetit."

Sincerely,

The Helpful '8' Committee:—

LESLEY BENNETT, GILLIAN BURR, GLORIA BROWN, CHARLOTTE DAVIS, FAITH DUKE, DOREEN GAINSFORD, VALERIE GREEN, RENATA KNOBIL, DIANA MARKS, VALERIA ROSS, KAROL SOLOMONS, YAFFA WAGNER, DIANNE ZIMMERMAN.

Dips and Starters ~

See Supper and Salad sections for extra ideas.

Cut tops from green peppers. Scoop out centres and use as containers for dips. All dips should be made at least 4 hours in advance.

Keep left-over rice. Fry and serve it with tomato ketchup and use instead of potatoes, or use to make risotto or cold salad.

If bread rolls have gone stale, sprinkle with a little water and put into a hot oven for about 10 minutes.

Speedy cocktail snacks: Scoop out seed from ½ inch slices of cucumber, and fill with seasoned cream cheese. Chill.

A substitute for pastry shells: Trim crust from slices of sandwich bread. Brush with melted butter and press into patty tins. Bake in moderate oven.

Sour cream will keep for two weeks if it is stored upside down in a refrigerator. This prevents the air from getting in.

To keep cut vegetables crisp for dips, fill large bowl with ice cubes, cover with transparent film wrap and arrange vegetables over.

When slicing avocado pears, squeeze with lemon juice to prevent discolouring.

Emergency starter: Prepare grapefruit as usual. Sprinkle each half with 1 dessertspoon brown sugar, 1 tablespoon sherry and ¼ oz. butter. Grill until caramelized.

Frosted Mint Sprigs: First dip in beaten egg-white and then in caster sugar. Spread the leaves into shape and put in refrigerator on greased paper to crystallize. Use to decorate grapefruit.

Accompaniments to Cocktails ~

AVOCADO DIP
Gillian Burr

1 medium avocado
1 carton sour cream

Juice of ½ lemon
Salt and black pepper to taste

Put all ingredients in blender and liquidize until smooth. (Can be made the day before and kept in refrigerator).

GREEN ONION DIP
Faith Duke

1 double packet of Green Onion dip mix
8 oz. cream cheese

Milk or single cream
as preferred

Put cheese in bowl and cream lightly with a fork. Sprinkle over green onion dip and mix thoroughly. Add sufficient cream or milk to make a light creamy consistency. Cover and put in refrigerator overnight to mature. Serve with carrot and celery fingers, raw cauliflower florets and crisps for dunking.

MEXICAN CHEESE DIP
Evelyn Rose

½ lb. cottage cheese
2 oz. butter
½ large green pepper
6 cocktail gherkins
Yoghurt or sour cream
8 drops tabasco or a pinch of cayenne

2 spring onions (green only)
or 2 tablespoons chives
Sprig of parsley
1 tablespoon mayonnaise
1 tablespoon French dressing
½ teaspoon salt

Cream the butter, beat in the cheese, chop finely the deseeded pepper, gherkins, spring onion tops or chives, and the parsley. Blend into the cheese mixture together with the mayonnaise, French dressing, salt, tabasco and enough yoghurt to make a creamy consistency. Put in a pottery dish, and surround with crisps or tiny biscuits for dunking. (The blending of butter into cream cheese heightens the flavour of the other ingredients to give this dip a unique and exciting flavour).

HOT CHEESE BISCUITS
Charlotte Davis

Savoury crackers
Cheddar cheese or Gruyére cheese

Black pepper

Cut slices of cheese to fit on top of crackers. Place under hot grill until cheese has melted. Serve hot, sprinkled with a little black pepper.

HOT CHEESE TARTS
Faith Duke

½ lb. shortcrust or cheese pastry
1 pint cheese sauce

2 beaten eggs
Parsley to garnish

Roll out pastry and cut to fit smallest patty tins. Prick the base of the pastry, then fill with a mixture of well flavoured cheese sauce and beaten eggs. Bake immediately near the top of oven Gas No. 6 (400°) for approximately 20 minutes. Serve as soon as possible garnished with parsley.

FRIED CHOPPED LIVER BALLS FOR COCKTAILS

Doreen Gainsford

¾ lb. chicken livers
2 hard boiled eggs
1 sliced stalk celery
1 beaten egg
Frying oil

4-6 tablespoons chicken fat
½ sliced Spanish onion
½ small green pepper
Fine matzo meal

Sauté liver, onion, celery and green pepper for a few minutes until soft. Put all ingredients including eggs through mincer. Season and add a little beaten egg. Roll into balls, dip into egg and then matzo meal. Deep fry until brown and serve hot.

AUBERGINE HORS D'OEUVRE

Betty Felitz

1 aubergine
4 tablespoons olive oil
Tomatoes and cucumber to garnish

1 small onion
Salt and pepper

Bake aubergine in oven until soft. Skin and peel. Place on board and chop with a wooden spoon until mashed. Add oil, salt and pepper. When cold add finely chopped onion. Garnish with tomatoes and cucumber. *Serves 2.*

AUBERGINE MAYONNAISE

Dianne Zimmerman

1 aubergine
1 tablespoon mayonnaise
Salt

1 hard boiled egg
1 clove garlic
Black pepper

Wrap aubergine in silver foil and place in medium oven for approximately 40 minutes. When soft remove from skin and chill. When cold chop well and add finely grated egg, crushed clove garlic, salt, pepper and mayonnaise. Mix well. *Serves 4.*

AVOCADO APPETISER

Lesley Bennett

2 large ripe avocado pears
½ chopped Spanish onion
4 large tomatoes
3 tablespoons chopped celery

1 crushed clove garlic
Juice of 1 lemon
1 tablespoon chopped parsley
Salt and black pepper

Mash avocado with wooden spoon, add lemon juice, garlic, tomatoes (chopped), onion, celery and parsley. Leave stone in mixture to keep from browning. *Serves 4.*

7

AVOCADO WITH EGG AND ONION
Maxine Davis

2 ripe avocado pears
6 - 8 large spring onions

2 hard boiled eggs
Vinaigrette dressing

Peel and remove stones from avocados, chop the flesh with the egg into bite-sized pieces, add finely chopped spring onions. Pour vinaigrette dressing over and pile on top of lettuce leaves on plates or in dishes. Serve with hot toast or French bread. *Serves 4.*

AVOCADO MOUSSE (1)
Sally Friend

2 ripe avocado pears
½ lb. cream cheese
2 spring onions

Salt and pepper
Lemon juice

Put all ingredients in blender and liquidize until smooth. Chill in refrigerator. Serve with hot toast. *Serves 4.*

AVOCADO MOUSSE (2)
Vivienne Barnett

2 large ripe avocado pears
2 finely chopped hard boiled eggs
Chopped lettuce

French dressing
½ lemon

Place all ingredients in blender and liquidize until smooth. Serve piled on lettuce in grapefruit dishes. Garnish with slices of stuffed olives and a little more French dressing. *Serves 4.*

AVOCADO ST. TROPEZ
Dianne Zimmerman

1 avocado pear
1 hard boiled egg
½ very finely grated medium onion

1 tablespoon thick cream
Salt and pepper

Carefully remove avocado from skin and sieve. Add onion to taste, sieved egg, cream, salt and pepper. Keep fresh in airtight container. To serve put a little shredded lettuce in avocado shell and pile mixture on top. *Serves 2.*

CALVES FOOT JELLY
Freida Stewart

2 calves feet
2 or 3 bay leaves
1 clove garlic
1 unskinned onion

1 hot red pepper
2 or 3 peppercorns
2 hard boiled eggs
Salt

Bring calves feet to boil. Skim, add all other ingredients except egg. Salt to taste and simmer for 3 — 4 hours. Test for setting by putting a tablespoon of liquid onto saucer. Strain bones into pyrex dish, add sliced egg when jelly is half set. Refrigerate until ready to serve. *Serves 4.*

COD'S ROE HORS D'OEUVRE

Joy Walker

4 ozs. skinned smoked cod's roe
2 tablespoons water
2 tablespoons olive oil
Juice of ½ lemon

2 cloves garlic
1 oz. white breadcrimbs
1 tablespoon water to be
poured over breadcrumbs

Put all ingredients in liquidizer and blend until a soft smooth paste. Serve with hot toast. *Serves 4.*

COURGETTE SOUFFLÉ

Marian Gold

2 whole eggs
2 egg whites
1 lb. courgettes
5 tablespoons grated Gruyére cheese

BÉCHAMEL SAUCE:
1 oz. butter
Scant ¼ pint warmed milk
2 tablespoons flour
Salt and pepper

Boil courgettes in a little water until soft. Sieve and add to Béchamel sauce, and cheese. Take off heat and add well beaten egg yolks. When cool fold in stiffly beaten egg whites. Turn into 1½ pint buttered souffle dish. Stand in baking tin in water in oven Gas No. 4 (350⁰) for approximately 40 minutes. *Serves 8.*

OEUFS EN COCOTTE

Pamela Kaye

6 eggs
½ lb. Cheddar cheese

BASIC WHITE SAUCE using
½ pint milk (see Sauces)

Hard boil eggs and allow to cool. Cut into smallish squares. Make white sauce and add 3 tablespoons grated cheese. Simmer for approximately 3 minutes. Add eggs to sauce. Put into individual shell dishes and sprinkle cheese on top. Grill for about 15 minutes until crisp. Serve immediately. *Serves 6.*

EGGS AND ONIONS

Freda Stewart

4 eggs
Chicken fat

1 medium onion
Salt and pepper

Hard boil eggs and grate. Add finely chopped onion, seasoning and chicken fat. Mix to a fairly good consistency. Serve garnished with either parsley or watercress. *Serves 4.*

EGGS AND TOMATOES BAKED IN THE OVEN

Gillian Burr

4 eggs
1 tomato
Margarine

2 slices Salami
Salt and pepper

Grease scallop dishes. Chop a little tomato in the bottom of each dish. Chop a little salami or vienna also (if desired). Break an egg on top, season with salt and pepper and dot with margarine. Bake in oven for approximately 15 minutes on Gas No. 4 (350⁰). *Serves 4.*

HADDOCK

Karol Solomons

1½ haddock fillets
¼ pint water
2 tomatoes
1 oz. butter
½ oz. flour

Lemon juice
6 peppercorns
1 wineglass dry white wine
1 dessertspoon chopped parsley
1 tablespoon double cream

Wash and dry fillets and put in buttered fireproof dish, sprinkle with salt. Add lemon and water and put peppercorns at one side. Cover with buttered paper and poach in oven Gas No. 4 (350°) for about 15 minutes. Work butter and flour into paste. Scald and skin tomatoes and remove seeds. Cut into slices. Boil wine and reduce quantity, strain on liquid from the fish and thicken with the kneaded butter. Simmer for 2 – 3 minutes. Adjust seasoning, add parsley, cream and tomatoes and reheat gently. Place fish on a hot serving dish and spoon over the sauce and garnish with pieces of toast spread with garlic butter. *Serves 4 – 6.*

CHOPPED HERRING

Lesley Bennett

1 large jar Wonderfood Herring
1 medium Spanish onion
4 – 6 ginger biscuits
Sugar to taste

4 hard boiled eggs
1 large eating apple
2 – 3 tablespoons wine vinegar
¼ teaspoon cinnamon

Put herring, eggs, onion, apple and biscuits through mincer. Add vinegar, sugar and cinnamon to taste. *Serves 6 – 8.*

HERRING HORS D'OEUVRE

Diane Krais

Shredded lettuce
2 avocado pears
1 medium jar Swedish Hors d'Oeuvre herrings
2 apples

Thousand Island dressing
Vinaigrette dressing
Mayonnaise

Dice avocados, apples and slice herrings thinly and mix together. Sprinkle with vinaigrette, add mayonnaise and dressing to sauce consistency. Place in glasses with layers of shredded lettuce. Top with black olives, a little paprika or a twisted slice of lemon. *Serves 5 – 6.*

HERRINGS IN SOUR CREAM

Valerie Ross

1 medium jar Luncheon herrings
Squeeze lemon juice

2 eating apples (optional)
1 carton sour cream

Spread half carton of sour cream over bottom of glass bowl. Cut tails off rollmops. Cut into pieces 2 inches long and spread over sour cream. Slice apples and lay over herrings. Squeeze a little lemon juice over to prevent apples browning. Cover with onions from herring jar. Top with remaining sour cream. Serve chilled. *Serves 3 – 4.*

KIPPER PÂTÉ

Joan Stiebel

2 x 6 oz. packets of boil-in-the-bag kipper fillets
Salt and pepper
Finely chopped parsley to garnish

6 oz. softened butter
Squeeze of lemon juice

Simmer kipper fillets as directed. When cool enough to handle remove skins and mash flesh with juice from packets. Liquidize ingredients and season to taste. (If packet contains butter, omit the 6 oz. from the recipe). *Serves 6.*

LEEK MAYONNAISE   Dianne Zimmerman

6 leeks
2 tablespoons tomato ketchup

4 large tablespoons mayonnaise
1 small tin baby carrots

Trim leeks to equal lengths. Put in boiling salted water and simmer till tender, approximately 12 minutes. Chill. Just before serving mix together mayonnaise, tomato ketchup and sieved carrots. Place leeks on a bed of lettuce and pour on the mayonnaise. *Serves 4 – 6.*

CHICKEN LIVER PÂTÉ (1)   Barbara Green

1 lb. chicken livers
1 small glass dry sherry
1 small glass brandy
2 oz. margarine

Salt and pepper
1 clove garlic
Pinch of mixed spice
Powdered thyme, basil and majoram

Clean livers well and sauté in margarine for 3 – 4 minutes. Remove the livers and add to the margarine the sherry and brandy. Mash the livers to a fine paste, with plenty of salt, black pepper and clove of garlic. Add 2 ozs. margarine and the powdered herbs. Add the liquid from the pan to form a very thick paste. Shape into the form of a smooth loaf and put on an oblong dish and place in the coldest part of the refrigerator. Prepare 24 hours before serving. It can then be properly sliced. (Do not keep in the deep freeze). *Serves 8.*

CHICKEN LIVER PÂTÉ (2)   Dianne Zimmerman

1 lb. chicken livers
6 oz. margarine
Parsley
2 dessertspoons brandy

1 large onion
1 clove of garlic
1 bay leaf
Salt and black pepper

Crush garlic and grate onion and soften in 2 ozs. margarine. Add liver and saute for 2 – 3 minutes. Add parsley, bay leaf, salt and pepper. Cook until liver is just cooked through. Mince finely and add remaining margarine (melted) also brandy, check seasoning and refrigerate in pâté mould. *Serves 8.*

CHOPPED LIVER   Naomi Naylor

½ lb. calves or chicken livers
2 large onions
Salt and pepper

¼ lb. chicken fat
3 eggs

Fry liver until lightly cooked. Allow to cool. Hard boil the eggs. Fry chopped onions until browned. Mince liver and eggs together, add salt and pepper to taste. Mix onions and hot fat with the liver and stir well. (Reserve some cooked egg yolk if desired to sieve and garnish liver). *Serves 4.*

MELON, CUCUMBER AND AVOCADO COCKTAIL   Helen Bloom

1 avocado
½ medium melon

½ cucumber
1 carton sour cream

Cut the avocado, melon and cucumber into cubes. Put into dishes and sprinkle with salt and pepper and pour over the sour cream. Sprinkle with parsley. *Serves 4.*

MOCK SHRIMP COCKTAIL   Pauline Israel

½ cup tomato ketchup
1 tablespoon lemon juice
1 tablespoon chopped parsley

½ pint home made mayonnaise
1 teaspoon salt

Mix all ingredients together very well. Serve over flaked haddock on shredded lettuce. Also tasty over artichokes. (This sauce freezes very well). *Serves 8.*

HOT MUSHROOM APPETISER   Sally Friend

½ lb. mushrooms
1 tablespoon finely minced onion
¼ teaspoon each salt and black pepper
1 cup double cream
2 lightly beaten eggs

2 teaspoons lemon juice
3 tablespoons butter
2 tablespoons grated parmesan cheese
2 tablespoons fine white breadcrumbs
1 tablespoon flour

Pre-heat oven on Gas No. 7 (435°). Butter ovenproof dish or individual dishes. Wash mushrooms and cut off stems. Slice thinly and sprinkle with lemon juice to prevent discolouration. Melt the butter in saucepan, add mushrooms and finely minced onion, cover with tight lid and simmer until soft. Season. Stir in flour and parmesan cheese. Cook for approximately 3 minutes. Place mushroom mixture in dish. Mix cream with egg yolks and pour over the mushrooms. Sprinkle with the breadcrumbs and dot with remaining butter. Bake until golden, approximately 15 minutes. Serve immediately. *Serves 4.*

MUSHROOM COCKTAIL   Faith Duke

½ lettuce
¼ pint double cream
2 tablespoons tomato sauce

½ lb. button mushrooms
2 tablespoons mayonnaise
1 tablespoon lemon juice

Half fill 4 wine glasses with washed, dried, shredded lettuce. Peel mushrooms. Cover mushrooms and stalks with boiling water for 2 minutes, drain and slice. Combine cream, mayonnaise, tomato sauce and lemon juice. Add mushrooms and chill slightly. Spoon into the 4 glasses and decorate side with ½ slice lemon. *Serves 4.*

ONION PIE   Shirley Byre

Shortcrust pastry
2 Spanish onions
1 tablespoon flour
¼ pint cream
Grated nutmeg

¼ pint milk
5 ozs. butter
3 eggs
Salt and freshly ground black pepper

Bake pastry blind in pie dish for 10 – 20 minutes. Chop onions finely and sauté in butter until transparent. Let onions cool then add rest of ingredients and mix well. Pour the mixture into pastry case and bake in oven at Gas No. 2 (300°) for 40–60 minutes. *Serves 6 – 8.*

PILCHARD PÂTÉ
Wendy Freilich

2 x 5½ oz. tins pilchards in natural brine
Pepper

1 dessertspoon grated onion
1 dessertspoon salad cream

Drain pilchards, remove main bones. Add onion, salad cream and a little pepper. Mash. Serve with crispbread as a pâté. (Quick starter for unexpected dinner guests). *Serves 2.*

PLAICE AUX CHAMPIGNONS
Jewels Leader-Cramer

1 medium plaice
½ lb. finely chopped mushrooms
¼ pint double cream

Butter
1 tin condensed mushroom soup

Skin and fillet plaice, wash and dry. Butter fireproof dish. Roll fish and place in dish. Season well and put a knob of butter on each fillet. Cook in oven on Gas No. 7 (425°). Sauté mushrooms in butter and then mix with mushroom soup and fold in cream. Season well. Pour sauce over fish and put back in oven for 5 minutes. (This is also delicious as a supper dish). *Serves 4 – 6.*

SMOKED SALMON PÂTÉ
Claire Jacobs

3 ozs. cream cheese
½ lemon grated rind only
1 egg yolk
¼ carton sour cream
Handful parsley

Salt and pepper
Garlic to taste
1 pinch cayenne pepper
3 ozs. smoked salmon
1 medium-thick slice bread

Put the cheese in the top of a double boiler, stir in the lemon rind, egg yolk and sour cream. Cook for about 5 minutes until thickened. Add the salt and put into blender followed by the salmon, seasonings, parsley and cut up bread. Blend until smooth. Spoon into a shallow dish, smooth top and cover tightly. Chill for 24 hours if possible. (For a coarser pâté do not liquidize smoked salmon, but chop it finely then add to the cream mixture). *Serves 12.*

SMOKED TROUT PÂTÉ
Claire Jacobs

2 skinned and boned smoked trout
12 ozs. cottage cheese
2 tablespoons creamed horseradish

4 tablespoons double cream
Salt and pepper to taste

Blend all ingredients in liquidizer until smooth. Chill. *Serves 8.*

PÂTÉ OF SMOKED TROUT
Lesley Bennett

4 smoked trout
Juice of a lemon
Black pepper

6 tablespoons double cream
2 tablespoons olive oil
Toast

Remove skin and bones from smoked trout and then place in bowl of electric mixing machine. Mix slowly with double cream and olive oil until it becomes a smooth paste. Season to taste with lemon juice and black pepper. Place in a small bowl ready to serve and chill. Serve with toast. *Serves 8.*

QUICK HOT GRAPEFRUIT

A Lazy Cook

2 grapefruit

3 tablespoons demerara sugar

Cut grapefruit in half and loosen segments with a sharp knife. Leave segments in skin. Sprinkle top of grapefruit halves with the sugar and place under medium grill until sugar has melted. *Serves 4.*

TROPICAL HORS D'OEUVRE

Faith Duke

15½oz. tin of palm hearts
Parsley
Paprika
Lettuce

Mayonnaise
Tomato Ketchup
Tabasco sauce
Salt and pepper

Arrange a bed of lettuce on each plate or dish. Put a drained palm heart on to lettuce. Make sauce to taste from mayonnaise, tomato ketchup, tabasco sauce, salt and pepper, and pour over. Decorate with parsley and a little paprika. *Serves 4.*

TUNA FISH PÂTÉ

Vera Gale

7 ozs. tuna fish
Lemon juice

2 ozs. butter
Garlic and pepper

Put fish, butter, 1 clove garlic in liquidizer and blend until smooth. Add lemon juice and pepper to taste. Put in refrigerator. *Serves 4.*

TUNA AND PINEAPPLE APPETISER

Sandra Granditer

1 x 7 oz. can tuna fish
1 small can pineapple

5 stalks celery
Empty pineapple shell

COCKTAIL SAUCE:
Equal amounts of mayonnaise and tomato ketchup, a few drops of tabasco sauce.

Dice celery and pineapple and mix together with flaked tuna. Add cocktail sauce and mix together. Place in empty pineapple shell. Serve with Melba toast or hot French bread. *Serves 4.*

STUFFED VINE LEAVES

Anonymous

½ lb. or 1 tin vine leaves
1 Spanish onion
Salt and black pepper

2 lbs. minced beef
2 eggs
Matzo meal to bind

Combine beef, onion and eggs, salt, pepper and matzo meal. Use fairly large vine leaves. Make meat into balls with wet hands and wrap in leaves. Place in large flat cooking dish. *Serves 6.*

SAUCE:

1 large tin tomato pureé
Juice of 2 lemons
4 tablespoons vinegar

Water
4 tablespoons brown sugar
Few handfuls sultanas

Add water to tomato pureé and make up to 1 pint. Add lemon juice, vinegar and sugar. Pour over meatballs and throw sultanas over. Cover and simmer on Gas No. 3 (325°) for 1 – 1½ hours.

NOTES

Soups and Accompaniments

Left-over soup can be put into an ice tray. When frozen, store cubes in a plastic bag and use for adding to gravies, etc.

If soup is too salty add a potato.

Cook soups in a very slow oven to prevent burning.

For richer coloured chicken soup, put in a washed unpeeled Spanish onion.

To remove fat from soup, place a lettuce leaf or a piece of kitchen paper on top to soak up the fat.

When using root in soup, keep the leaves on for added flavour.

Save vegetables from chicken soup. Liquidize and add a prepared stock cube. This makes a tasty economical soup.

When freezing soups allow 2 inches at top of the container for expansion.

To make fancy croûtons, cut bread with shaped cocktail biscuit cutters.

Always keep various packets of dehydrated vegetables handy for emergencies.

Keep fat from chicken soup to roast potatoes in. Fattening, but worth it!

Quick tomato soup. Fry a chopped onion until golden, add a tin of tomatoes and a tin of cream of tomato soup. Stir and bring to the boil.

Accompaniments ~

EGG MANDEL FOR SOUP
Hannah Mintz

8 eggs
1 cup water
1 lb. approximately self raising flour

Salt
Hot oil

Beat eggs with water and salt. Gradually add flour until ready to roll out as dough. Knead with hands. Flour board and roll dough to 1/8" thick. Cut into strips then cut across (making squares or shapes). Drop into hot oil in deep chip pan, one at a time (so as not to stick together), Fry as chips shaking after a few minutes until golden. They should rise. Place on wire to cool. Store in airtight tin.

KNEIDLACH
Sally Bloom

2 beaten eggs
2 tablespoons chicken fat
1½ cups medium Matzo meal
1 dessertspoon ground almonds

1 cup boiling water
1 teaspoon salt
Pepper

Mix thoroughly together, softened fat and eggs, add boiling water, matzo meal, ground almonds and seasoning and mix well. When cool refrigerate for several hours. Wet hands, roll into balls and cook gently in boiling chicken soup for 15 minutes.

For stuffed Kneidlach: Mixture as before plus ¼lb cooked meat finely minced plus one small grated onion seasoned and lightly fried together. Put in centre of Kneidlach and cook as before.

MATZO BALLS
Lesley Bennett

1 cup medium Matzo meal
1 cup boiling water
1 egg

1 tablespoon melted chicken fat
1 teaspoon cinnamon
Salt and black pepper

Combine all ingredients. Roll into balls and drop into boiling chicken soup.

MATZO KNEIDLACH
Marion Segall

3 eggs
1 cup medium Matzo meal
1 cup warm water

Pinch ground ginger
1 dessertspoon ground almonds
2 dessertspoons chicken fat

Beat eggs together with the water, add ginger, ground almonds and matzo meal, lastly the chicken fat. Make to a soft consistency, roll into balls and put in the chicken soup for about 7 minutes.

18

Soups ~

AVOCADO SOUP
Yaffa Wagner

5 cups hot chicken stock
1 lb. sliced avocado pear
Salt and pepper

1 cup dry white wine
Juice of ½ lemon

Put hot stock, avocado pears and seasoning in the blender until smooth. Add the wine and lemon juice and heat. Do not boil. Stir while heating. Serve with a slice of lemon. *Serves 8.*

BARLEY SOUP
Gillian Burr

1½ lbs. beef bones
Piece of stewing meat or shin
1 leek
1 root
2 large carrots
2 eating carrots

6 ozs. haricot or butter beans
(soaked in water overnight)
6 ozs. pearl barley
Salt and pepper
2 lumps sugar
1 large onion

Put bones and meat in large saucepan and practically fill with cold water. Let it come to the boil and remove scum, add salt, pepper and sugar. Add beans and cook gently on moderate heat for 1 hour. Add large onion, carrots, leek and root, cook slowly for 2 hours and remove vegetables. Add barley, cook for ½ hour and taste to check seasoning. Add eating carrots and cook for further ½ hour. (Meat balls may be added to this soup if desired). *Serves 8 – 9.*

BEETROOT BORSHT
Fanny Morris

3 lbs. uncooked beetroot
Water
2 carrots
1 onion

Sultanas
Brown sugar
Salt and pepper
Juice of 3 – 4 lemons

Peel and slice beetroots and cover with water, bring to boil, skim and simmer. Add salt, black pepper and brown sugar to taste. Add carrots and onion, cook for 1 – 2 hours. ½ hour before cooked add lemon juice and 1 – 2 handfuls of sultanas and continue simmering. Serve hot or cold with 1 or 2 teaspoons sour cream per person. *Serves 8.*

SWEET AND SOUR CABBAGE SOUP
Faith Duke

2 chicken stock cubes
2 pints water
1 pint tomato juice
1 medium cabbage

Lemon juice
Castor sugar
Salt and pepper

Put water, stock cubes and tomato juice into saucepan, bring to the boil then simmer. Add finely shredded cabbage. Simmer until cabbage is tender. Season to taste with lemon juice, sugar, salt and pepper. *Serves 6.*

CAULIFLOWER SOUP

Betty Feltz

1 cauliflower
2 tablespoons margarine
2 tablespoons flour
1 Spanish Onion
1 stick celery

Parsley
Salt and pepper
1 chicken stock cube
2 pints water

Poach cauliflower in boiling water for 5 minutes and drain. Melt margarine in a saucepan and add flour stirring until smooth paste. Gradually add 2 pints water, with dissolved chicken cube, all vegetables and cook for 30 minutes. Liquidize. Add salt and pepper to taste. Serve with croûtons. *Serves 4–5.*

CREAM OF CELERY SOUP

Karol Solomons

1 head sliced celery
1 finely chopped onion
1 pint water
Salt and pepper
1 oz. butter

1 tablespoon flour
½ pint milk
2 beaten egg yolks
4 – 5 tablespoons single cream
Croûtons

Put celery and onion in saucepan with water. Season and simmer gently for about 30 minutes until soft. Put in liquidizer. Make a roux with butter and flour, remove roux from heat and mix in milk and celery purée. Return to heat and stir until boiling. Simmer 2 – 3 minutes and check seasoning. Add 2 tablespoons of hot soup to egg yolks mix with cream, stir slowly into soup. Reheat gently until soup is thickened. Serve with croûtons. *Serves 6.*

CHICKEN SOUP

Charlotte Davis

1 x 4–5 lb. fowl and giblets
4 carrots
1 leek
2 large onions
1 small turnip

1 small swede
1 root
2 stalks celery
Parsley
Salt and pepper

Clean fowl, and prepare vegetables, put in a large saucepan and cover with cold water, bring to the boil and remove scum. Add seasoning. Simmer for 2½ – 3 hours. Strain but retain fowl, giblets and carrots. Allow soup to cool and refrigerate. Before reheating remove fat from top of soup. If not strong enough add 1 stock cube. *Serves 8.*

ICED CUCUMBER SOUP

Claire Jacobs

1 very large cucumber
¼ pint yoghurt
Salt and pepper
1 tablespoon finely chopped gherkin

½ pint double cream
2 tablespoons tarragon vinegar
Garlic to taste
2 tablespoons chopped mint

Wash and coarsely grate the unpeeled cucumber. Stir in the cream, and yoghurt. Add the seasonings and stir in the gherkins. Chill. Before serving, stir in the chopped mint. (Serve with a sprig of mint in each bowl, on a warm summer evening. Delicious!) *Serves 4 – 6.*

EGG AND LEMON SOUP
Marilyn Ford

1 pint chicken stock
2 lemons (squeezed)
1 tablespoon cold water

2 tablespoons sugar
Pinch salt
4 eggs

Mix eggs, lemon juice, sugar, water and salt, beat well. Put on heat and bring to simmer, add the chicken stock, stirring all the time. Simmer, stirring until soup thickens. DO NOT ALLOW to boil as it will curdle. *Serves 3–4.*

GAZPACHO 1
Hedy Rabin

1 lb. tomatoes
1 clove garlic
1 green pepper
1 onion
1 tablespoon vinegar

2 tablespoons salad oil
Juice of ½ lemon
Salt, pepper and sugar to taste
1 cup cold water or tomato juice
Toast

Liquidize halved tomatoes, crushed garlic and green pepper. Strain into a bowl. Stir in lemon juice, add salt, pepper and sugar. Add cold water or tomato juice for thick consistency, or more if desired. For garnish finely chop onion, cucumber, green pepper, tomato and toast. *Serves 4.*

GAZPACHO 2
Madeline Cope-Thompson

1½ lbs. ripe tomatoes
1 tablespoon chopped onion
2 cloves garlic
Salt and black pepper
Squeeze of lemon juice
3 tablespoons oil
1 tablespoon wine vinegar
Crushed ice

1 large diced green pepper
¼ pint iced water
Finely chopped parsley
¼ diced cucumber
3 diced tomatoes
2 slices diced bread
Oil (for frying)

Plunge tomatoes in boiling water for 1 minute. Drain and remove skin, place in liquidizer with onion and crushed garlic. Season and stir in lemon juice, olive oil, vinegar and water. Chill. Add crushed ice. Serve with diced cucumber, pepper, tomatoes and bread croutons and sprinkle each serving with chopped parsley. *Serves 6–8.*

LEEK AND POTATO SOUP
Lesley Bennett

6 leeks
4 tablespoons butter
4 medium potatoes
1½ pints water
1 vegetable cube

Salt and black pepper
Nutmeg
½ pint cream
Chopped chives

Remove green tops from leeks, cut the remainder into small pieces and sauté in butter until soft, do not brown. Peel and slice potatoes, add to leeks with water, stock cube, salt, pepper and nutmeg to taste and simmer until vegetables are cooked. Place in liquidizer to purée. Add cream and serve sprinkled with chopped chives. *Serves 6–8.*

LEEK AND POTATO SOUP
Ellissa Bennett

3 large leeks
½ lb. peeled potatoes
2 – 3 ozs. butter

1 small can condensed milk
Approximately ¾ pint fresh milk
Salt and pepper to taste

Thoroughly wash and drain leeks and cut into rings. Discard dark green leaves. Melt butter in fairly large saucepan and add leeks and finely sliced potatoes. 'Sweat' until tender, stirring occasionally. Place cooked mixture, condensed milk and some of the fresh milk in liquidizer and blend until smooth. Taste and add seasoning as required. Pour into double saucepan and add remaining milk until required consistency. Heat and serve. *Serves 4.*

LENTIL SOUP WITH FRANKFURTERS
Renata Knobil

13 ozs. lentils
2 large raw potatoes
1 oz. smoked beef
1 tablespoon flour
2 beef cubes

½ onion
Salt
Ground nutmeg
1 clove garlic

Wash the lentils and completely cover them with cold water and leave to soak overnight. Cook the lentils. Glaze the finely chopped onions and garlic, and add diced beef. Add these to the lentils and cook for 1 hour. Add the beef cubes, salt, nutmeg and grated potatoes. Cook the soup for a further ½ hour, and if it is not thick enough add the flour. Just before serving add the sausages (as many as you need) whole or cut up, simmer and serve very hot. *Serves 4.*

MINESTRONE
Patricia Miller

1 finely chopped onion
4 small carrots
4 sticks celery
1 courgette
1 tablespoon haricot beans (soaked for 2 hours)
1 medium tin of tomatoes

2 tablespoons macaroni
1 very small white cabbage
2½ pints stock (preferably veal broth)
2 tablespoons oil
Salt and pepper

Fry onion gently in oil until soft but not brown (about 5 minutes). Add diced carrot, celery, tomatoes, courgette and beans, cook for another 5 minutes (covered). Add stock and cook for about 2½ hours. Add shredded cabbage and macaroni and cook for further 20-30 minutes. *Serves 10.*

MUSHROOM SOUP
Lesley Bennett

4 tablespoons butter
3 tablespoons flour
1 pint water
1 vegetable cube (made up with water)
½ pint milk

½ lb. mushrooms
2 tablespoons chopped parsley
¼ pint double cream
Salt and black pepper

Liquidize raw mushrooms. Melt butter, add flour and cook gently for 3 minutes. Add vegetable stock, blend and bring to boil stirring constantly. Add milk, mushrooms and parsley. Simmer for 5 minutes. Stir in cream and season to taste. This is nice hot or cold. *Serves 4–6.*

MUSHROOM SOUP
Sally Friend

1 lb. mushrooms	Salt and pepper
2 ozs. butter	¼ pint single cream
1 oz. flour	1 pint milk
1 chopped onion	

Fry onion in butter. Add mushrooms, flour, milk, salt and pepper. Cook 20-30 minutes, add cream and serve. *Serves 4–6.*

MUSHROOM SOUP WITH RICE
Gina Marks

8 ozs. flat mushrooms	1 tablespoon rice
2 medium onions	1 bayleaf
1½ ozs. corn oil or margarine	1 tablespoon chopped parsley
1 oz. flour	and mint (mixed)
2 pints strong chicken stock	Salt and pepper

Peel and stalk mushrooms, wash and slice thinly. Chop onions, soften in 1 oz. of fat, then add mushrooms. Press a piece of paper on top and cover for 5 minutes. Take off heat and add rest of fat. Stir in the flour and pour on the stock. Season and return to heat stirring until boiling. Add the rice and bayleaf. Simmer for 15-20 minutes. Remove bayleaf, adjust seasoning, add herbs and serve. *Serves 8.*

ONION SOUP
Madeline Cope-Thompson

½ oz. margarine	½ – 1 oz. grated cheese
1 medium to large onion	½ inch slice of French bread
½ pint vegetable stock	French mustard
Salt and black pepper	

Melt fat. Sauté peeled sliced onion. Cover and cook gently until tender (about 15 minutes). Add stock and season to taste. Bring to boil and simmer for 20 minutes. Spread bread with mustard and cover with cheese. Place under hot grill until brown and crisp. Place on top of soup immediately before serving. Serve extra grated Parmesan cheese at supper table if desired. *Serves 1 portion.*

SOUP A L'OIGNON
Doreen Gainsford

24 small onions	4 – 6 rounds toasted French bread
4 tablespoons butter or margarine	Salt and black pepper
Sugar	FOR MILK MEAL:
2½ pints beef or vegetable stock	Grated Gruyère cheese
4 fluid ozs. cognac	

Peel and thinly slice the onions. Heat margarine or butter with a little sugar in a large saucepan. Add onions and cook gently stirring with a wooden spoon until onion is golden brown. Add stock and continue stirring until soup boils. Lower heat and simmer covered for 1 hour. Before serving add cognac, salt and pepper. Serve in large tureen or individual bowls, placing toasted French bread on top. If using for a milk meal, gruyère cheese can be placed on the bread before toasting. *Serves 6.*

QUICK ONION SOUP
Shirley Young

2 chicken stock cubes
(made up as directed)

Salt and pepper
5 onions

Slice the onions, put into prepared stock and boil for 20 minutes. Liquidize before serving. *Serves 6–8.*

OXTAIL SOUP
Dianne Zimmerman

1 oxtail
4 ozs. sliced onions
4 ozs. sliced carrots
3 ozs. turnip
1 stick celery
¾ pint good stock
1 glass sherry

3 quarts water
Salt
Parsley
Bayleaf
4 – 6 peppercorns
1 oz. margarine

Wash tail well, cut into pieces and crush slightly with chopper. Put margarine in a thick pan and add vegetables, simmer gently for 10 minutes. Add tail and continue to simmer for about 10 minutes. Add stock and sherry and cook until liquid has reduced by half. Add water and salt, peppercorns and herbs, bring slowly to boil, skim, simmer 2-3 hours. Strain. Chill to remove fat. Reheat, and just before serving add another glass of sherry. *Serves 10 – 12.*

QUICK PEA SOUP
Shirley Young

1 large packet frozen peas
2 pints chicken stock or 2 cubes
(made up as directed)

1 large onion
Salt and pepper

Boil all ingredients for 5 minutes. Liquidize before serving. *Serves 6–8.*

SAINT GERMAINE PEA SOUP
Diana Marks

2 – 2½ cups split green peas
2 large carrots
1 large onion

Salt and pepper
1 beef or chicken stock cube
2 pints water

Put peas in saucepan and cover with 2 pints of water, add onion and carrots. Bring to boil and skim. Allow to simmer for 1 hour and add seasoning to taste plus stock cube. Strain or liquidize and serve with croûtons. This soup may be made the day before use. *Serves 6–8.*

GREEN PEPPER SOUP
Dianne Zimmerman

2 medium green peppers
¼ cup onion
2 tablespoons butter
1 pint water

¼ teaspoon oregano
1 tablespoon flour
¼ teaspoon salt
½ pint milk

Sauté chopped pepper and onion in half the butter, until onion is golden. Add water and oregano and simmer for 10 minutes. Purée soup in liquidizer. In a clean saucepan melt the rest of the butter and blend in flour and salt, cook until bubbly and remove from heat. Gradually add milk and return to heat and cook stirring until thick and smooth. Stir in pepper mixture. Refrigerate. Serve with chopped pepper garnish. *Serves 6.*

SCOTCH BROTH
Dianne Zimmerman

2 lbs. mutton scrag	1 turnip
3 pints water	2 ozs. onion
1½ ozs. pearl barley	2 ozs. celery
1 carrot	Salt and pepper
1 leek	Parsley

Remove as much fat as possible from meat, cut into small pieces. Put into cold water and bring to boil. Skim well. When all the scum is removed add barley and salt. Simmer for ½ hour. Add diced vegetables and pepper. Cook for 1½ hours with lid on. Remove meat and cut a few pieces from the bone and return cut meat to pan. Chill to remove fat. Reheat, add parsley and serve. *Serves 10–12.*

SPINACH SOUP
Marion Segall

2 tins clear chicken soup	1 large tablespoon coriander
1 large packet chopped frozen spinach	1 teaspoon garlic powder
3 tablespoons oil	Salt and pepper

Defrost the spinach in the soup. In a small saucepan gently fry onion for 2-3 minutes, add coriander, garlic powder, pepper and salt. Add carefully to the soup and serve with cooked rice. *Serves 4.*

SPINACH SOUP
Penny Marks

2 packets frozen chopped spinach	2 ozs. butter
½ – ¾ pint milk	2 vegetable cubes
2 ozs. flour	Garlic
½ pint cream	

Melt butter and stir in flour until it forms a ball. Slowly add the milk stirring all the time, until it is of a smooth consistency. Add defrosted spinach, garlic and stock cubes which have been dissolved in about ½ pint water. Cook for ½ hour. Add cream, do not boil. *Serves 6–8.*

SUMMER SOUP
Judith Solomon

1 lb. tomatoes	½ teaspoon sugar
1 x 4 inch piece of peeled cucumber	2 ozs. sherry
1 teaspoon chopped onion	4 tablespoons cream
½ teaspoon celery salt	Salt and pepper

Place quartered tomatoes with the diced onion and cucumber into a saucepan and cook covered over a low heat until onion is soft. Liquidize, add seasoning and sugar and blend again. Pour through a strainer into a bowl, stir in sherry and put in refrigerator to chill. Just before serving stir in the cream. *Serves 3 – 4.*

HOME MADE TOMATO SOUP
Janet Nathan

7 lbs. cooking tomatoes
1 large sliced onion
Lemon juice

Salt and pepper
Little butter or margarine
Sugar

Sauté the onion in butter or margarine, then add the washed tomatoes, salt and pepper. Cook over a low heat until the tomatoes are soft. Sieve, add lemon juice and sugar to taste. This soup can be made two days before it is needed. *Serves 6.*

TOMATO AND ORANGE SOUP
Karol Solomons

2 lbs. tomatoes
1 sliced onion
1 sliced carrot
1 strip lemon rind
1 bayleaf
6 peppercorns
Salt
1 vegetable cube

2 pints water
1½ ozs. butter
3 – 4 tablespoons flour
Rind and juice of ½ orange
Pepper
Sugar (to taste)
¼ pint single cream

Wipe the tomatoes and halve. Squeeze to remove seeds. Put tomatoes, onion and carrot into pan with lemon rind, bayleaf, peppercorns and a good pinch of salt. Make stock with vegetable cube, water and salt and add to tomato mixture. Put lid on and simmer for about 30 minutes. Rub through sieve and set aside. In clean pan, melt butter and stir in flour. Pour on tomato mixture, blend and bring to the boil. Shred the orange rind (blanch by cooking in boiling water for 1 minute) rinse well with cold water. Add orange juice to soup with seasoning and sugar to taste. Stir in the cream at the last moment and finally add orange rind. Serve immediately. (If serving for meat meal use chicken stock cube and omit cream). *Serves 6.*

VEGETABLE SOUP
Valerie Halpern

2 pints water or stock
4 sticks celery
½ medium cabbage
4 medium carrots
4 medium onions

2 large leeks
Salt and pepper
Knob of butter or margarine
Lemon juice

Cut up vegetables and cook in 2 pints water or stock. Bring to boil and simmer for 20 minutes. Drain liquid into bowl, Add knob of butter or margarine, salt, pepper and lemon juice to vegetables. Purée vegetables and combine with liquid. Reheat and serve. *Serves 8.*

WATERCRESS SOUP
Karol Solomons

2 bunches watercress
1 oz. butter
1 chopped onion
1 tablespoon flour
1½ pints milk

Salt and pepper
Stale bread for croûtons
2 egg yolks
5 tablespoons single cream

Wash and finely shred the watercress. Melt butter in pan, add cress and onion, cover with greased paper and lid, and stew for 10 minutes. Blend in flour. Boil milk and pour on to cress mixture and season. Simmer for 15 minutes, liquidize. Return to pan and thicken with egg yolks and cream. To do this, work yolks and cream together in small basin and stir in 2 tablespoons hot soup, return to pan and reheat slowly, stirring all the time. DO NOT LET THIS SOUP BOIL AFTER ADDING YOLKS. *Serves 6.*

WATERCRESS SOUP   Joan Edwards

¼ lb. butter or margarine
1 cup flour
2 cups chicken stock or water

2 bunches watercress
(drained and chopped)
Cream (optional)

Melt butter or fat, stir in flour, slowly add water or stock. Allow to simmer then drop in watercress and cook gently for ½ hour. (If milk soup, add cream, but this is not necessary). Season with salt, pepper and a pinch of nutmeg if desired. Add more butter or margarine, then liquidize. Garnish with croûtons and a little fresh watercress. *Serves 4.*

QUICK WATERCRESS SOUP   Shirley Young

3 potatoes
2 bunches watercress
Salt and pepper

2 chicken stock cubes
(made up with 2 pints water)

Boil all ingredients together for 20 minutes. Liquidize. *Serves 6.*

YOGHURT SOUP WITH NUTS   Yaffa Wagner

1 small cucumber
Salt
Olive oil
Dill

6 cloves crushed garlic
3 cups yoghurt
2 ozs. minced nuts
Mint

Peel cucumber and cut into tiny cubes, season with salt and add a few drops of oil, pinch of dill (chopped) and garlic. Mix well, add yoghurt and continue to stir. If mixture is too thick, add a small quantity of water until desired consistency is reached. Refrigerate. Before serving add the chopped nuts and a few drops of olive oil. Garnish with a sprig of mint. *Serves 6.*

NOTES

Fish ~

To avoid fishy hands, chill fish thoroughly in cold water before handling

Frozen fish need not be thawed before cooking.

When frying fish wash first in cold water, put in a colander, sprinkle lightly with salt and leave for one hour, then dry with kitchen paper. Do not rinse. Further seasoning is unnecessary.

Freeze salmon uncleaned to retain more flavout.

Do not scale salmon before cooking as the scales will keep it extra moist.

When grilling soles, first dip in flour, dot with butter, season with salt and pepper then place under the grill.

When making fish balls dip hands frequently in cold water.

Keep whole cold halibut or salmon moist by removing skin and using it again to cover fish.

To stop poached fish breaking keep the cooking liquid below simmering point. The water should just "tremble".

Freeze any left-over fish stock for next time.

CARP

Marie Duke

1 carp
1 large sliced Spanish onion
3 sliced carrots
Salt

½ teaspoon pepper
4 teaspoons sugar
2—3 sticks celery

Have carp cleaned and sliced. Wash well and salt. Leave in salt for about 1 hour. Fill a medium saucepan a third full of water. Add onion, carrots and a little salt and pepper. It should not be too salty. Bring to the boil. Add the slices of carp and the head, with the sugar and celery. Simmer for 2-2½ hours approximately on a very small heat until tender. Taste occasionally and should it become too salty add more boiling water. Leave in the pan to cool. Take out and put into a large shallow 1½ inch deep glass dish. Pour stock over, garnish with cooked carrots and chopped parsley. When quite cold put into fridge.
STUFFED CARP: Cook as above and stuff with Gefilte Fish. *Serves 6—8.*

CARP IN PAPRIKA

Yaffa Wagner

4 lbs. carp
4 green peppers
1 lb. fresh tomatoes
5 ozs. finely chopped onion

1½ teaspoons salt
4 ozs. margarine
2 teaspoons paprika
4 tablespoons water

Chop the green peppers and tomatoes, cut the carp into serving pieces. Sprinkle the fish with salt. Fry the onions in margarine stirring often. Sprinkle with paprika and add water. Cook until the onions become mushy. Add the pepper and tomatoes, bring to the boil. Place the fish in a baking dish and pour on the paprika sauce. Bake for 45 minutes in oven Gas No. 4 (350°) basting from time to time. *Serves 8.*

FISH POACHED IN MILK

Stella Mayoram

4 pieces skinned bream, haddock or cod
Potatoes
½ pint milk
Salt and pepper
Parsley

2 ozs. butter
Carrot
Onion
Celery

Boil sliced carrot, onion, celery and parsley together in large saucepan with about 3 pints water. Add potatoes and par-boil. Place fish on top of potatoes. Add milk and butter. Cover with lid and turn heat to simmer. Taste for seasoning. *Serves 4.*

BAKED FISH IN TOMATO SAUCE

Valerie Green

2½—3 lbs cod, hake or halibut
TOMATO SAUCE: 1 chopped Spanish onion
1 medium size tin tomatoes
2 cloves
Freshly ground black pepper
1 tablespoon water
1 level tablespoon chopped parsley

2 tablespoons olive oil
¼ pint dry white wine
Salt
1 level tablespoon cornflour
12 green olives
2 level tablespoons capers

To make tomato sauce: Sauté chopped onions in olive oil till soft. Add tomatoes, white wine and cloves with salt and pepper to taste. Cover pan and simmer for 20 minutes. Mix cornflour and water to a paste. Add to the tomato mixture. Simmer for further 5 minutes. Add olives, parsley and capers.

Fish: Wash, dry and place in well-greased baking dish. Pour the tomato sauce over and bake for 35 minutes in oven Gas No. 5 (375°) until fish flakes easily. Serve hot with sauce. *Serves 4−6.*

FISH PIE
Doreen Gainsford

1 lb. cod or haddock (or any fish that
flakes well)
1 packet shortcrust pastry
4 egg yolks
½ pint single cream

Grated nutmeg
2 tablespoons butter
6 ozs. diced Gruyère cheese
2 ozs. chopped mushrooms
Salt and black pepper

Line two 8 inch pie dishes with pastry, prick bottoms with fork. Cover with greaseproof paper and bake blind for 15 minutes, Gas No. 5 (375°). Cool slightly. Meanwhile boil fish for five minutes, flake and season. Whisk egg yolks then add cream and continue whisking or beating until thicker. Season with salt, pepper and nutmeg to taste. Arrange diced cheese and flaked fish in two dishes. (If preparing in advance pie can be left like this until needed). Pour cream and egg mixture over. Sprinkle with mushrooms. Bake in moderate oven Gas No. 4 (350°) for 35 minutes. Serve hot. Can be frozen in tin foil pie dish preferably without cream mixture. *Serves 4−6.*

POTATO FISH PIE
Sally Friend

2 lbs. filleted fresh haddock
1 lb. smoked haddock
Cheese sauce to cover

Mashed potatoes
Sliced hard boiled eggs
Milk

Cook fish in milk for a few minutes. Season. Strain and put in bottom of fireproof dish. Cover with cheese sauce and arrange sliced egg on top. Cover with mashed potato, dot with butter and cook for 30-40 minutes in oven Gas No. 5 (375°) until brown. This is delicious! *Serves 4−6.*

FISH — PROVENCAL STYLE
Bernice Sion

1 lb. white fish
3 cloves garlic
1 large onion
¾ lb. tomatoes
4 tablespoons oil

3 fl. ozs. white wine (optional) or
little water
½ lemon
Salt and pepper

Cut fish into steaks — sprinkle with lemon, salt and pepper and leave for 15 minutes. Fry finely chopped garlic and onion in oil to colour, add chopped skinned tomatoes and cook for a few minutes. Add wine or water, cook another few minutes. Lay fish in casserole and cover with Sauce. Cook, covered, for 20-25 minutes in oven Gas No. 5 (375°). *Serves 2.*

GEFILTE FISH

Marie Duke

1 lb. minced hake
3 grated hard boiled eggs
1 large grated Spanish onion
Salt, pepper, sugar
1 raw egg
½ egg shell of water

STOCK:
1 sliced Spanish onion
2 sliced carrots
2 sticks celery
4 teaspoons sugar

Mix hake, hard-boiled eggs, onion, seasoning and raw egg. If too dry add ½ egg shell of cold water. Taste and adjust seasoning. Take a large pan one third full of water, a little salt and half teaspoon of pepper. Add onion, carrots, celery and sugar. Bring water to the boil. Make balls of the fish and drop into boiling water. Simmer for 2-2½ hours. Leave in the pan to cool. Take out and put into a large glass dish. Pour stock over. Garnish with carrots and chopped parsley. *Makes 6 balls.*

FRIED GEFILTE FISH

Gloria Brown

3 lbs. chopped minced fish (mixed)
1 lb. grated onions
6 ozs. coarse breadcrumbs
2 tablespoons Coffee Mate
2 tablespoons boiling water

½ cup cold water
3 eggs
Salt and pepper
1 teaspoon cinnamon
Sugar to taste

Soak breadcrumbs in Coffee-Mate dissolved in boiling water and the added quarter cup cold water. Add beaten eggs, onions, salt, pepper, sugar and seasonings. Gradually add in chopped fish and mix well until blended. Dampen hands and form into balls for deep frying. (Freezes well in plastic freezer bags. Takes 2½ hours to defrost). *Makes 18–20 balls.*

HADDOCK WITH AVOCADO PEAR

Jo Smith

2 ozs. cooked haddock
(filleted baby ones are best)
1 avocado
Lemon juice
Salt and pepper
Tomato

SAUCE:
6 ozs. thick home made mayonnaise
Tomato ketchup to colour
1 good tablespoon horseradish cream
2 drops tabasco

Bone fish well using fingers preferably and place in a covered oven dish. Season with salt and pepper and cook in a moderate oven for about 30 minutes or until fish flakes easily, allow to cool. Cut avocado in half, coat surface with lemon juice. Mix sauce ingredients together. Mix with fish, saving a little sauce. Fill avocado with fish mixture. Place a teaspoon of sauce on top. Cut a thin slice of tomato lengthways and place one strip on stalk end to garnish. *Serves 1.*

BARBECUED HALIBUT

Karol Solomons

1½ lbs. halibut
2 gills boiling water
Salt and pepper
½ teaspoon French mustard
Juice of ½ lemon

1 dessertspoon A.1. sauce
A good pinch of sugar
A few capers
A good-sized leaf of fennel

Heat butter in frying pan. Dip fish in flour, cook and brown on both sides. Put remaining ingredients in saucepan and bring to the boil. Reduce a little and pour over fish which has been kept on a hot dish.

HALIBUT, HAKE OR HADDOCK CRÉOLE
Evelyn Rose

1½ lbs. fish cut into 4 large steaks
2 large skinned and chopped tomatoes
1 small seeded and chopped green pepper
2 heaped tablespoons dry breadcrumbs
1 oz. melted butter
Few grinds black pepper

1 pinch oregano
1 crushed clove of garlic
1 level teaspoon salt
1 tablespoon finely chopped onion
½ oz. butter
1 tablespoon Parmesan cheese

Toss the breadcrumbs in 1 oz. melted butter. Melt the ½ oz. butter and cook the onion till golden, then add the tomatoes and green pepper, and cook for 2-3 minutes until the butter has been absorbed. Butter well a shallow oven-to-table casserole and arrange the steaks in it. Add the seasonings to the buttered vegetables and spread them over the fish steaks. Cover with a layer of buttered crumbs. Refrigerate. Bake for half-an-hour near the top of a quick oven Gas No. 6 (400°) till the fish flakes easily with a fork and the topping is golden. (Buttered-sautéed vegetables will enhance the flavour of a baked fish dish; a "gratin" topping finishes the dish without the need for further garnishing after baking). *Serves 4.*

SWEET AND SOUR HALIBUT
Lesley Bennett

1½ – 2 lbs. halibut
1 sliced Spanish onion

Juice of 3 lemons
3 eggs

Barely cover the bottom of a large frying pan with water, juice of one lemon, sliced onion, salt and black pepper. Bring to boil and simmer for 5 minutes. Add fish and cook over a low heat on both sides until fish flakes easily. Remove fish. Beat the eggs with the juice of 2 lemons. Add the juices from the fish and cook gently until sauce thickens. Do not boil. Pour sauce over fish. Serve cold. If desired add sugar to taste. *Serves 4–6.*

FRIED MACKEREL
Charlotte Davis

1 mackerel
1 egg
Fine Matzo meal

Corn oil for frying
Salt and pepper

Split fish in two from head to tail – cut off little fins. Wash and dry very well. Dip into seasoned beaten egg and dip in fine matzo meal. Fry in hot corn oil. Keep turning till golden brown on both sides. Turn out on greaseproof paper. When bottom is dry turn over to fresh piece of paper. Brown paper is better than greaseproof if available. *Serves 2.*

QUENELLES OF PIKE
Gloria Brown

2 lbs. pike
9 whole eggs
2 egg whites
1¾ cups sifted plain flour
¾ lb. butter

2 pints fish stock
1 cup milk
1 cup water
Salt and black pepper
Nutmeg to taste

33

Boil the water and milk with one tablespoon of butter and ½ teaspoon of salt. Remove from heat and gradually add the sifted flour. Add five eggs, one at a time beating well until mixture comes away from sides of saucepan. Cool paste. Mix paste with pike, and put in blender a little at a time, with four whole eggs and two whites (beaten); add remainder of butter. This should become very creamy. Season with 2 teaspoons of salt, ½ teaspoon freshly ground black pepper and pinch of nutmeg. Freeze overnight and remove one hour before use. Form desired shape, place in fish boiler and poach in a well seasoned fish stock for 40 minutes. Make a sauce by reducing stock and add sour cream to taste. *Serves 10.*

FRIED PLAICE WITH BANANAS   Betty Feltz

1 plaice – 4 fillets   Fine Matzo meal
¼ lb. butter   2 bananas halved lengthwise

Wash and salt plaice. Dry, dip in fine matzo meal and fry in butter until golden brown. Fry bananas and serve on top of the fish. *Serves 2.*

OVEN FRIED PLAICE   A Fish Fancier

4 – 6 plaice fillets   Grated rind of ½ lemon
1 tablespoon salt   Little thyme
½ pint milk   4 tablespoons melted butter
¼ lb. dry breadcrumbs   Lemon to decorate
2 tablespoons chopped parsley

Heat oven. Add salt to milk. Dip fish in milk then in breadcrumbs mixed with parsley, lemon peel and thyme. Place fish in well buttered baking dish and pour over the melted butter. Put in oven on top shelf for about 12 minutes Gas No. 7 (425°). Serve with lemon. *Serves 4–6.*

PLAICE FILLETS IN MUSHROOM SAUCE   Myrna R. Sayers

6 small plaice fillets   ¼ lb. mushrooms (optional)
1 can condensed mushroom soup

Cut fish lengthwise and roll. Place in an ovenproof dish so that it cannot unroll. Slice mushrooms and lay them on top. Spoon over condensed soup undiluted. Cook for 20 minutes in oven Gas No. 4 (350°). These quantities are for a starter course – as a main dish increase accordingly. *Serves 6.*

GRILLED FRESH SALMON WITH CUCUMBER   Barbara Davison

1 slice of fresh salmon (approx. ½ lb.)   Fresh sliced cucumber
Salted butter   Salt and black pepper

Wash and clean fish and sprinkle with salt at least one hour before cooking. Remove tray from grill pan and if desired cover tray with silver foil. Preheat pan and grill. Place slice of salmon on pan and dot with slivers of butter and put under grill for 3 or 4 minutes to seal the surface of fish. Remove from grill. Turn fish over carefully. Cover completely with over-lapping slices of finely cut cucumber, peeled or unpeeled as desired. (A mandoline cutter is a useful tool for this). Then dot cucumber with slivers of butter and season with pepper. Return pan to grill and grill slowly without turning, but basting occasionally with pan juices, until fish is cooked through. (Test by inserting fork between fish and bone – if they part cleanly fish should be sufficiently cooked). Serve immediately. Hollandaise sauce can accompany this dish. *Serves 1.*

SALMON KEDGEREE
Lesley Bennett

1 lb. poached salmon
3 oz. rice
4 tablespoons butter
1 teaspoon curry powder

2 hard boiled eggs
Salt and black pepper
½ pint hot cream sauce (see sauces)

Cook rice in boiling salted water, until tender but not mushy. Drain and keep warm. Flake salmon, removing all bones and skin. Melt butter in saucepan and blend in the curry powder. Add fish and sauté. Combine chopped whites of hard-boiled eggs with rice and fish. Season to taste with salt and black pepper. Fold in hot cream sauce. Serve on a platter with yolks of hard-boiled eggs finely chopped or sieved over the top. This is a super way of using up left over salmon! *Serves 4.*

SALMON MOUSSE
Jacky Bennett

¾ lb. fresh salmon
¼ pint mayonnaise
¼ pint double cream

Black pepper
Chives
1 packet gelatine dissolved in 1 cup hot water

Butter six individual pots. Cook salmon then flake into liquidizer, omitting bones and skin. Add all other ingredients except the chives. Switch on and liquidize until creamy then add chives and blend for another few seconds. Pour into pots. Refrigerate. When set turn out and serve with hot buttered toast. *Serves 6.*

POACHED SALMON WITH EGG AND LEMON SAUCE
Fay Carr

4 – 5 lbs piece of salmon with scales on
4 – 5 sliced onions
Salt and pepper

1 bayleaf
2 peppercorns

Wash and salt the fish. Wash salt off. Invert enamel plate at the bottom of a pan, cover the whole base with sliced onions then just cover onions with water. Add the bayleaf and peppercorns and bring to the boil. Add the salmon and pepper to taste. Simmer 5-7 minutes Turn off heat and leave to cool with lid on until cold, Take out, skin, and put on dish. Retain stock for sauce

SAUCE: Stock
9 whole eggs

Juice of 2 lemons
Sugar to taste

Strain stock. Beat eggs and add to stock with lemon juice and sugar. Stir constantly over a tiny light until it thickens, leave to cool. (Cover salmon with a little sauce to keep it moist. Put into a covered casserole and it will keep moist for the next day). *Serves 10.*

SALMON RISSOLES
Freida Stewart

1 medium tin red salmon
1 medium tin pink salmon
1 small onion

1 egg
2 ozs. fine Matzo meal
Oil for frying

Strain, bone and skin the salmon. Add egg, grated onion and matzo meal and mix well. Mould into round cakes and fry in small quantities of oil. *Makes 10 rissoles.*

SALMON STEAKS IN CREAM

Bernice Sion

1 salmon steak per person about 1 inch thick
Single cream
1 bayleaf

Salt and pepper
Butter

Season steaks well with salt and freshly ground black pepper. Choose oven dish into which steak fits closely but not jammed. Butter dish well, put in steak and pour over enough cream to cover. Add bayleaf and bake in oven Gas No. 5 (375°) for 20-25 minutes until cooked. Baste once or twice with cream and add more cream if it reduces. *Serves 1.*

BAKED SALMON TROUT

Barbara Davison

2½ − 3 lbs. salmon trout
Butter

Fresh lemon juice
Salt and black pepper

Clean the salmon trout and notch the skin in a few places. Sprinkle with salt and lemon juice inside and out. Leave for one hour. Take a piece of silver foil large enough to completely envelope the fish and carefully butter one side of the foil. Then sprinkle buttered foil with pepper and a little lemon juice. Wrap fish so that the packet will not leak and place on a flat baking tray or dish in a preheated oven Gas No. 4 (350°) and cook for 45-75 minutes according to size and thickness. Open packet carefully to avoid burning by steam, test fish and then serve hot accompanied by Hollandaise sauce or mayonnaise. Fish may be skinned quickly before serving if desired. *Serves 5−7.*

SOLE GOUJON

Valerie Ross

Dover or lemon sole (your fishmonger will
prepare the fish for you)
Fine Matzo meal (seasoned)

Oil for frying
2 eggs (more if there is more fish)
Salt and pepper

Wash and dry pieces of fish. Dip in beaten egg. Toss pieces in seasoned matzo meal and fry in deep oil for a few minutes until golden brown. Drain on fish paper. Serve with tartare sauce. For hors d'oeuvre allow 8 pieces per person and for a main course allow more as required. (Dover Sole is naturally best but Lemon Sole is perfectly adequate).

FILLET OF SOLE MEUNIÈRE

Doreen Gainsford

2 x 1¼ lb. Dover soles − skinned and filleted
A small quantity of seasoned flour
2 ozs. butter
Mushrooms for garnishing − optional

1 large teaspoon chopped mixed herbs
including parsley
1 teaspoon lemon juice

If using mushroom garnish prepare first and keep hot as fish only takes a few minutes. Wash and dry fish thoroughly. Roll in seasoned flour. Heat a thick frying pan and drop on a little less than half the butter, when foaming lay in the fillets skinned side uppermost. Cook over a moderate heat until golden brown, then brown the other side. Lay fillets without draining in a hot dish allowing them to overlap slightly. Add garnish, if required, and keep hot. Wipe out frying pan. Reheat and drop in rest of butter. Allow to colour a delicate nut brown then quickly add herbs and lemon juice. Pour over fish and serve immediately. *Serves 4.*

FILLETS OF SOLE MORNAY
Doreen Gainsford

2½ lb. Lemon or Dover sole (ask fishmonger to skin both sides, fillet and retain bones)
½ sliced onion
6 peppercorns
½ bayleaf
6 tablespoons water

MORNAY SAUCE:
1½ ozs. butter
2 tablespoons flour
½ pint milk
Salt and pepper
4 ozs. button mushrooms
2 tablespoons grated cheese

Wash and dry fish very thoroughly and trim the fillets. Fold the ends of the fillets under, put in fireproof dish with a little salt, onion, peppercorns, bayleaf and water. Place washed bones on top, cover and cook 10-12 minutes in oven Gas No. 4 (350°).
Sauce: Melt 1 oz. butter in pan, remove from heat and blend in flour and milk. Season lightly return pan to heat and bring slowly to boil, stirring all the time. Strain liquid from fish, add to sauce and cook 2-3 minutes more. Wash mushrooms, trim and slice. Cook in remaining butter. Arrange fish and spoon over mushrooms. Remove sauce and beat in cheese keeping 1 tablespoon for top. Cover fish and brown lightly under grill. *Serves 6*. (This recipe can be used with Haddock and Bechamel Sauce).

TROUT WITH ALMONDS
Lesley Bennett

4 – 6 fresh trout
Salt and pepper
Milk
Flour
¼ lb. butter

1 tablespoon oil
4 – 6 tablespoons slivered blanched almonds
Juice of ½ lemon
2 – 4 tablespoons chopped parsley

Season washed trout with salt and black pepper. Dip them in milk and then in flour. Sauté fish in half the butter and 1 tablespoon oil until golden on both sides. Drain fat from the pan and wipe out with kitchen paper. Melt the remaining butter and cook almonds, shaking pan continuously until they are golden brown. Add lemon juice and chopped parsley and pour the sauce over the trout which have been placed on a heated platter. *Serves 4–6.*

TROUT CASALINGA
Helene Littlestone

2 trout
1 large tin tomatoes
1 small tin tomato purée
1 large onion
Capers

Black olives
Olive oil
Lemon juice
Salt and pepper
(Garlic salt if liked)

Heat oil in fireproof dish, put in trout; add seasoning and lemon juice. Bake in hot oven Gas No. 8 (400°) for 20 minutes.
Sauce: Heat oil in saucepan. Slice onions and fry till slightly golden. Add tin of tomatoes (don't put in all the liquid), add tomato purée. Simmer gently for 20 minutes. Lastly season to taste, add capers and olives. Pour over trout after removing excess liquid from dish. Serve at once. *Serves 2.*

TROUT IN FOIL
Monica Morris

2 trout
Butter
1 small sliced shallot
1 sprig of rosemary, fennel or tarragon

Sliver of lemon peel
Salt and pepper
Cooking foil

Butter pieces of foil well and parcel up each trout together with shallots, herbs, seasoning and lemon peel. Close parcels completely. Cook on a baking sheet in a preheated oven Gas No. 2 (300°) for 30 minutes. *Serves 2.*

TROUT MEUNIÈRE

6 rainbow trout (2 extra for second helping!)
4 tablespoons flour — seasoned
Salt and pepper
1½ ozs. butter

TO FINISH:
1 oz. butter
Juice of ½ lemon
Salt and pepper
1 dessertspoon finely chopped parsley

Wash trout and check that they have been cleaned thoroughly, dry with absorbent paper. Cut off fins and trim the tail. If the fish are large, score them once or twice on either side and then roll in seasoned flour. Heat a **heavy** frying pan, drop in 1½ oz. butter, when foaming put in the fish and cook until golden brown on either side, turning once — about 12 minutes in all. Place the trout, without draining, on a hot dish and keep warm. Wipe out frying pan, add remaining butter and cook slowly until brown. Add the lemon juice with herbs and while still foaming pour over the trout. Serve immediately. (Do not use dried parsley — this spoils the flavour). *Serves 4.*

SOUSED TROUT
Mrs. Poster

6 freshwater trout
2 medium onions
2 bayleaves
12 peppercorns

1 cup brown vinegar
Salt and pepper
1 cup of water

Place half the onions on bottom of baking tin, then lay fish across. Cover with rest of onions, bayleaves and peppercorns, salt and pepper to taste. Cover with water and vinegar and cook in oven Gas No. 4 (350°) for ¾–1 hour. *Serves 6.*

STEAMED TURBOT WITH PARSLEY SAUCE
Judy Solomon

4 cutlets turbot approx. ¾ lb. each
1 dessertspoon cornflour
2 tablespoons finely chopped parsley
Butter

½ pint milk
½ pint fish stock
Salt

Wash cutlets and place in roomy aluminium fish kettle with a drainer. Just cover with water and add 1½ tablespoons salt. Bring to boil and simmer very gently, for about 20 minutes. As soon as knife goes through the fish near the bone without resistance, it is cooked. Let stand for five minutes to set then lift out on drainer. Keep fish stock.
Parsley Sauce: Mix cornflour with ½ pint cold milk. Put into pan with ½ pint of fish stock and a little butter, stir ingredients and bring to boil, add parsley and stir in quickly, remove from heat. *Serves 4.*

38

WHITING A LA COLBERT

A Good Housekeeper

1 whiting per person
A little milk

White pepper and salt
Flour

Anchovy sauce
Egg and breadcrumbs

Lemon and parsley
Maitre d'hotel butter

Fish should be skinned, cleaned and head removed. Make a slit down the back of fish, forming a pocket. Dip the fish in seasoned milk then flour. Next dip them in egg and breadcrumbs, pressing the breadcrumbs on firmly. Fry the fish in hot fat until golden brown. Slip a good pat of butter into each pocket of fish. Lay fish on plate and serve with slices of lemon around. Serve with anchovy sauce over if desired.

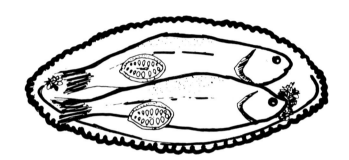

NOTES

Meat ~

Steaks which are to be grilled do **NOT** need to be soaked and salted. The grilling process draws out the blood from the meat and this is considered to satisfy the requirements of Kashrut.

Meat should be kashered by soaking in cold water for ½ an hour, rinsed thoroughly and placed on a wooden board with holes in it, lightly sprinkled with salt and drained for 1 hour, then rinsed thoroughly in cold water.

Add a tablespoon of vinegar to a tongue whilst cooking to facilitate easy skinning.

Rub roast beef with dry mustard before cooking, for added flavour.

An easy way to coat meat with seasoned flour, is to put all ingredients into a plastic bag and shake well. Keep remains of ingredients for thickening gravies and stews.

For richer gravy, crush a meat cube into the roasting tin and add ½ pint of water.

Make a variety of stews for freezing by braising meat in the usual manner, divide into required amounts, adding tomatoes, mushrooms and green peppers, or baked beans, peas and carrots, or artichokes, celery and green beans.

For juicy hamburgers add a 1/3 cup of apple sauce per pound to your usual recipe.

Beef ~

TO PICKLE BRISKET

Mrs. E. Silver

5 – 6 lbs. boned and trimmed fresh brisket
1 clove garlic (optional)
2 large handfuls of salt

1 bayleaf
2 teaspoons saltpetre
3 peppercorns

Stab the brisket with a large fork and place in a large saucepan with the saltpetre, salt and water to cover. Weigh down with a plate and leave for 4-5 days, turning the meat each day. Before cooking wash off the pickling liquid. Add the bayleaf and peppercorns to fresh water and cook for 2½-3 hours. Eat hot or cold. *Serves 10–12.*

HICKORY CURED SALT BEEF

Gloria Brown

5 lbs. pickled brisket
¼ lb. heavy marmalade
¼ lb. pineapple jam

Equal amounts of prepared
mild mustard and
Soft brown sugar

Cook salt beef in the usual way. Pat dry and place on a roasting tin. Mix together the mustard and sugar and spoon over the top of the beef. Melt the marmalade and the jam together in a saucepan and pour over the beef. Put in a moderate oven for 1 hour and keep basting. Keep in a warm place after removing from the oven. (Suitable for a buffet table). *Serves 10.*

BEEF CASSEROLE

Mrs. E. Silver

2 lbs. stewing steak
1 oz. margarine
2 tablespoons olive oil
14 oz. tin of tomatoes
1 tablespoon tomato purée
¼ lb. sliced mushrooms

Salt and pepper
A pinch of oregano or thyme
½ bayleaf
1 clove garlic
½ pint of water or stock

Cut the beef into cubes and sauté with the mushrooms in the oil and margarine until brown. Add the tomatoes, tomato purée, seasoning and spices. Put into a casserole and cook in a slow oven for 3 hours. *Serves 6.*

BEEF GOULASH

Gerda Dell-Steinberg

2 lbs. cubed stewing steak
Salt and black pepper
4 medium onions
Plain flour

Cold water
Large tin tomato purée
Bouquet garni

Season the flour and roll the meat in it. Heat the margarine in a large frying pan and brown the meat. Add the sliced onions and brown with the meat. Add cold water to cover and bring to the boil. Remove the meat and add enough flour to the pan juices and thicken to gravy consistency. Add the tin of tomato purée, bouquet garni, and salt and pepper to taste. Put everything into a casserole and cook for 2½ hours at Gas No. ½ (275°). If desired, add mushrooms. Serve on a bed of rice. *Serves 4–6.*

BRAISED BOLA PRINTANIES
Miriam Margolin

4 – 5 lbs. corner of bola
1 teaspoon salt
Few grinds black pepper
1 teaspoon paprika
1 teaspoon dry mustard
1 large onion
A handful of parsley
1 – 2 tablespoons oil

1 crushed clove of garlic
3 soft tomatoes
1 large carrot
2 stalks celery
1 turnip
1 bayleaf
A few peppercorns
1 tablespoon flour

Mix together the flour, mustard, paprika, salt and pepper, and roll the meat in it. Heat the oil in a heavy casserole and brown the meat thoroughly on all sides. Lift out, and in the same fat put in all the chopped vegetables. Stir them well into the fat until it is absorbed, then add the bayleaf, peppercorns and parsley. Sprinkle with salt and pepper and lay the meat back on top. Cover, bring to the boil, then transfer to a slow oven on Gas No. 1 (300°) for 2½-3 hours, or until the meat feels very tender when prodded. Pour off the gravy and remove any fat. Either serve the gravy as it is or sieve it and thicken with a teaspoon of cornflour. For easier carving leave the meat in a warmed oven for 15-20 minutes. *Serves 10–12.*

BRAISED STEAK AMERICAINE
Vivian Seymour

2 lbs. steak in ¾ inch slices
1 oz. flour
2 ozs. fat
1 sliced green pepper
2 diced stalks celery
2 sliced onions
10 oz. tin of tomatoes
1 tablespoon tomato purée
A pinch of paprika

1 cup beef stock
1 bouquet garni
1 teaspoon Worcestershire sauce
1 small tin mushrooms
Generous pinch oregano
Salt
Pepper
½ teaspoon sugar

Cut the meat into serving pieces, sprinkle with salt and pepper and dust with flour. Fry in fat to seal, and remove to a casserole. Sauté the onion, green pepper and celery and pour over the meat. Drain the tomatoes and mushrooms and add to the meat. Make a gravy by adding the Worcestershire sauce to the tomato liquor with the beef stock, paprika, oregano and salt and sugar to taste. Pour over the meat and cook covered for 2½ hours in a slow oven Gas No. ¼ (250°). Cook uncovered for the last ½ hour. *Serves 4–6.*

SWEET AND SOUR MEAT (ACIC FLEISH)
A Good Cook

1½ lbs. cubed chuck steak
2 tablespoons sugar
1 teaspoon white acid

½ Spanish onion
2 tablespoons lemon juice

Chop the onion, add the sugar and cook on a slow heat until brown but not burnt. Add the lemon juice, acid and meat. Barely cover with water and add a pinch of salt. Bring to the boil and then simmer with the lid tightly on for 2½-3 hours, until the gravy has been reduced by half. Adjust seasoning according to taste. Serve piping hot, in plenty of gravy with fresh rye bread or chola for dunking! *Serves 4–6.*

STUFFED CABBAGE
Valerie Green

10 – 12 large cabbage leaves
1 lb. minced beef
½ cup cooked rice
1 egg
1 teaspoon salt
⅛ teaspoon pepper
Wooden toothpicks

½ cup raisins
1 thinly sliced onion
Juice of 1 lemon
¼ cup brown sugar
2 cups tinned tomatoes
1 cup water

Use large whole outside leaves of cabbage. Place in boiling water for 5 minutes to soften. Combine the meat, rice, egg, salt, pepper and half the raisins. Put a generous amount on each leaf. Fold in the sides, roll up and fasten with a toothpick. Shred the heart of the cabbage. Line the bottom of a pot with the shredded cabbage, put the cabbage parcels close together on top. Add the remaining cabbage, onion, raisins, lemon juice, sugar, tomatoes and water, and simmer gently for 2½-3 hours. *Serves 6–8.*

PUFF PASTRY LOAF
Marian Goodman

1 packet frozen puff pastry
2 lbs. minced meat
1 chopped green pepper
2 chopped onions
2 eggs
½ cup Matzo meal

1 small tin pimentoes
Salt
Pepper
Worcestershire sauce
Beef cube

Fry the onions, peppers and pimentoes together. Mix all the other ingredients with the cooked vegetables. Form into a loaf shape, and cover in puff pastry. Bake in a tin on Gas No. 7 (425°) for 5 minutes, then reduce to Gas No. 3 (325°) for 1 hour. This can be eaten hot or cold and cut in slices. *Serves 6.*

SHEPHERDS PIE
Lesley Bennett

1 finely chopped Spanish onion
2 tablespoons olive oil
1 lb. cooked minced beef
½ pint rich beef gravy
2 teaspoons Worcestershire sauce
1 tablespoon chopped parsley

¼ teaspoon mixed herbs
Salt and black pepper
Margarine
1 lightly beaten egg
Mashed potatoes

Sauté the onion in olive oil until transparent and soft. Add the minced beef, gravy, Worcestershire sauce, parsley, mixed herbs, salt and pepper and keep warm. Add the beaten egg and margarine to the mashed potatoes. Place the meat in a deep well greased oven proof dish and cover with the mashed potato. Bake for 15-20 minutes on Gas No. 5 (400°) until golden brown. *Serves 6.*

BEEF IN PASTRY
Diana Marks

4 lbs. ball of the rib
1 lb. Spanish onions
½ lb. button mushrooms
2 packets puff pastry
Red wine

Margarine
1 egg
Salt
Black pepper
Garlic

Fry the finely chopped onions and mushrooms with seasoning. Strain the juice and allow to cool. Season the meat and add a little wine. Place in the oven on Gas No. 8 (450°) for 20 minutes. Remove the meat from the oven and strain the juices into the onion juice, and allow the meat to cool. Roll out the pastry quite thick, and put on a greased and floured baking tin. Put the mushroom mixture on the pastry and place the meat on top, cover with more of the mixture but reserve a little for the gravy. Wrap the pastry around the meat and press down the seams with a little water. Turn over so that the seam is underneath. Place in the oven Gas No. 3 (325°) for 15 minutes, then remove, brush lightly with egg and decorate with pastry flowers. Put back into the oven until golden brown, about another 10 minutes. Make a thick sauce from the pan juices and add the reserved mushroom mixture. This is good for a dinner party if individual ones are made, allowing ½ lb. of meat per person. *Serves 6.*

INDIVIDUAL MEAT PIES FOR FREEZING   A Freezer Owner

½ lb. diced braising meat
Sliced onion (optional)
Salt and pepper

Short or puff pastry
Mushrooms (optional)

Season the meat and braise with the vegetables. Leave to cool. Put into a foil dish and cover with the preferred pastry. Freeze until wanted. Defrost overnight in the refrigerator for use the following day. Bake for 35-40 minutes on Gas No. 7 (425°). If baking frozen, lower the oven temperature and cook 10 minutes longer. *Serves 1.*

SWEET SOUR MEAT BALLS   Gloria Brown

3 lbs. minced meat
Small tin of tomato juice or
Small tin vegetable juice

Medium tin sauerkraut
½ cup brown sugar
½ cup white sugar

Prepare the meat balls in the usual way — i.e. 2 eggs, salt and pepper, breadcrumbs and water. Mix all together and form into balls. Put in a saucepan with the tomato juice, sauerkraut, brown and white sugar, and boil together for 45 minutes. Serve with rice. *Serves 10.*

MEAT LOAF   Jenny Green

2 lbs. minced meat
1 packet onion soup
2 beaten eggs
¼ cup barbecue sauce

¼ cup warm water
1½ cups bread crumbs
4 hard boiled eggs

Mix all the ingredients except the hard boiled eggs, together. Place half the mixture in a loaf tin. Put the hard boiled eggs lengthways on the mixture and cover with the remainder of the meat mixture. Bake for 1 hour in oven on Gas No. 6 (400°). *Serves 6.*

STEAK PIE   Valerie Ross

1½ lbs. diced chuck steak
4 medium carrots
1 large onion
1 small tin peeled tomatoes
¼ lb. mushrooms
A little flour

Salt and pepper
Worcestershire sauce
1 beaten egg
1 pint stock or water
1 packet frozen puff pastry
A little margarine or fat

Wash the meat and dip in seasoned flour. Peel and dice all the vegetables except the tomatoes. Fry meat and vegetables in a little fat for a few minutes only, to seal in the juices. Strain the meat and vegetables and put in a deep casserole with a little more salt and pepper, a good sprinkling of worcestershire sauce and the peeled tomatoes. Cover this with stock or water, and cook in a slow oven on Gas No. 2 (300°) for 3 hours until tender. Remove from the oven and allow to cool. Strain of nearly all the liquid and put everything else into a pie dish. Keep the juices as this makes a delicious gravy. Roll out the pastry quite thinly. Make a collar to fit over the edge of the pie approximately 1 inch wide, leaving quite a large hole in the centre of the pie, then roll out the pastry again. Dampen the collar and place the pie top over this, making 2 layers all around the edge of the pie, but only one in the centre. Brush with beaten egg and decorate or crimp as required. Bake for 40 minutes on Gas No. 4 (350°). *Serves 4.*

OXTAIL CASSEROLE
Dianne Zimmerman

1 oxtail	Salt
2 ozs. flour	Pepper
1 large onion	Beef stock
Paprika	2 ozs. margarine

Chop the oxtail into portions and blanch. Melt the fat in a thick pan. Mix together the flour, paprika, pepper and salt and dip in the oxtail pieces. Slice the onion and soften in the fat, add the meat and seal all round. Add the stock to cover, and simmer for approximately 2 hours until very tender. Serve with rice. *Serves 4.*

OX TONGUE
Gillian Burr

1 pickled tongue	2 carrots
12 peppercorns	1 bayleaf
1 onion	1 lump of sugar

Wash the tongue thoroughly, put in a pan and cover with cold water. Bring slowly to the boil and remove scum. Add the peppercorns, onions, carrots, sugar and bayleaf and cook gently for 1¼-1½ hours. Turn over and cook for a further 1¼-1½ hours. Skin whilst still hot with a sharp knife. If serving cold put tongue in a round bowl and cover with a plate that fits into the bowl. Put a heavy weight on the top and refrigerate until set, and required. *Serves 8.*

TOURNEDOS STEAKS
Gillian Burr

4 steaks	2 ozs. margarine
4 pieces of toast	1 oz. flour
1 lb. mushrooms	Salt
½ pint madeira wine	Pepper

Grill the toast, fry the steaks lightly, then put the steaks on the toast and keep hot. Fry the mushrooms and put on top of the steaks. Add the flour to the margarine, stir in the madeira wine and bring to the boil. Simmer for 1 minute and season to taste. Serve the sauce over the steaks. *Serves 4.*

Lamb ~

LAMB CURRY
Gina Marks

2 lbs. middle neck of lamb
1 clove garlic
1 oz. margarine
1 tablespoon curry powder
1 tablespoon sweet pickle
½ pint stock or water
2 medium onions
1 tablespoon of flour

2 large skinned and chopped tomatoes
1 bayleaf
4 cloves
1 teaspoon cinnamon
1 teaspoon salt
1 oz. sultanas or seedless raisins
1 cooking apple (peeled and grated)

Cut the lamb into pieces removing fat. Slice onions and garlic and fry until golden brown, stir in all ingredients except stock and lamb. Blend in stock and add lamb slowly bringing mixture to boil. Lower heat, cover pan and simmer for 1¼-1¾ hours. Serve with ¾ lb. boiled rice, to which can be added salted peanuts, sliced cucumber and chutney. *Serves 4.*

HONEY GLAZED LAMB
Gillian Burr

1 shoulder of lamb
1 heaped tablespoon flour
½ teaspoon cinnamon
Rosemary (to taste)
1 large carrot
1 large onion
Salt and pepper

GLAZE:
1 heaped tablespoon thick honey
½ pint cider
GRAVY:
4 tablespoons stock or water
1 tablespoon cornflour
GARNISH:
1 medium tin apricot halves
4 tablespoons vinegar
1 teaspoon honey

Mix together the flour, salt, pepper, cinnamon and rosemary, and rub well into the meat on all sides. Skin the onion and carrot and cut into thick slices, lay this on the bottom of a roasting tin. Place the meat on top and roast on Gas No. 4 (350°) allowing 30 minutes per pound. Half an hour before serving, lift out the meat and strain off all the fat leaving the vegetables. Replace the meat, spread the honey over it and pour on the cider. Increase the oven heat to Gas No. 5 (375°) and continue cooking, basting once or twice. Dish up the meat, and if desired add the cornflour with the stock or water to the liquor in the pan and boil stirring carefully for a few minutes. Strain into a sauceboat. Serve with SWEET AND SOUR APRICOTS: Drain the syrup from a tin of apricots, put the vinegar and honey in a pan and boil for 2 minutes. Add the apricots and turn to glaze and heat. *Serves 6.*

LAMB IN PASTRY
Anne Moss

1 boned shoulder of lamb
2 ozs. chicken livers
2 ozs. margarine
2 ozs. mushrooms

Salt and pepper
2 tablespoons brandy
1 egg
1 packet puff pastry

Cut the liver finely and fry gently, add the sliced mushrooms and season. Fry until soft. Add the brandy and cook for about 3 minutes. Stuff the lamb with this mixture and sew up the hole at both ends. Place in a baking tray and cook in a hot oven on Gas No. 5 (375°) for about 1¼ hours. Remove, allow to cool and dry well. Roll out the pastry and wrap the meat in it, making a neat parcel. Decorate with pastry leaves. Make sure the meat is well enclosed. Bake on Gas No. 6 (400°) for about 10 minutes then paint with beaten egg and cook for a further 20 minutes or until the pastry is golden brown. Serve with a well flavoured tomato sauce. *Serves 8.*

47

STUFFED SHOULDER OF LAMB

Gillian Burr

1 small boned shoulder of lamb
Salt and pepper
1 oz. margarine
4 ozs. liver
1 finely chopped large onion
1 large handful stoned raisins
Majoram and parsley

3 ozs. boiled rice
Rosemary (to taste)
1 heaped teaspoon flour
1 teaspoon tomato purée
¼ pint stock or water
1 dessertspoon mixed thyme

Season the inside of the lamb well. Cut the liver into small squares. Melt the fat and sauté the liver briskly for a few minutes. Remove the liver and sauté the onion until soft but not brown. Replace the liver and add the herbs **except the rosemary** and shake together for half a minute. Turn into a bowl, mix with the rice and season. Cool a little then put the stuffing into the lamb and sew up securely. Put the joint into a roasting tin, pour over a little melted fat if desired, sprinkle with rosemary and cook in the oven on Gas No. 4 (350°) for 1½-2 hours or until tender. *Serves 5.*

LAMB SURPRISE

Vikki Kovler

2½ − 3 lbs. shoulder of lamb
1 teaspoon dry mustard
½ − 1 glass fresh orange juice

Black pepper
Salt
Rosemary

Sprinkle the lamb with seasoning and place in a casserole with a lid. Put in the centre of a moderate oven on Gas No. 4 (350°) for approximately 1 hour. Mix in a glass the orange juice, mustard and rosemary, and baste the lamb with this from time to time. (This sauce is also delicious with roast chicken). *Serves 5−6.*

LAMB IRISH STEW

Penny Marks

2 − 3 lbs. middle neck chops
1 cup barley
1 large onion
4 carrots
Flour
Salt
Mushrooms (optional)

1 pint chicken stock
1 large tin peeled tomatoes
1 dessertspoon tomato purée
Oil
Margarine
Pepper

Season and flour the meat. Fry the onions in a mixture of oil and margarine, add the meat and fry to seal. Add the barley and cover with the chicken stock. Put into a large saucepan and cook for approximately 1 hour, then add the carrots, tomatoes and tomato purée. Cook for a further hour. Add a little more water if necessary and mushrooms if desired. *Serves 4.*

RIBS IN BEER AND HONEY

Valerie Green

4 ribs or 2 chops per person
½ pint brown ale
¼ lb. clear honey or golden syrup
1 teaspoon tabasco

1 tablespoon mixed herbs
1 tablespoon lemon juice
1 dessertspoon salt
2 teaspoons dry mustard

Mix together all ingredients and leave the ribs to marinade for 2 hours or more. **FOR BARBECUE:** Thread the ribs on skewers and place over hot coals turning frequently **and** basting as often as you like. These can cook for as long as you like. FOR THE OVEN: Cook the ribs in the marinade for 1¼ hours on Gas No. 4 (350°). Put the heat up for the last 15 minutes to glaze the ribs. *Serves 8.*

STICKY CHOPS   Marian Gold

8 neck of lamb chops
¼ cup finely chopped onion
Lemon juice
Brown sugar

2 tablespoons Worcestershire sauce
2 tablespoons tomato ketchup
2 tablespoons vinegar
2 tablespoons soy sauce

Place the chops in a roasting tin, add all the ingredients and sprinkle with a little lemon juice and brown sugar. Bake in the oven on Gas No. 5 (375°) for 1½ hours. The chops must be turned and basted every 15-20 minutes so that the sauce sticks to the chops. If the juice becomes too greasy, pour some away. *Serves 4.*

STUFFED CROWN OF LAMB   A Well-wisher

1 large crown of lamb (allow 3 chops per person)
2 ozs. margarine
1 large onion
8 ozs. fresh breadcrumbs
2 oranges

2 eggs
1 dessertspoon finely chopped parsley
Salt
Black pepper
Bayleaves (optional)

Season the meat and add the bayleaves if desired. Sauté the finely chopped onions, and add to the breadcrumbs with the grated rind and juice of the oranges and all the other ingredients. Mix these to a smooth consistency and then stuff the crown. Roast for 1½ hours on Gas No. 4 (350°). Decorate the chops with paper hat frills and serve with redcurrant jelly and mint sauce. *Serves 6.*

Liver ~

FRIED LIVER WITH ONIONS   Susan Mandell

1 lb. finely sliced best calves liver
1 large Spanish onion
Flour
Gravy mix

Salt
Black pepper
Oil

Wash and dry the liver, season and cover finely in flour. Heat the oil and fry the onions until golden brown. Keep them hot in the oven on a separate plate. Fry the liver for about 6 minutes on each side. Make a thick gravy mix and pour over the liver, simmer for 2 minutes then add the onions and serve. This is delicious with mashed potato. *Serves 2.*

LIVER RISOTTO
Gillian Berman

1½ pints cooked rice
3 medium onions
1 clove crushed garlic
½ lb. mushrooms
3 tablespoons olive oil
¾ lb. calves liver

1 diced pepper
1 large tin tomatoes
2 tins sliced red pimentoes
1 tablespoon chopped mixed herbs
Salt
Pepper

Slice the onions, add the garlic and fry until golden brown in the olive oil. Put on a low heat and add the mushrooms and pepper. Cook for 15 minutes. Add all the remaining ingredients except the liver and adjust the seasoning. Turn this mixture into a fireproof dish and keep warm. Cut the liver into cubes and coat lightly in seasoned flour, fry gently until tender and add to the rice. Serve straight away. *Serves 4–6.*

Veal ~

HUNGARIAN VEAL GOULASH (STEW)
Mrs. A. Balint

2 lbs. stewing veal
3 ozs. dripping
1 large onion very finely chopped
1 green pepper

1 tablespoon tomato purée
1 teaspoon sweet red pepper
Salt

Fry onion until light yellow in hot fat, cut the meat into cubes, add cooked onion, the sweet red pepper and salt, fry in fat for a few minutes. Add tomato purée and stew slowly in covered casserole on top of cooker for approximately 45 minutes or until tender. No extra water is necessary as the meat makes its own juices, but if it does become a little dry add a few teaspoons of water. Serve with boiled new potatoes or boiled rice. *Serves 4–6.*

SICILIAN CASSEROLE OF VEAL
Bobby Collins

1½ lbs. stewing veal
3 dessertspoons oil
1 aubergine
4 fluid ozs. white or rosé wine
14 oz. tin of tomatoes
Lemon juice

1 large green pepper
½ lb. sliced onions
4 ozs. mushrooms
1 - 2 cloves crushed garlic
Salt
Black pepper

Heat the oil and fry the onions until transparent. Add the meat and continue frying until it is nicely coloured. Deseed and slice the pepper and add to the casserole. Slice the unpeeled aubergine, halving the slices if too large, add with the whole mushrooms. Cook lightly, pour in the wine and simmer for 2-3 minutes. Add the herbs, garlic and tomatoes and season to taste with salt and black pepper, and a little lemon juice. Cover and cook gently over a low heat or in a slow oven on Gas No. 3 (325°) for about 2 hours or until the meat is tender. Adjust the seasoning and stir well before serving with fluffy boiled rice or potatoes. *Serves 4.*

VEAL MARSALA
Yaffa Wagner

Veal escalopes
Flour
Salt and pepper
Boiling water

Chicken stock cubes
Marsala wine
Corn oil

Dip each escalope into seasoned flour. Fry in shallow oil till brown on both sides. Make a strong stock with the stock cubes and water. Add 1 tablespoon of Marsala to 2 tablespoons of stock for each escalope and allow to cook in this for 1 minute. If there is not enough gravy make more with the wine and stock. Cook in the oven at Gas No. 4 (350°) for 10-15 minutes.

ESCALOPES À L'ORANGE
Rosalyn Nathan

5 escalopes
2 ozs. margarine
1 dessertspoon flour
2 oranges
Chopped parsley

1 tablespoon brandy
¼ pint stock
Salt
Pepper

Sauté the escalopes in margarine until nicely brown. Take them out and draw the pan aside. Stir in the flour, grate the rind of 1 orange into the pan and add the strained juice, brandy and stock. Bring to the boil and season well. Replace the escalopes, cover and simmer for 10 minutes. In the meantime, slice the peel and pith from the second orange, cut the flesh into rounds, one for each escalope. Warm these between two plates. Put the escalopes on to a serving plate, put a slice of orange on top of each escalope, spoon over the sauce and sprinkle with parsley. *Serves 5.*

WIENER SCHNITZEL
Charlotte Davis

1 escalope per person
1 – 2 eggs
Corn oil

Golden breadcrumbs
Salt
Pepper

Wash and dry the escalopes well. Season the beaten eggs with salt and pepper. Dip the escalopes first in the beaten egg and then in the breadcrumbs, and fry in hot oil until golden brown on both sides. Serve immediately.

FILLET OF VEAL
Barbara Green

2 lbs. fillet of veal
1 carrot
1 onion
½ stick celery
2 egg yolks
Salt and pepper
1 glass oil

3 ozs. tinned tuna fish
3 anchovies
1½ ozs. capers
Lemon juice from 2 small lemons
Small gherkins
Twisted lemon peel
Capers

Put the veal in cold water with the carrot, onion, celery and salt. Bring to the boil and simmer until tender, approximately 1½-2 hours. Let it get cold, then cut into thin regular slices. Finely chop the tuna fish, anchovies and 1½ oz. of capers then pound or liquidize until it is a paste. Make a mayonnaise with the egg yolks, oil, salt, pepper and lemon juice, and when completed add the paste. Cover the veal with this thick sauce. Garnish with the lemon peel, capers and gherkins, which have been sliced lengthways almost to the end, then spread out like a fan. (Do not serve vegetables or a salad with this dish. In Italy only plain meat is served with salad, but never meat which has a sauce over it). *Serves 4–6.*

VEAL LOAF

Vikki Kovler

8 ozs. pastry (shortcrust or puff),
or 1 packet frozen pastry
1 lb. minced veal
1 small chopped onion
1 egg (optional for binding)

Sprinkling of rosemary, parsley
1 bayleaf (optional)
1 sliced tomato
Salt
Pepper
Paprika

Mix together meat, onion, seasoning and herbs. Roll out cold pastry, place meat mixture in the centre of pastry, garnish with sliced tomato, fold pastry over, dampening edges before sealing. Brush over pastry with mixture of egg and water and sprinkle with paprika. Place in greased open baking dish and cook in oven on Gas No. 1-2 (300⁰) for ¾-1 hour or until golden brown. *Serves 4–6.*

VEAL PINEAPPLE ROLL

Gillian Burr

4 lbs boned and rolled breast or shoulder of veal
2 tablespoons chopped parsley
3 tablespoons chopped mushrooms
3 tablespoons chopped celery
1 teaspoon salt

¼ pint drained crushed pineapple
½ lb. dry breadcrumbs
½ teaspoon mixed herbs
2 ozs. margarine

Unroll the veal and sprinkle with salt. Cook the celery and mushrooms with the parsley in margarine for 10 minutes, stirring often. Mix in the pineapple, breadcrumbs and herbs. Spread the stuffing on the veal, roll up and tie or skewer securely. Spread with a little margarine. Place on a baking tray and pour on the pineapple syrup. Brown in a hot oven on Gas No. 8 (450⁰) for 15 minutes and reduce heat to Gas No. 4 (350⁰) and cook for 2 hours basting frequently. *Serves 6.*

ROAST VEAL

Dianne Zimmerman

1 breast of veal
Salt
Pepper

STUFFING:
½ lb. sausage meat
½ Spanish onion
2 tablespoons margarine
1 tablespoon chopped parsley
1 beaten egg
½ lb. chopped spinach
Margarine and oil

Wash and dry the veal and season with salt and pepper. Sauté the chopped onion in margarine, then mix with the sautéed spinach, parsley, beaten egg, salt and pepper. Put the stuffing in the veal and sew up. Dust the meat with the flour and cook in a roasting tin with a mixture of margarine and oil. Cook on Gas No. 2 (300⁰) for 1½-2 hours basting frequently. *Serves 4.*

SWEETBREADS

Lily Cappin

2 lbs sweetbreads
1 large Spanish onion
6 quartered tomatoes
½ lb. sliced mushrooms
Flour

Salt
Pepper
A pinch of sugar (optional)
Margarine or chicken fat
Gravy browning

Scald the sweetbreads with boiling water, then remove all the skin and veins. Fry the onion in margarine or chicken fat until transparent. Season to taste and add sugar if desired. Add the tomatoes and mushrooms and cook for a few minutes. Transfer the mixture to a casserole and put to one side. Season the sweetbreads and dry in a little more fat until slightly brown, and add these to the casserole. In the same pan make some gravy with a little flour, seasoning and gravy browning and pour over the sweetbreads. Cook in a slow oven on Gas No.1-2 (300°) for approximately 2 hours. If the gravy gets too thick add a little more water. 15 minutes before completion add a few frozen peas for colour. *Serves 4—5.*

NOTES

NOTES

NOTES

Poultry ~

Rub poultry with ½ a lemon before scalding to remove the odour.

Always season the cavity of a bird as well as the skin.

If freezing left over stuffed poultry, always remove the stuffing immediately after the meal. Freeze it separately to avoid food poisoning.

Prevent splitting when roasting poultry by putting a tablespoon of water in the bottom of the tin.

Ideas for left over poultry:

Chicken and Mushroom Pie

Chicken Risotto

Chicken Curry

Chicken Vol au Vent

Chicken Croquettes

Chicken Salad

To clean a chicken more easily use a pair of tweezers.

To render chicken fat without burning, put it in the oven in a covered dish.

Place an apple or a stick of celery in the cavity of a duck or goose before roasting. This will remove excess fat. Prick skin frequently.

Garnish cold turkey with thick slices of cranberry jelly cut into decorative shapes.

Chicken

BARBECUED CHICKEN
Stephanie Carson

1 tin tomato juice
1¼ teaspoons cayenne pepper
2 teaspoons mustard powder
1 teaspoon caster sugar
1 bay leaf
1 tablespoon Worcestershire sauce

¾ pint cider vinegar
2 – 3 cloves chopped garlic
1½ ozs. salad oil or margarine
2 – 3 lbs. quartered chicken
3 medium sized, thinly sliced onions
Salt and pepper

Combine first 9 ingredients in saucepan. Stir and simmer for 10 minutes. Chill. Preheat oven Gas No. 7 (425°). Arrange skinned chicken pieces in a single layer, tuck onion rings under wings and legs. Pour sauce over, and cook 30 minutes either side, basting from time to time. *Serves 8.*

CASSEROLED CHICKEN (1)
B. B. Green

3 lb. chicken
4 tablespoons cooking oil
3 diced tomatoes
7 cloves garlic
½ cup brandy
2½ cups dry white wine
1 teaspoon salt

4 bay leaves
½ bunch celery with leaves
¼ teaspoon ginger
12 green olives
5 peppercorns
2 oranges

Cut chicken into small pieces, brown well in oil, add diced tomatoes and 2 cloves garlic. Cook on low heat for 20 minutes. Add brandy, wine, salt, bay leaves, celery, ginger, olives, peppercorns and rest of garlic. Cook for another 20 – 30 minutes until chicken is tender. Slice the oranges with the peel, place round the chicken and heat for a few more minutes. *Serves 3 – 4.*

CASSEROLED CHICKEN (2)
Sandra Hirsh

6 chicken breasts
¼ lb. olives
2 ozs. capers
1 large Spanish onion
½ lb. mushrooms

2 – 3 cloves garlic
1 small bottle white wine
1 small tin tomato purée
½ pint stock
Salt and pepper

Fry floured chicken breast lightly in fat until golden. Sauté onions and mushrooms in separate pan, add olives, capers, garlic seasoning, stock and purée, lastly put in wine and bring to boil. Transfer chicken to casserole dish, cover with sauce and put in the oven for approximately 1 hour. (This dish is better prepared the previous day and reheated). *Serves 6.*

CURRIED CHICKEN
Wendy Sheinman

1 roasting chicken
Salt
Curry powder
6 small potatoes
Vegetable oil

SAUCE:
1 oz. margarine
¾ teaspoon black pepper
2½ teaspoons curry powder
1 dessertspoon mixed herbs
½ teaspoon white pepper
¼ teaspoon onion powder
½ teaspoon garlic salt
1 medium sliced onion
4 medium cut tomatoes
1½ teaspoons salt
Dash tabasco
2 tablespoons cold water

Dissect the chicken into suitable portions, season and coat with curry powder and fry in oil until beautifully brown but not cooked through. Meantime place all the sauce ingredients in a small pan and let it simmer for about 20 minutes. Place the browned chicken in an oven to table casserole, cover with water and allow to boil quickly to reduce the liquid to half, then add the small potatoes and the sauce and allow to cook slowly for about 1 hour, or until the chicken is really tender. Serve with rice. *Serves 4–6.*

FAZZI CHICKEN CASSEROLE
Marian Cohen

4½ lb. chicken
5 cups vertically sliced strong onions
1 tablespoon grated lemon rind
4 slices lemon
15 black olives
½ teaspoon cinnamon
¼ teaspoon clove or allspice
¼ teaspoon ginger

¼ teaspoon hot paprika
½ teaspoon coarse black pepper
3 pinches saffron shreds
12 crushed coriander seeds
1/3 cup olive oil
2 ozs. margarine
3 tablespoons honey
2 large tomatoes (optional)

Place all the ingredients, except the chicken and honey in a large flame-proof casserole. Cover tightly and put over a low heat until the onions soften and become translucent. Snuggle the chicken down into the onions, add ¼ cup of water and cover. Turn the chicken regularly, stirring the onions and if necessary adding more water, but do not let it become too soupy. When the chicken is very tender add the honey. Two large seeded skinned and quartered tomatoes heated in margarine may be added at the same time if desired. Serve with PITA (Arab bread), if not available French or Italian bread is better with this dish than rice or potatoes. (If you wish to be really authentic, serve in a wide low bowl without carving the bird and eat with fingers of the right hand only). *Serves 4–5.*

ITALIAN CHICKEN CASSEROLE
Lorice Lazarus

3 x 3½ lb. chicken jointed
2 ozs. oil
8 button onions or
1 medium chopped onion
½ lb. button mushrooms

4 tablespoons chicken stock
1 clove garlic crushed
Flour seasoned with garlic
1 glass sherry
Salt and pepper

Melt oil in thick pan or casserole. Dip the chicken joints in seasoned flour and sauté to golden brown. Remove chicken to one side, add onions, mushrooms and garlic and sauté gently. Then add tomato purée, stock and sherry. Replace chicken pieces, cover, and simmer gently until chicken is tender. About 2 hours. *Serves 4.*

CHICKEN AND ALMONDS
Gina Marks

4 lb. boned chicken in sections
2 medium Spanish onions
2 lbs. potatoes
1 pint chicken stock

3 tablespoons sherry
Flour
Flaked or whole roasted almonds
Yolk of egg, hard boiled

Fry sliced onions in oil, put aside. Sauté potatoes in same oil. Dip the chicken in flour and fry until golden brown. Pour away most of excess oil. Place chicken in bottom of pan skin side up, cover with onions and potatoes. Sprinkle roasted almonds over, reserving a few per portion for decoration. Add stock to cover chicken, bring to the boil and simmer for 10 minutes, add sherry and bring to boil again. Cook covered, until chicken is tender for approximately ¾ hour. To garnish, rub egg yolk through sieve, and sprinkle egg and almonds over each portion. *Serves 6.*

ROAST CHICKEN WITH APRICOT STUFFING AND RICE
Faith Duke

4½ lb. roasting chicken
6 ozs. margarine
STUFFING:
8 ozs. dried apricots
2 ozs. margarine
4 ozs. fresh white breadcrumbs
Salt, pepper and nutmeg

RICE:
12 ozs. long grain rice
2 ozs. sultanas
4 ozs. flaked almonds

Mince unsoaked apricots. Melt margarine in frying pan. Stir in breadcrumbs and apricots. Season to taste with salt, pepper and nutmeg. Stuff chicken and truss. Brush chicken with melted margarine, season with salt and pepper. Roast in oven on Gas No. 5 (375°) for 20 minutes per pound plus 20 minutes over. Cook 1/3 of the time on each side and last 1/3 breast uppermost. Baste once during cooking. Remove from pan, remove trussing and keep warm. Stir flaked almonds and sultanas in the roasting tin retaining juices from roasted chicken. Fold into freshly cooked rice. Season to taste. Arrange almond rice mixture on a hot platter and place chicken in centre. *Serves 4.*

CHICKEN WITH CHERRIES
Gillian Burr

3 x 2 lb. quartered chickens
2 cups black pitted cherries
3 ozs. margarine
1 tablespoon flour
1 teaspoon sugar
½ teaspoon allspice
½ teaspoon cinnamon
½ teaspoon powder mustard

8 ozs. drained crushed pineapple
2 – 3 tablespoons rum
1 chicken stock cube
1 teaspoon red vegetable colouring
1 teaspoon salt
1½ lbs. cooked rice
Paprika

Season chicken with paprika and salt and sauté until brown in deep saucepan. Remove chicken and blend flour, sugar and spices in fat remaining in saucepan, drain cherries and reserve. Add liquor to saucepan and return chicken. Add pineapple, rum, chicken cube and food colouring. Cover and simmer for 30 – 45 minutes until soft. Add cherries and simmer for a further 10 minutes. Serve on a bed of rice. *Serves 12.*

CRISPY ROAST CHICKEN

Faith Duke

1 large roasting chicken
1 large Spanish onion
1 chicken stock cube

Salt and pepper
½ pint of water

Heat oven at Gas No. 9 (475°). Put the chicken in a roasting tin. Slice the onion and put ½ inside the bird and ½ around it. Dissolve the stock cube in the water and pour around the chicken. Season with salt and pepper. Roast chicken breast up for 15 minutes. Turn onto breast and baste and continue cooking for 15 minutes. Baste and lower heat to Gas No. 7 (425°). Roast for a further 35 minutes. Baste again and turn breast side up cooking for 25 minutes more. (This will be lovely and crispy all over and very juicy). *Serves 6.*

GRILLED CHICKEN

Ruth Hilton

2 small chickens
½ head garlic
Salt and pepper
Chicken cube

Olive oil
Lemon juice
1 teaspoon gravy powder

Cut chickens into serving portions. Pound garlic cloves and rub some of it into the pieces of chicken. Sprinkle on olive oil and lemon juice and allow to marinate for 1 hour. Make grill hot and cook chicken on both sides. When cooked pour off excess fat and make a gravy by mixing together the gravy powder, rest of garlic and lemon juice, water and chicken cube. Cooking time approximately 20 – 30 minutes. *Serves 4.*

CHICKEN WITH HONEY

Audrey Stone

1 roasting chicken
1 tablespoon honey
¼ lb. margarine

Salt and pepper
¼ lb. sliced almonds

Prepare the chicken and put into a roasting tin with honey and margarine. Season to taste. Place in warmed oven at Gas No. 6 (400°) for 1½ hours, until sauce is dark brown. Garnish with sliced almonds. *Serves 4.*

LEMON FLAVOURED CHICKEN

Barbara Froomberg

5 lb. roasting chicken
6 ozs. margarine
2 tablespoons lemon juice
2 tablespoons sherry

1 teaspoon Worcestershire sauce
1 clove whole garlic
½ teaspoon salt

Put chicken in roasting tin. Boil the remaining ingredients together, and pour over chicken, breast side down. Keep basting and turn breast side up for last ½ hour of cooking. Cook in oven on Gas No. 5 (375°) for approximately 2 hours. *Serves 6.*

OVEN FRIED CHICKEN
Dianne Zimmerman

3 lb. roasting chicken
2 ozs. flour
Salt and black pepper
1 tablespoon chopped parsley
1 teaspoon tarragon
4 tablespoons margarine

1 teaspoon rosemary
Grated rind 1 lemon
1 beaten egg
2 tablespoons water
4 tablespoons olive oil

Cut chicken into serving pieces. Mix together flour, salt, pepper, chopped parsley, tarragon, rosemary and lemon rind. In another bowl, mix together beaten egg and water. Dip chicken pieces into egg and then into flour mixture, chill well. Put oil and margarine in baking tin and heat in oven. When sizzling add chicken pieces and spoon fat over. Cook for 45 – 50 minutes until chicken is tender and brown in oven Gas No. 5 (375°). Turn once or twice during cooking. *Serves 4.*

BAKED CHICKEN WITH PEACHES
Angela Howard

4 ozs. margarine
½ level teaspoon salt
Freshly milled pepper
4 chicken joints

3 teaspoons crushed cornflakes
1 x 16 oz. tin peach halves
Rosemary or thyme

Melt margarine in large saucepan and add salt and a little pepper. Dip each chicken joint in the melted margarine, then in crushed cornflakes and press coating on firmly. Place joints in shallow roasting tin, skin sides up and not touching each other. Pour over any remaining margarine and bake until tender in oven Gas No. 6 (400°). To test whether it is tender enough, push point of sharp knife into thickest part of joint. Juices which come out should be clear and not tinged pink. During baking baste, do not turn joints. If browning too fast, cover with greased paper. Approximately 15 minutes before end of baking time put chicken to one side of tin, add peach halves. Spoon over a little juice from can and return to oven. Just before serving sprinkle peaches with pinch of crushed rosemary or thyme. *Serves 4.*

CHICKEN WITH PINEAPPLE AND ALMONDS
Faith Duke

4 lb. roasting chicken
1 x 8 oz. tine pineapple slices
Salt and pepper

Whole roasted almonds
Watercress
½ lemon

Rub the chicken with lemon, season with salt and pepper and roast in oven Gas No. 3 (325°). Half an hour before the bird is done pour over the juice from the tinned pineapple and baste frequently. Keep the chicken hot on a serving dish, heat pineapple slices in roasting tin while reducing gravy. Surround chicken with pineapple rings, pour gravy over, scatter with almonds and garnish with watercress. *Serves 6.*

ROAST CHICKEN

Charlotte Davis

1 large chicken
12 fl. ozs. corn oil
6 fl. oz. water

Salt
Ground black pepper
1 lb. onions

Pre-heat oven. Prepare chicken and place the water in a roasting tin and cover with oil breast downwards. Salt and pepper (always do this as it allows the juices to run out and makes the breast more tender). Cook in oven on Gas No. 7 (425°) for 20 minutes. Turn the bird over, season again and tuck the onions under the wings and legs. Turn down oven to Gas No. 6 (400°), turn the bird every half hour, finish breast side up. Tip away most of the fat. Cook for 2 – 2½ hours. *Serves 6.*

CHICKEN BAKED IN SALT

Anonymous

3 – 4 lb. chicken
4 lbs. coarse sea salt
Olive oil

STUFFING:
½ lb. chicken livers
1 clove garlic
¼ lb. breadcrumbs
2 eggs
Salt and pepper

Black pepper
Salt
Greaseproof paper
Chicken Stock:
4 tablespoons chopped parsley
½ teaspoon tarragon
Pinch mixed spice
Margarine

For the stuffing:– put livers and garlic through the mincer, moisten the breadcrumbs with a little stock. Mix all the stuffing ingredients together except the eggs, adding more stock to make fairly loose mixture. Simmer in a little margarine until it is partially cooked, remove from heat and beat in eggs. Stuff this into the chicken by loosening the skin from around the breast and inserting as much stuffing as possible, put remainder in cavity.

To bake chicken:– Spread sea salt 1 inch thick on bottom of casserole, rub chicken with oil and season generously. Wrap chicken lightly in greaseproof paper and place on bed of salt. Pour sea salt round chicken to completely cover bird. Place lid on and put in preheated oven on Gas No. 5 (375°) for 1½ hours.

To serve: – Remove casserole cover, break salt crust, lift chicken out and remove paper. Place on serving plate. *Serves 4 – 5.*

BABY CHICKEN WITH SHALLOTS AND MUSHROOMS

Susan Mandell

3 baby chickens
1½ lbs. baby shallots
1 clove garlic

Salt and black pepper
Paprika
Rosemary

Cut chicken into halves and place on large baking dish with onions and about ½ pint water. Season chickens well and put knob of margarine or chicken fat on top of each portion. Roast in oven on Gas No. 3 (325°) for 2 hours basting constantly. (A little honey and orange juice gives nice added flavour). Serve and garnish with watercress. *Serves 6.*

63

LEFT-OVER BOILED CHICKEN

Mrs. E. Silver

1½ pints chicken soup
Juice of lemon
4 eggs

Left-over diced chicken
Cooked rice

Add to chicken soup the juice of lemon (or more according to taste). Beat the eggs and gradually add them to the soup. Put into double saucepan and stir over low heat until thick. Do not boil. Put cooked rice and chicken into ring mould, pour sauce over, plate and serve. *Serves 4.*

LEFT-OVER COLD CHICKEN RISOTTO Dianne Zimmerman

2 cups cold cooked rice
1 small chopped green pepper
Vinaigrette dressing

3 chopped tomatoes
Diced chicken or fowl
½ small chopped cucumber

Mix all ingredients together with vinaigrette dressing. *Serves 4.*

ROAST DUCK WITH APPLES IN CALVADOS Barbara Davison

1 roasting duck
1 eating apple per serving

Several tablespoons Calvados

In a separate ovenproof dish or plate, place 1 washed eating apple (red looks nicer) per serving. Slit skin around the centre of apple and core. Sprinkle the calvados over the apple so that some runs inside then cook in the oven at the same time as the duck. As an optional addition the duck may be flavoured with calvados before serving. Each serving of duck should be accompanied by an apple which may be eaten, skin and all. *Serves 4.*

DUCK WITH APRICOTS

Paula Goldring

4 lb. duckling
¾ lb. apricots, fresh or tinned
½ teaspoon rosemary
½ teaspoon fennel seeds

½ pint apricot wine
1 tablespoon cornflour
1 liqueur glass apricot brandy

Stone the apricots, add rosemary and fennel and stuff the prepared duck. Cook for 1½ hours on Gas No. 4 (350°). Take bird from oven and remove apricots and rub through sieve. Quarter the duck and place in casserole. Mix wine with cornflour, add to apricot purée and bring to boil for 1 minute. Pour over duck. Cover and cook for 30 minutes more or until tender. Just before serving pour over apricot brandy. (You can substitute medium white wine with 1 tablespoon apricot brandy instead of apricot wine). *Serves 4.*

DUCK WITH CITRUS AND LIQUEUR
Letitia Leigh

1 duckling	Juice of orange
2 ozs. corn oil or	Juice of ½ lemon
2 ozs. margarine	Orange and lemon peel
Seasoned flour	Salt and pepper
2 tablespoons wine vinegar	1 teaspoon orange curaçao
2 lumps of sugar	1 teaspoon brandy

Roll duckling in seasoned flour and brown all over in frying pan in hot oil or margarine. Put in casserole and pour over liquid from pan. Cover and cook for 1½ − 2 hours. When cooked put vinegar and sugar in small saucepan until sugar is melted. Add juices from casserole to pan. Put duck on dish and keep warm. Add the orange and lemon juice to the other juices and cook briskly until syrupy. Toss in strips of orange and lemon peel. Season to taste and add curaçao and brandy. Pour over duck with strips of peel spread over the top. Garnish with watercress. Gas No. 3 (325°). Cooking time 2 − 2¼ hours.

To make orange and lemon peel: Take sharp knife and cut 4 sections from orange and lemon taking the peel off the fruit with as little pith on as possible, remove with the knife any remaining pith. Then slice peel into fine strips. Put in pan and cover in cold water. Bring to boil and drain off. Repeat 2 − 3 times more to remove all bitterness. Then add to sauce. *Serves 4 − 5.*

BRAISED DUCK WITH ORANGE AND CHERRY SAUCE
Dianne Zimmerman

1 duck trussed with giblets	¼ pint white wine
Rind of 1 orange	1 pint water
1½ ozs. fat	Salt and pepper
1 medium onion sliced	12 maraschino cherries
2 carrots	Juice of 1 orange
1 clove garlic	1 tablespoon maraschino syrup
2 ozs. mushroom stalks	Watercress
Thyme	Orange and cherries
Mace blade	

Put rind in prepared duck. Melt fat, fry duck quickly to brown, put in casserole. Fry onion until brown, add carrots and mushroom stalks and garlic. Add thyme, mace, water and wine. Season and bring lightly to boil. Pour round duck in roasting tin and cook for 2½ hours in oven on Gas No. 2 (300°). Lift out duck, giblets, mace and thyme and put sauce through sieve or vegetable mill. Put back into pan and boil. Skim off fat and add the orange juice and maraschino syrup, boil rapidly without lid allowing liquid to become more concentrated and reducing the liquid to approximately ¾ pint. Add cherries and check seasoning, replace duck and heat gently for ½ hour. Serve on a heated plate with sauce poured over, garnish with sliced oranges and cherries and watercress. (This may be cooked in advance). *Serves 4.*

DUCK IN ORANGE
Maxine Davis

5 lb. duck	SAUCE:
1 large onion	2 oranges
1 clove garlic	1 lemon
Honey	1 tablespoon brandy
Salt and pepper	1 teaspoon arrowroot
	¼ pint chicken stock

Set oven on Gas No. 7 (425°). Roast duck for ¾ hour with a little water pricking skin frequently to reduce fat. Pour off all the fat. Rub duck with honey and season with salt and pepper. Slice onion and crush garlic and add to duck with a little more water. Roast for further 1¾ hours. **Sauce:—** Squeeze oranges and lemon and place with brandy and chicken stock in saucepan. Bring to boil and thicken with arrowroot mixed with a little cold water. Cut duck into quarters and pour over sauce. *Serves 4.*

DUCK WITH PINEAPPLE, GINGER AND CHINESE RICE   Ghita Tarn

3 lb. duck
1 small tin of pineapple
6 pieces of tinned ginger
1 teaspoon salt
Pepper
SAUCE:
1½ teaspoons cornflour
1 cup tinned pineapple juice
½ cup tinned ginger juice

CHINESE RICE:
1 cup patna rice
¼ cup raisins
2 cups stock
1 small grated onion
¼ cup cashew nuts
Salt and pepper
¼ teaspoon cinnamon

Rub salt and pepper into the duck and roast as usual. Allow to cool then cut into large slices and arrange in the centre of a big dish. Cut the pineapple and ginger into slices and arrange them alternately around the duck. **Sauce:** Heat the juices in a frying pan, add the cornflour, mixed with a little cold water, to thicken the juices. Pour the sauce on top of the duck before serving. Serve with **Chinese Rice** made as follows:— Brown the onion in oil or fat, add the rice and brown for 10 minutes stirring constantly. Remove from the heat and add the seasoning, chopped nuts, raisins and stock. Place in a fire-proof glass dish and bake for 35 minutes on Gas No. 6 (400°). *Serves 4.*

ROAST GOOSE   Ilse Edwards

1 goose
Salt

Boiling water

After cleaning and washing well, salt the goose inside only. Prick the outside all over with a fork. Put the goose in an oven dish, breast down, and pour over approximately 2 pints of boiling water. It should be 1½ inches high in the pan. Put in a hot oven on Gas No. 7 (425°) for 1 hour. Discard all the water and add the same quantity of fresh boiling water. Return to the oven for a further ½ hour. Turn over and cook for another 2 hours and 40 minutes. Throw away half the liquid and pour a glass of cold water over the bird. Leave for a further 20 minutes until crisp. *Serves 6 – 8.*

TURKEY SOUTH AFRICAN STYLE   Ghita Tarn

12 – 14 lbs. turkey
2 cups tomato juice
1 cup sherry
1 dessertspoon paprika
6 cups water.

2 dessertspoons salt
½ teaspoon pepper
2 carrots cut lengthways
4 stalks celery

Place the turkey in a large roasting tin. Stuff with the carrots and celery. Mix all the other ingredients together and pour over the turkey. Cook on Gas No. 5 (375°) for 3 hours. Baste the turkey every ½ hour. The skin will be crisp, and the meat moist, exactly as a delicious turkey should be. *Serves 12.*

CRISPY ROAST TURKEY

Gillian Burr

16 lb turkey
Salt and pepper
2 onions
2 bay leaves

Lemon juice
Margarine
2 carrots
2 sorts stuffing

Thoroughly clean and dry turkey. Salt and pepper inside and stuff with sausage-meat stuffing at one end and chestnut at the other. Sew meat in order that stuffing cannot fall out. Season with salt, pepper and a little lemon juice, and cover with bay leaves, sliced onion and carrots. Put dots of margarine on top, carefully putting some on legs to stop them burning. Wrap whole turkey in silver foil. Place in large roasting tin with ¼ pint water on bottom to make a good gravy. Cook in oven on Gas No. 6 (400°) for 3½ hours, turning turkey after 2 hours, then remove silver foil except on legs, which are liable to burn if left uncovered. Baste frequently for last hour, lowering oven to Gas No. 5 (375°). Pour off most of juices to make gravy. *Serves 20.*

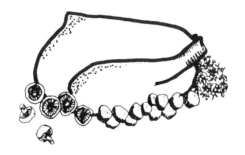

NOTES

Vegetables ~

To bring out the flavour of any vegetable add a lump of sugar whilst cooking.

Prevent jacket potatoes from bursting by slitting the skin before baking.

When coating vegetables in flour for deep frying i.e. onion rings or fried courgettes, put flour into a plastic bag and shake well to coat evenly.

Sautéed onions will brown quicker if sprinkled with a little sugar.

Remember that all vegetables growing underground should be cooked with the lid on, and those growing above with the lid off.

No tears! When peeling onions chill well before mincing or slicing.

Save the liquid from cooked or canned vegetables and use for making sauce or soup. It can also be frozen for a later use.

To avoid breaking the tips of tinned asparagus open the tin from the bottom.

Make a change! Use fennel as you would cauliflower. Serve with butter or a well seasoned cream sauce.

When cooking green vegetables add a pinch of bicarbonate of soda to maintain a good colour.

AUBERGINES AU GRATIN

Anne Moss

2 aubergines
1 small tin pimento – sweet red pepper
1 tablespoon tomato sauce
¾ oz. flour

¾ oz. butter
½ pint milk
2 ozs. grated Parmesan cheese
Salt and pepper

Peel aubergines and cut them into strips about 2 – 3 inches long and ½ inch thick and sprinkle with salt. Leave for about ½ hour then wash in cold water, drain and dry well. Heat oil in frying pan and fry aubergine until golden brown. Transfer into fireproof dish. Cover with red peppers cut into strips and then tomato sauce. Make a Béchamel sauce by melting the butter then adding the flour. Carefully mix in milk and cook gently until sauce is smooth. Pour sauce over vegetables and sprinkle with cheese. Cook in hot oven Gas No. 5 (400°) for about 20 minutes. Brown under grill until golden. *Serves 4.*

AUBERGINES (ISRAELI FASHION)

An Aubergine Lover

2 large aubergines
Salt and pepper
Oil

1 –2 cloves garlic
Tomato purée – small tin
Vinegar

Slice aubergines into rounds. Wash, drain and salt. Leave in colander to drain for 1 hour. Heat oil in frying pan, dry each slice of aubergine and fry well on both sides. Drain in colander or on kitchen paper. Make dressing with spot of oil, half a cup of vinegar, the garlic and small tin of tomato purée. Put aubergines into bowl and cover with dressing. This can be eaten hot (put in oven until ready for use) with any type of meat dish, or cold with meat or fish as a pickle. Will keep fresh for some time. *Serves 4.*

AUBERGINES IN TOMATO SAUCE

Yaffa Wagner

2 large aubergines
Salt and pepper
4 ozs. flour
½ cup water
Oil for frying
2 cloves crushed garlic
2 eggs

SAUCE:
1 lb. ripe tomatoes or medium tin
peeled tomatoes
1 clove crushed garlic
4 teaspoons sugar
Dash of chilli sauce

Slice aubergines (peeled or unpeeled) into ½ inch thick pieces. Sprinkle with salt and leave for 1 – 2 hours. Make a batter with flour, water and eggs. Dry sliced aubergines. Dip in batter and fry in hot oil. Arrange slices in casserole and sprinkle with pepper and garlic. Mince all the ingredients for the sauce and pour over the aubergines and bake in oven Gas No. 4 (350°) for 30 minutes. Serve hot or cold. *Serves 6 – 8.*

STUFFED AUBERGINES

Yaffa Wagner

2 lbs. aubergines (small)
8 ozs. lamb – minced
2 medium onions – chopped
4 tablespoons cooking oil
1 teaspoon salt
¼ teaspoon black pepper
1 tin peeled tomatoes (small)

2 tablespoons chopped parsley
2 teaspoons sugar
4 teaspoons melted margarine
1 teaspoon chilli sauce
5¼ ozs. rice
3 tablespoons tomato purée

Cut aubergines in half lengthwise and scoop out almost all the flesh. Fry the meat. Then cut up aubergine flesh and onion and fry in half the oil. Remove from heat and add half the salt, pepper, peeled tomato, parsley, 1 tablespoon margarine and the chilli sauce. Add rice and 1 tablespoon tomato purée. Half fill the aubergines with the mixture. With the remaining oil fry them in a shallow pan. Add water to reach the rim of the aubergines. Mix together the remaining margarine, chilli sauce, salt, sugar and tomato purée etc. and add to pan. Cook over medium heat for about 30 minutes then place in baking dish and cook in oven Gas No. 6 (400°) for about 20 minutes basting from time to time. *Serves 6.*

BROCCOLI AMANDINE
A Broccoli Lover

2 x 10 ozs. packets broccoli spears
½ cup butter or margarine
3 tablespoons lemon juice

½ teaspoon salt
½ cup slivered almonds

Cook broccoli as package label directs. Meanwhile melt butter in small saucepan. Add rest of ingredients, simmer, stirring occasionally, for 5 minutes. Drain broccoli, arrange in serving dish and top with the sauce. *Serves 6.*

BRUSSELS IN BREADCRUMBS
Bernice Sion

1 lb. brussels sprouts (baby Kroren sprouts
are ideal)
Salt and pepper

4 — 6 tablespoons toasted fresh breadcrumbs
½ clove chopped garlic
4 tablespoons butter

Cook sprouts in salted water for a few minutes. Strain. Toast fresh breadcrumbs until golden. Melt butter in frying pan, add garlic and fry for a few seconds. Add sprouts and breadcrumbs and sauté for a few more seconds. *Serves 4.*

CABBAGE À LA CRÊME
Bernice Sion

1 medium white cabbage
3 fl. ozs. single or double cream
Fresh ground black pepper

Salt
2 ozs. butter

Shred cabbage and cook in salted water until soft (about 8 minutes). Strain. Add butter and seasoning and stir in cream. Mix well. This is a nice accompaniment to all hot fish dishes, and this method can be applied to most vegetables. *Serves 4 — 6.*

STUFFED CABBAGE
Thea Singer

12 cabbage leaves
1 lb. rice
8 tablespoons sugar

2 oz. raisins or sultanas
3 ozs. margarine chopped into small pieces

Boil rice in salted water. Drain well. Add sugar, margarine and raisins. Scald cabbage leaves with boiling water for 2 — 3 minutes. Drain well, then place a ball of rice mixture in centre of leaf and roll up, tucking in the ends to make a parcel. Arrange side by side in greased baking tin. Dot with margarine and cook in oven on Gas No. 4 (350°) for 1½ hours. Serve with meat dishes, especially those with gravy such as gedempte beef or casserole chicken etc. *Serves 4.*

RED CABBAGE

Sally Bloom

1 medium red cabbage – shredded
2 ozs. margarine
1 chopped onion
2 chopped cooking apples

2 bayleaves
2 cloves
1 cup water
Sugar and salt to taste
Vinegar

Fry onion until golden brown. Add apples, then cabbage, water and seasoning. Cook until soft 1 – 2 hours. If desired a little vinegar can be added.

RED CABBAGE

Charlotte Davis

1 whole red cabbage
2 large cooking apples
Lemon juice

Sultanas (optional)
Margarine
Sugar, salt and pepper

Slice red cabbage and boil in a little salted water until soft. Add the diced apples and lemon juice and re-cook until tender. Toss in margarine and add suagr, more salt and pepper to taste. *Serves 4–6.*

SWEET AND SOUR RED CABBAGE

Diane Krais

1 medium red cabbage
1 onion
2 cooking apples
Wine vinegar

Salt
Pepper
Sugar
Water

Slice cabbage, onion and apple, put in layers in fireproof dish. Sprinkle each layer with salt, pepper and sugar, pour over equal amounts of vinegar and water to cover. Cover and cook in oven on Gas No. 2½ (315°) for 3 hours. Adjust seasoning if necessary.

GLAZED CARROTS

Betty Feltz

1 large tin baby carrots
2 ozs. brown sugar

1 medium sliced Spanish onion
1 oz. margarine

Fry the onions in margarine until transparent. Strain the carrots and toss into the brown sugar, add to the onion and cook until warmed through. Keeps well in the oven until needed. *Serves 4.*

GLAZED CARROTS

Bernice Sion

1 large tin baby carrots
3 tablespoons brown sugar

2 ozs. butter or margarine

Heat carrots in juice, strain and remove from pan. Melt butter in saucepan, add sugar on fairly high heat until dissolved. Throw in carrots, turn off heat and toss. *Serves 4–6.*

QUICK CAULIFLOWER WITH BREADCRUMBS   Valerie Green

1 cauliflower   Butter or margarine
Shake and Bake breadcrumbs (gives best flavour)

Boil cauliflower until nearly cooked in salt water. Cut and put in casserole dish and arrange nicely. Sprinkle breadcrumbs over. Add knobs of butter or margarine. Bake for 15 minutes in oven on Gas No. 3—4 (325^0—350^0). Looks like fried cauliflower! *Serves 4.*

CAULIFLOWER IN TOMATO SAUCE   Lesley Bennett

1 cauliflower   1 tin Italian peeled tomatoes
1 Spanish onion — finely chopped   2 tablespoons parsley — finely chopped
2 cloves garlic — finely chopped   Salt and black pepper
3 tablespoons olive oil   1 tablespoon breadcrumbs
2 tablespoons butter

Cut cauliflower into flowerets and cook in boiling salted water for 5 minutes. Sauté onion and garlic until transparent in the olive oil. Add diced peeled tomatoes and parsley. Season with salt and pepper. Add cooked cauliflower and breadcrumbs and simmer for further 10 minutes or until tender. *Serves 4.*

FRIED CAULIFLOWER   Ruth Phillips

1 cauliflower   Breadcrumbs
Butter

Cut cauliflower into flowerets. Cook in boiling salt water until just soft. Drain completely dry. Fry in butter. Sprinkle with breadcrumbs whilst frying. Serve immediately. *Serves 4.*

FRIED CAULIFLOWER IN TOMATO SAUCE   Cauli Cooker

1 cauliflower   4 ozs. plain flour
Oil   Salt
1 egg   1 tin peeled tomatoes
¼ pint milk

Make batter with egg and milk. Beat in flour and salt until smooth. Break cauliflower into flowerets and boil for 5 minutes. Dip into batter. Deep fry until brown. Drain and serve with mashed tinned tomatoes if desired.

COURGETTES PROVENÇAL   Diana Marks

1½ lbs. courgettes   2 ozs. margarine
1 small tin peeled tomatoes   Salt and black pepper

Peel and cook courgettes whole for 20 minutes. When soft cut into slices, add tinned tomatoes, margarine, salt and pepper. Simmer on low light until ready to serve, or can be kept in oven and served in ovenproof dish. *Serves 4.*

FRIED ZUCCHINI

Diana Marks

1 lb. baby courgettes
Oil

Flour
Salt and black pepper

Wash and slice courgettes into lengthways sections. Season and cover in plain flour. Deep fry in hot oil for 5 minutes each side. These may be kept in hot oven until needed. (Hint: An easy way to cover completely in flour is to shake courgettes and flour in plastic bag). *Serves 4 – 6.*

KEIRECH

Gourmet Cook

3 medium potatoes
1 tin peas
2 courgettes
1 aubergine sliced

1 red pepper
1 tin tomato purée (250 grams)
2 green peppers
150 grams beans

Put everything in saucepan on top of stove for about 15 minutes and then in medium oven on Gas No. 5 (375°) for 90 minutes until dry. *Serves 2.*

LEEKS AU GRATIN

Barbara Sandler

8 leeks approximately same size

SAUCE:
1 oz. butter
1 tablespoon flour
1 pint milk
3 ozs. grated cheese
Salt
Freshly ground pepper

Wash the leeks and cut lengthwise. Lay in a buttered fireproof dish. Melt butter in saucepan, add flour and slowly add the milk – stir until the sauce thickens. Add 2 ozs grated cheese and the salt and pepper to taste. Pour the sauce over the leeks and sprinkle the rest of the cheese on top and place in oven on Gas No. 4 (350°) and cook for approximately 30 minutes. (Celery can be substituted for leeks). *Serves 4.*

POIREAUX À LA PROVENÇALE

Myra Round

3 lbs. leeks
½ lb. tomatoes
1 dozen black olives
2 tablespoons olive oil

Juice of 1 lemon
1 dessertspoon grated lemon peel
Salt
Black pepper

Cut cleaned leeks into ½ inch lengths. Put oil into a shallow heatproof dish and add leeks when oil is warm, but not smoking. Add salt and pepper, cover pan and simmer for 10 minutes. Add peeled tomatoes cut in halves, stoned olives, lemon juice and peel. Cook slowly for a further 10 minutes. This is excellent with lamb also cold as a salad. *Serves 6.*

PETITS POIS À LA FRANCAISE

Karol Solomons

1 pint shelled green peas
Heart of lettuce — shredded
6-8 spring onions
¾ cup cold water

Pinch of salt, pepper and sugar
Parsley and mint stalks in bouquet
1 large spoon oil

Put all ingredients into a medium size pan with half the butter. Cover tightly or set a soup-plate filled with hot water on top of the pan. (This water may be used for adding to the peas if additional liquid is required during the cooking). Cook on moderate heat until peas are just tender approximately 15 − 20 minutes. Draw aside, remove the bouquet, adjust seasoning and add the remaining oil. Turn into hot dish. *Serves 6.*

STUFFED PEPPERS

Yaffa Wagner

6 green peppers
9 ozs. minced beef
1 small can tomato purée (4 ozs.)
Chopped parsley
2 tablespoons rice
1 teaspoon paprika

1 egg
Salt and pepper
3 tablespoons oil
1 medium onion
½ teaspoon sugar

Discard stems, cores and seeds of green peppers. Rinse in cold water and let dry. Add 2 tablespoons water to the minced meat and mix well adding ¼ the can of tomato purée and parsley, rice and salt and pepper. Put 3 tablespoons oil in a medium size saucepan. Stuff peppers with meat mixture. Arrange in saucepan with cut end uppermost. Slice onion, divide into quarters and place a quarter slice on each pepper. Dilute the remaining tomato purée with water and pour into saucepan until peppers are almost covered. Add sugar and pinch of salt. Boil over medium heat for 40 − 50 minutes, occasionally adding water to keep level. Beat egg in medium size bowl until creamy. Carefully spoon by spoon add gravy from saucepan until all liquid is transferred to bowl. Return mixture to saucepan and simmer on low heat for 5 − 10 minutes, adding 1 teaspoon of paprika powder. *Serves 6.*

BAKED POTATOES

Doreen Gainsford

For Dinner Parties or discerning baked potato eaters : −

Cut potatoes into attractive sizes. If potatoes are too large cut appropriately, but round off sharp edges. Put into boiling salted water for 4 − 5 minutes. Drain. Hold pan with potatoes over heat and shake to dry for a few more minutes. Scrape potatoes with fork to roughen. Place with seasoning into really hot fat in baking tin at top of oven and regularly shake to turn and avoid sticking. Cook for 1 hour Gas No. 6 or 7 (400°−425°).

BAKED POTATOES

Charlotte Davis

Potatoes
Corn oil
Onion

Salt
Ground pepper

Peel and dry potatoes well. Put a shallow dish with corn oil on top shelf of the oven, when oil is hot add potatoes, salt and freshly ground pepper and slice onion over them. Cook for 2 − 2½ hours on Gas No. 6 (400°).

CHEESY POTATO BALLS

Dianne Zimmerman

1½ lbs. potatoes	Salt
2 egg yolks	Black pepper
4 tablespoons chopped onion	2 eggs
1 tablespoon butter	Flour
2 tablespoons chopped parsley	Breadcrumbs
4 tablespoons grated parmesan cheese	Oil for frying

Peel and cook potatoes in salted water. Mash and mix in egg yolks and cheese. Fry chopped onion in butter until golden, add to potato mixture with salt, pepper and parsley. Mix until smooth and form into small balls — about 24. Beat eggs with fork. Roll potato balls in flour, then into eggs. Coat with breadcrumbs and refrigerate until needed. Heat oil and fry a few balls at a time until golden brown. *Serves 6.*

GRATIN DAUPHINOIS

Lesley Bennett

1 lb. new potatoes	4 tablespoons grated Parmesan cheese
¼ pint double cream	Butter
8 tablespoons grated Gruyère cheese	Salt and black pepper

Butter a shallow fireproof casserole dish. Peel and slice potatoes thinly and soak in cold water for a few minutes. Drain thoroughly with a clean tea towel. Place a layer of potatoes on bottom of dish in overlapping rows. Pour over a quarter of the cream. Sprinkle over 2 tablespoons of grated cheeses. Dot with butter and season to taste. Continue the layers as before ending with a layer of cheese. Dot with butter and cook for about 1 hour on Gas No. 3 (350°). Potatoes should then be cooked and the top brown. Serve very hot. *Serves 4.*

CRISPY TOPPED MASHED POTATO

Faith Duke

Potatoes	Margarine
Salt and pepper	

Cook the potatoes in the usual way with salt and pepper to taste. When cooked, drain well. Return to pan and dry over a low heat for a few minutes. Remove from gas and add margarine. Mash until smooth with as much margarine as is necessary. Put into ovenproof dish and decorate the top with a fork. Put into a hot oven for approximately 1 hour on Gas No. 6-7 (400°-425°) until golden brown and crisp on top. If you are cooking something on a low heat, cook for longer.

CROQUETTE POTATOES WITH ALMONDS

Barbara Sandler

2 lbs. potatoes	Flaked almonds or toasted breadcrumbs
½ oz. margarine	for coating
2 eggs	Oil for deep frying
Salt and freshly ground pepper	Flour

Boil potatoes until soft, do not overcook. Drain well and return to hot pan, dry over low heat. Put through sieve. Heat margarine in saucepan, when melted mix in potatoes and season well. Separate eggs, beat in yolks and place whites in shallow dish. Turn potato mixture onto a floured working surface, shape neatly and divide into small balls, dusting with flour. Makes approximately 24 potatoes. Lightly beat egg whites. Roll each potato first in egg white and then in either almonds or breadcrumbs. Fry potatoes a few at a time in deep oil. Turn potatoes so that they brown evenly. Drain on absorbent paper and keep warm until ready to serve. These potatoes can be prepared in advance ready for frying. They also keep well in the freezer. *Serves 6.*

FRENCH POTATOES OR CROQUETTES   Sylvia Boston

3 lbs. potatoes
¼ lb. margarine
3 eggs

½ teaspoon salt
¼ teaspoon pepper
2-3 ozs. medium Matzo meal

Boil potatoes gently until cooked and mash with the above ingredients using sufficient matzo meal to bind together. Roll into little balls or fingers. Fry for a few minutes. Can be heated in the oven the following day. *Serves 8.*

POTATO LATKES   Lesley Bennett

4 large potatoes
1 Spanish onion
2 eggs
2 tablespoons fine Matzo meal

½ teaspoon baking powder
Salt
Black pepper
Oil for frying

Peel and grate potatoes. Grate onion. Combine in a bowl. Add beaten eggs, matzo meal and baking powder. Add salt and pepper to taste. Heat oil in frying pan. Drop potato mixture in spoonfuls and fry until brown on both sides. Drain well and serve hot.
A little tip from an Israeli friend: Make smaller latkes and serve for cocktails sprinkled with cinnamon and sugar — This was really delicious! *Serves 6–8.*

POTATOES LYONNAISE   Diana Marks

Potatoes
Onions

Oil
Salt and pepper

Peel potatoes, cut in half and boil for about 10 minutes until soft. Fry finely sliced onions in oil. Add sliced potatoes and fry until golden brown. Add seasoning — garlic can be used if desired.

POMMES À L'ORANGE   B. B. Green

6 large potatoes
2 teaspoons salt
2 cloves garlic
5 tablespoons margarine

2 whole eggs
4 egg yolks
Grated rind of 4 oranges

Boil potatoes in normal way, putting salt and garlic in pan. When cooked drain and dry potatoes. Beat potatoes in mixer until smooth. Add margarine, whole eggs, egg yolks and grated rind. Beat well. Place mixture in piping bag and pipe into large rosettes on well-greased tin. Add a little melted margarine on top and brown under grill. Slide a spatula carefully under rosettes and place round chicken on a hot dish. *Serves 6.*

POTATO PUDDING
Mrs. M. Solomons

6 large potatoes
2 eggs
1 large grated onion

Salt
Pepper
2 tablespoons fine Matzo meal

Grate potatoes into colander and drain well. Mix all ingredients well and bind together to a medium consistency. Grease a 10 inch flat baking tin and put mixture in and flatten. Bake about 2 hours on Gas No. 4 (350°). *Serves 4–6.*

POTATO PUDDING
Diana Marks

Potatoes
Onion
Butter

Salt
Black pepper
Little milk

Slice potatoes thinly and dry in tea towel. Butter ovenproof dish and make a layer of potatoes. Add salt and black pepper, butter, thinly sliced onion and a little milk. Make 4 – 6 layers in the same way and place in oven on Gas No. 3 (325°) for approximately 2 hours. Serve direct from dish. *Serves 4–6.*

RATATOUILLE
Bernice Sion

2 aubergines
2 medium courgettes
2 large green peppers
2 onions
4 tomatoes

¼ pint olive oil
1 clove garlic
2 tablespoons chopped parsley
Salt and pepper

Chop aubergines and courgettes, sprinkle with salt and leave to drain for 30 minutes. Chop peppers, removing seeds, and onions, skin and de-seed the tomatoes and chop coarsely. Heat oil in large frying pan and cook peppers and onions for a few minutes. Add dried aubergines and courgettes. Cover and simmer for 30 minutes, add tomatoes and crushed garlic, cook for another 10 minutes. Stir in chopped parsley and serve. Can be served cold as an hors d'oeuvre. *Serves 6.*

RATATOUILLE
Doreen Gainsford

2 sliced Spanish onions
1 diced green pepper
1 diced red pepper
2 diced aubergines
2 sliced baby marrows
8 sliced tomatoes (or 1 large tin)
¼ lb. diced mushrooms

8 tablespoons olive oil
Salt and pepper
1 tablespoon chopped parsley
1 pinch oregano
1 pinch basil
1 large clove garlic

Using large casserole suitable for top of cooker or frying pan, sauté onions in hot olive oil. When transparent add all the other vegetables and stew on top of cooker or in oven Gas No. 4 (350°) for 1 hour. It is important that the vegetables cook slowly. Add salt, pepper, all herbs and crushed garlic and simmer or continue in oven for 15 minutes. Serve hot or cold as a starter, or vegetable dish. *Serves 4–8.*

SPANISH RICE   Vivien Seymour

½ cup uncooked rice
1 tin tomatoes
Paprika
Seasoning

2 small onions
¼ lb. mushrooms
1 green pepper

Sauté diced onion, mushrooms and green pepper. Add rice, seasoning, paprika. Add tomatoes and simmer. Then cook in oven on Gas No. 3 (325°) for approximately 1 hour. *Serves 3.*

SAUERKRAUT   Ilse Robert

1 tin sauerkraut
1 sliced cooking apple
1 level teaspoon caraway seed

1 level tablespoon meat fat
1 pinch sugar
1 large fresh pineapple

Put the sauerkraut, apple, fat and sugar into a pan and cook for 1 hour. Scoop out the centre of a pineapple, cut and dice 2 slices. Cook with the other ingredients for 15 minutes. Place in the pineapple shell and serve with the top replaced. *Serves 4.*

SPINACH MOULD   Beryl Kramer U.S.A.

2 lbs. frozen spinach
1 cup milk
5 eggs
2 tablespoons butter

2/3 cup stale white breadcrumbs
(homemade or french bread)
½ cup grated Swiss cheese
Salt and pepper

A 6-American cup ring mould or soufflé dish or 4 ramekins of 1½ cup capacity.

Cook spinach, stir in additional butter and milk. Beat the eggs, then gradually beat into them the warm spinach mixture. Stir in the breadcrumbs and cheese and season. (Butter the side of the mould heavily and line the bottom with buttered waxpaper). Pour into mould. (It can be refrigerated until needed but cooking will take 10 minutes longer). Preheat oven to Gas No. 3 (325°). Set mould in a pan of 1½ inches boiling water (the water should come half to two-thirds way up the mould) and place in bottom third of oven. Bake 30 – 40 minutes, depending on shape of mould, until a knife plunged into centre comes out clean. Let settle for 5 minutes before unmoulding or keep warm in a pan of water in oven Gas No. ¼ (150°). To unmould, run a knife around the edge of custard, turn a hot serving dish upside down over the mould, reverse the two, and custard will drop onto dish. Peel waxed paper off top. No sauce is needed if the spinach mould is to take the place of a vegetable. If it is to be a first or main course then serve with a cream sauce, a light cheese sauce or a hollandaise sauce. *Serves 4–6.*

SWEETCORN FRITTERS

Faith Duke

10 — 11 oz. tin of sweetcorn
2 ozs. plain flour
Cooking oil

1 large egg
Salt and pepper

Drain corn well, lightly beat egg into flour, season and mix in corn. Heat a little oil in thick frying pan and drop spoonfuls of the mixture into frying pan, cooking until golden brown on both sides. *Serves 5-6.*

TSIMMES

Janis Brown

2 medium white potatoes
2 medium sweet potatoes
2 large carrots

½ cup shortening
1 cup chopped onion
1 teaspoon salt

Wash and peel vegetables and cook until tender. Heat shortening in frying pan, add onions and cook until golden brown. Mash vegetables together, add browned onion and any remaining melted shortening and salt. Turn into baking dish and put under grill until top of Tsimmes is golden brown. *Serves 4–6.*

TSIMMES

Betty Feltz

Small piece of top rib
2 lbs. carrots
Salt and pepper
1 tablespoon chicken fat
¼ lb. self-raising flour

1 large Spanish onion
1 large potato
3 tablespoons brown sugar
Water

Cook the rib with the onion, potato and diced carrots in slow oven for 5 — 6 hours. When nearly done, remove the onion. Mix all the remaining ingredients and cover the entire top with the dumpling mixture, return to oven and cook for further hour. *Serves 4.*

WASHINGTON RICE

An American Friend

¾ lb. rice
2 cloves garlic
Salt and black pepper
6 tablespoons margarine
2 sliced bananas

½ pint chicken stock
1 onion
Juice of 1 orange
2 teaspoons grated orange rind
2 tablespoons finely chopped parsley

Melt 4 tablespoons margarine and saute finely chopped onion and garlic in it until soft but not brown. Add rice and fry, stirring continuously until golden. Add parsley, season to taste and add orange juice and chicken stock. Cover and simmer for 12—15 minutes until rice is cooked but still firm. Melt remaining margarine and in it saute bananas until golden, sprinkle with orange rind and stir gently into rice mixture. *Serves 4.*

WILD RICE

Sally Bloom

½ lb. wild rice   Salt
Cold water

Wash rice thoroughly. Cover with cold water and bring to boil. Drain off water. Cover again with cold water, add salt to taste. Cook until done — approximately 30 minutes. Serve with any meat or chicken. Delicious but very expensive. *Serves 4.*

NOTES

Salads ~

Keep green salads fresher, sprinkle with the juice of lemon.

When making salad in advance leave out egg whites. Add at the last moment as they tend to go rubbery.

Making salad dressing. Double your quantity and store ½ in an airtight jar.

To improve the flavour of French or Italian dressing, insert a halved clove of garlic in the bottle and let stand for 1 day.

Get rid of summer greenfly — leave lettuce to soak in cold salted water, or water with vinegar added. They will rise to the top.

For prettier rice salad, put into a ring mould, turn out and garnish.

Remove skin of tomatoes more easily. Hold over a flame with the prong of a fork. Or immerse in boiling water for a few seconds.

Homemade tomato juice — purée tomatoes, add Worcestershire sauce, sugar, salt and pepper to taste, and thin with iced water.

Interesting containers for salads. Scooped out pineapple for chicken, orange shells for chicory and orange salad and red cabbage for cole slaw.

When jars of olives or cucumber go white, do not throw away. Wash well and re-cover with slightly salted water.

BEETROOT AND APPLE SALAD

Sally Bloom

2 large cooked beetroots
½ teaspoon salt

2 medium hard eating apples
Salad cream

Dice beetroot and apple into a bowl, sprinkle with salt then stir in salad cream to cover. Make the same day as being eaten. *Serves 6.*

BEETROOT AND CELERY SALAD

Diana Marks

1 head celery
2 small cooked beetroots
Vinegar
Mayonnaise

2 sour apples
3 tablespoons raisins
Sugar

Dice celery, peeled apples and beetroots into a bowl, add raisins and mix well. Dress with a mixture of vinegar diluted with a little water, salad cream and sugar to taste. Refrigerate. (This keeps well for a couple of days.) *Serves 6.*

BEETROOT JELLY SALAD

Doreen Gainsford

2 large cooked beetroots
Juice of ½ lemon

1 red jelly
1 jelly mould or bowl

Peel and grate beetroots. Melt jelly in ¼ pint of water. When cool, add beetroot, lemon juice and mix well. Pour mixture into jelly mould. Refrigerate until set and then turn onto a plate. Leave in refrigerator until required. *Serves 6.*

BEETROOT MOULD

Valerie Ross

1 dark red jelly
1 tablespoon white vinegar
2 medium cooked beetroots

½ pint boiling water
¼ pint cold water
1 Angel cake tin

Dissolve jelly in the boiling water then add cold water and vinegar. Dice the beetroots and add to jelly. Pour all into wetted Angel cake tin. Leave to set. This looks very pretty, if when turned out, the jelly is filled with sweetcorn or some other colourful salad. *Serves 4.*

CABBAGE SALAD

Beryl Kramer U.S.A.

1 head white cabbage
1 small head red cabbage
2 green peppers
1 cucumber
2 onions
1 bunch radishes.

DRESSING:
1/3 cup oil
½ cup white vinegar
2 cloves garlic
3 tablespoons sugar
2 teaspoons salt
½ teaspoon pepper

Slice all the vegetables on a thin slicer. Let stand then squeeze out excess water. Mix together the oil, vinegar, garlic, sugar, salt and pepper. Pour over the cabbage mixture. Let stand for a few hours before serving. (This keeps for 2 weeks in a refrigerator). *Serves 6.*

CABBAGE AND PINEAPPLE SLAW   Charlotte Davis

1 large head white cabbage
1 medium tin crushed pineapple

4 – 5 teaspoons salt
Mayonnaise

Shred cabbage as for Cole Slaw. Add salt and mix in thoroughly. Drain pineapple, (retaining liquid) add to cabbage and mix in well. Dress salad with mayonnaise mixed with 2 teaspoons pineapple juice. Stir thoroughly. Allow to stand for at least 2 hours before serving so that the cabbage can absorb the flavour of the dressing. *Serves 6.*

RED PICKLED CABBAGE   Benita Silverman

1 head red cabbage (2 lbs. approx.)
½ pint brown vinegar
½ pint water
Large screw top jar

Pickling spice
Sugar
1 teaspoon salt

Shred cabbage and put layer of it in bottom of jar. Sprinkle with a teaspoon of pickling spice, and a teaspoon of sugar. Continue in this way until jar is nearly full then add salt. Pour in vinegar and water, if liquid does not cover cabbage, add some more water. Screw lid on tightly and shake well. Put in refrigerator for 2 – 3 days. *Serves 4.*

CARROT AND ORANGE SALAD   Gloria Brown

1 lb. grated carrots
Juice of an orange

2 oranges
Watercress

Peel and cut oranges into skinless sections, mix with carrot. Pour over orange juice. Garnish with watercress. *Serves 6.*

CHICORY AND ORANGE SALAD   Esther Taub

4 heads chicory
3 oranges
Grated carrot

FRENCH DRESSING (Shake well):
3 tablespoons nut oil
1 tablespoon red wine vinegar
Pinch of salt, pepper, sugar and dry mustard

Wash chicory and separate leaves. Break leaves into manageable pieces 1½ inches long. Pare orange and carefully remove segments. Mix together with chicory, toss in French dressing and sprinkle with grated carrot. *Serves 6.*

CORN SALAD   Faith Duke

1 x 11 oz. tin of sweetcorn
2 ozs. chopped green peppers
1 –2 ozs. finely cut spring onions
2 ozs. chopped hard, white cabbage

The chopped white of a hard-boiled egg
2 – 3 tablespoons mayonnaise
Salt and pepper
Lettuce leaves and watercress

Combine all the ingredients, add mayonnaise, salt and pepper to taste and mix thoroughly. Serve piled on a bed of lettuce leaves and garnish with watercress sprigs. *Serves 4 – 5.*

CRANBERRY MOULD

Valerie Green
U.S.A. cups

1 lb. fresh cranberries
1 cup sugar
½ cup orange juice
½ oz. gelatine

1 cup chopped celery
1 cup chopped, peeled apple
1 cup pecan nuts or walnuts
1 quart mould

Wash and drain cranberries — remove stems. Put through food chopper. Add sugar. Let stand for 15 minutes stirring occasionally. Sprinkle gelatine over orange juice in saucepan to soften. Place over low heat until dissolved. Add gelatine mixture, celery, apple and nuts to cranberries. Mix well. Pour into 1 quart mould. Refrigerate until firm, 6 – 8 hours approximately. Serve with turkey. *Serves 6 – 8.*

CREAMY FRUIT SLAW

Anita Herson

1 white cabbage
2 ozs. raisins
1 tin pineapple
½ cup chopped celery
4 tablespoons mayonnaise

1 carton sour cream
1 tablespoon malt vinegar
½ teaspoon salt
½ teaspoon sugar

Shred cabbage and mix with raisins, celery and chopped pineapple. Mix all other ingredients together and toss cabbage mixture into it. This improves if left overnight in refrigerator. *Serves 6.*

PICKLED CUCUMBER

Benita Silverman

1 lb. cucumbers or 1 large cucumber
3 peppercorns
2 bay leaves
3 chilli peppers

Water
2 teaspoons acetic acid
1 dessertspoon sugar
Salt

Cut cucumbers according to size preferred and fill glass jar to 1 inch from top. Fill with water. Add acetic acid, sugar, dash of salt, peppercorns, bay leaves and chilli peppers. Close lid and give jar a good shake. Taste liquid for flavour (if not sharp enough add more acid etc.) Refrigerate for 2 to 3 days. *Serves 6.*

CUCUMBER AND PIMENTO SALAD

Lily Mallerman

Cucumber
Green pepper
Ground black pepper

White acid
Sugar
Water

Peel and slice cucumber very thinly. Cut and core pimento into long thin strips. Place in dish and make dressing with acid diluted with water and sugar to taste. Add a little black pepper. *Serves 4.*

CUCUMBER AND SOUR CREAM SALAD — Gloria Brown

1 cucumber	Salt
2 cartons sour cream	Black pepper

Half peel cucumber — i.e. leave a few strips of peel around. Slice very thinly and put into a container of well salted water for 20 minutes. Strain well, and pour the sour cream over. Place in refrigerator for at least 2 hours before using. *Serves 4.*

GREAT CAESAR SALAD — Jayne Drucker U.S.A.

2 Romaine or Webb's Wonder lettuces	Freshly ground black pepper
¾ cup salad oil	2 eggs — boiled 1 minute
1 clove garlic	¼ cup lemon juice
1½ cups diced dry bread	4 — 6 chopped anchovy fillets
½ teaspoon salt	½ cup grated Parmesan cheese

Combine garlic and oil. Let stand at room temperature for 15 minutes, or if you are a gourmet and want the very utmost in flavour — 3 hours. Place washed and dried salad leaves in a large bowl lined with paper towels. Cover and chill. Brown the bread cubes in 3 tablespoons of the flavoured oil. Remove paper towels from the bowl, tear the lettuce leaves into bite-sized pieces and salt and pepper them. Pour on remaining oil and toss. Add eggs and lemon juice, toss again. Sprinkle on cheese and chopped anchovies, toss lightly. Add bread cubes just before serving. *Serves 6 — 8.*

HAWAIIAN SALAD — Gillian Burr

Smallest tin pineapple titbits	12 walnuts
2 bananas	1 cucumber
3 pieces of celery	Mayonnaise

Chop each walnut into 2 — 3 pieces. Slice bananas and squeeze a little lemon juice over them. Slice celery and cucumber and add drained pineapple titbits. Cover with mayonnaise. *Serves 8.*

LEEKS VINAIGRETTE — Myrna Sayers

1 lb. leeks	Vinaigrette (see dressings)
Salt	Water

Trim and cut leeks into 4 inch lengths. Do not split. Wash well. Boil in salted water for 15 minutes. Cool. Cut into strips lengthwise and place on suitable serving dish. Pour over vinaigrette dressing. Serves 4.

MUSHROOMS A LA GRECQUE

Myra Round

8 ozs. mushrooms
1 gill dry white wine
½ pint white stock
12 small pickling onions
1 gill olive oil

1 tomato
Juice of 1 lemon
1 bay leaf
Salt and pepper

Cut mushrooms into quarters (if you can get small button mushrooms it is nicer to leave them whole), halve tomato. Put them in a saucepan together with the onions, oil, wine, stock, lemon juice and bay leaf. Season well. Cover the pan with a lid and cook quickly for 5 minutes. Allow them to cool in liquor. Remove the bay leaf. Adjust seasoning. Place in a dish, sprinkle with very finely chopped parsley and serve very cold with liquor. I find this is best made the night before and left in refrigerator until needed. This makes an excellent hors d'oeuvre, in which case I add 1 tomato per person. Serve with French bread or rolls. *Serves 4 – 5.*

MUSHROOM SALAD

Hilda Drapkin

8 ozs. mushrooms
1 tablespoon lemon juice
2 tablespoons chopped parsley
2 tablespoons chives

5 ozs. plain yoghurt
Small clove of garlic
Salt
Pepper

Wipe and slice mushrooms. Mix other ingredients together and then marinade mushrooms in the mixture for at least two hours. *Serves 4 – 6.*

SPICED MUSHROOMS

Evelyn Rose

½ lb. small mushrooms (left whole)
Squeeze of lemon juice

DRESSING:
2 tablespoons wine vinegar
1 level teaspoon grated onion
10 grinds black pepper
4 tablespoons salad oil
1 teaspoon salt
1 crushed clove of garlic
1 level dessertspoon chopped parsley

Simmer the mushrooms in a squeeze of lemon juice and salted water to cover for five minutes. Drain well and mix with salad dressing ingredients which have been shaken together to form an emulsion. Cover and leave until quite cold.
(Canned broiling mushrooms can be used instead of fresh ones. Tasty and very low in calories).
Serves 4 – 6.

SALAD NIÇOISE

Diana Marks

1 head lettuce
4 stalks celery
1 cucumber
¼ lb. cooked green beans
12 stuffed olives
2 hard boiled eggs
French dressing

1 head chicory
1 green pepper
6 tomatoes
3 gherkins
1 large tin tuna fish
1 tin anchovies

Wash and drain all salad. Cut lettuce in quite small pieces and place in large salad bowl and then arrange rest of salad ingredients on top. Half an hour before serving place tuna fish around bowl and arrange anchovies and sliced eggs on the top of them. Sprinkle with black pepper and pour over salad dressing. Leave in refrigerator until needed. Serve with hot French bread. *Serves 4 – 6.*

NUTTY COLE SLAW

Faith Duke

12 ozs. finely shredded white cabbage
2 – 4 ozs. salted peanuts

DRESSING:
1 tablespoon white wine vinegar
3 tablespoons oil
2 tablespoons freshly chopped parsley
1 level teaspoon French mustard
Grated rind of 1 lemon
Juice of ½ lemon
¼ teaspoon salt
Pepper

Put all dressing ingredients into screw top jar and shake until well mixed. Pour over cabbage and add nuts. Mix and chill for 30 minutes before serving. *Serves 4 – 5.*

GREEN PEA SALAD

Gloria Brown

2 tins of good quality peas
1 small finely chopped onion
2 tablespoons of chopped relish

Pinch of salt and pepper
2 finely chopped stalks of celery
Mayonnaise

Chill and drain peas, then add other ingredients using a little of the Relish pickle juice and cover with mayonnaise to bind. Chill and serve in lettuce cups. Sprinkle over a little paprika for decoration. *Serves 4 – 6.*

PEPPER AND ONION SALAD

Faith Duke

2 green peppers
2 red peppers
1 Spanish onion

White wine vinegar
Castor sugar
Hot water

Cut peppers in half and remove the seeds. Wash, then slice finely. Cut onion in half and slice finely, add to peppers and put in airtight container. Make sweet and sour dressing to taste by melting castor sugar in hot water and adding wine vinegar. Cover peppers and onion completely with dressing, cover and leave out of refrigerator for 12 hours to pickle. *Serves 4 – 6.*

POTATO AND CARROT SALAD

Faith Duke

2 lbs. new potatoes
1 lb. peeled carrots
¼ pint mayonnaise

6 tablespoons French dressing
2 – 4 ozs. spring onions
Watercress

Rinse the potatoes in cold running water. Put into a pan and cover with salted water, bring to the boil and simmer gently until largest potato is cooked, then put under cold water to cool the potatoes quickly. When cold, drain and peel. Grate the carrots into a bowl and marinate in the French dressing for 30 minutes. Dice potatoes, add chopped spring onions. Drain excess dressing from carrots, add to the potatoes with mayonnaise and mix with a fork. Spoon into a 3 pint ring mould and leave in a cool place until required. Turn out and fill the centre with watercress sprigs. *Serves 8.*

PROVENÇAL SALAD

Lesley Bennett

3 green peppers
6 hard boiled eggs
Black olives
6 firm tomatoes
Anchovy fillets

HERB DRESSING:
1 tablespoon chopped parsley
8 tablespoons oil
3 tablespoons wine vinegar
2 cloves crushed garlic
Tarragon and chives
Salt and pepper

Peel peppers by placing under grill until skin is charred all over. Remove skin under cold water. Slice peppers lengthwise and remove all seeds. Drain on kitchen paper. Slice tomatoes thickly and cover bottom of a large shallow serving dish with them. Sprinkle with a quarter of dressing, add a layer of pepper slices and cover with dressing. Shell and slice eggs and place on top of peppers. Pour over the rest of the dressing. Arrange anchovy fillets in a lattice design on top and place an olive in the centre of each lattice square. Chill in refrigerator for at least 1 hour. (This recipe can also be served as an appetiser). *Serves 6.*

RICE SALAD

Shirley Kanter

1 lb. cooked rice
8 oz. jar of stuffed olives
8 oz. jar of pickled cucumbers
4 ozs. sultanas
8 ozs. blanched almonds
1 lb. eating apples
1 stalk celery

2 green peppers
1 red pepper
8 oz. jar of button mushrooms
1 bunch spring onions
½ pint vinaigrette dressing
Mint leaves for decoration

Chop all ingredients and add vinaigrette sauce, leave to marinate for 2 hours. Add warmed rice and put into mould and refrigerate until used. Before serving, turn rice mould onto plate and decorate with mint leaves. *Serves 10.*

RUSSIAN SALAD
Rosita Green

3 hard boiled eggs
Salt
Black pepper
Spring onion

1 cup of diced cucumber
1 cup of diced tomatoes
1 cup of diced radishes
Salad oil

Dice eggs and mix with diced salad, add chopped spring onion to taste. Just before serving season with salt and black pepper and toss in a little oil. *Serves 4.*

SAUERKRAUT SALAD
Stella Mayoram

½ lb. sauerkraut
1 small tin pineapple pieces or
small tin of crushed pineapple

1 large diced cooking apple
Juice of ½ lemon
Stalk of celery with green leafy top

Prepare ingredients night before required. Wash sauerkraut well. Chop celery into small pieces. Mix all ingredients including the juice of the pineapple and keep in refrigerator until required. *Serves 6.*

TECHINA AND AUBERGINE SALAD
Rosita Green

1 tin Israeli Techina
1 tin water
1 large aubergine

2 cloves garlic
Juice of 1 lemon
Salt and pepper

Place Techina in mixing bowl. Add water very slowly beating vigorously with a fork. Mixture will become hard and will look curdled. Do not worry, just continue working water into Techina until thick and creamy. Add lemon juice, salt and pepper to taste. Bake aubergine in a cool oven being careful that it does not burn. Turn occasionally until soft. When cooked, skin and seed. Chop and add to Techina mixture. Put in a serving bowl and sprinkle with chopped parsley. Serve with hot Pittas (available from Greek delicatessens). *Serves 4 – 6.·*

WALDORF SALAD
Dianne Zimmerman

1 head of celery
2 eating apples
Mayonnaise
Salt

1 tablespoon crushed walnuts
1 tablespoon sultanas
2 tablespoons mandarin oranges

Chop celery finely and add crushed walnuts, also chopped eating apples, sultanas, mandarins, a little salt and bind with mayonnaise. *Serves 6 – 8.*

WELLINGTON CABBAGE SALAD

A Hungry Friend

2 lbs. red cabbage
Tarragon or wine vinegar
Salt and pepper
4 hard-boiled egg yolks

½ pint single cream
Juice of large lemon
Handful of raisins
½ cucumber, thinly sliced

Shred cabbage, wash and drain it, then marinate in vinegar, salt and pepper for approximately 1 hour. Drain well. Combine finely chopped egg yolks with cream and lemon juice. Add raisins and more seasoning. Pour dressing over cabbage. Mix well and serve decorated with cucumber slices. *Serves 6-8.*

FRENCH DRESSING

Yaffa Wagner

3 parts oil to 1 part vinegar or lemon juice
Pinch mustard

Salt and black pepper
Finely chopped garlic

Place oil with the vinegar in liquidizer, add other ingredients and mix for 2 minutes. Place in large container and keep in refrigerator. Use as required.

Mix all ingredients well together. Very good on green salad.

GREEN GODDESS DRESSING

Gloria Brown

1 pint mayonnaise
4 spring onions
Garlic powder and pepper

1 tin anchovies
1 tablespoon chopped parsley
1 pint sour cream

Put all ingredients into blender except sour cream, pulverise for 5 minutes then add the sour cream and blend for further 2 minutes. This dressing is delicious for green salads. The dressing should be made at least 4 hours before use and refrigerated. (To use as a dip double the quantities of anchovies and onions).

PEAR DRESSING

Gillian Burr

3 ozs. cream cheese
3 tablespoons redcurrant jelly

1 teaspoon lemon juice

Beat the redcurrant jelly until smooth and add lemon juice. Beat in cream cheese, cover and keep in refrigerator until thick (a few hours). Peel and core pears (one per person), arrange on lettuce leaves just before serving and coat quickly with the dressing.

YOGHURT AND MINT SALAD DRESSING   Anonymous

5 ozs. plain yoghurt
1 tablespoon chopped mint

Salt and pepper

Mix all ingredients well together. Very good on green salad.

NOTES

Sauces and Stuffings ~

When making sauces, rinse pan first in cold water. It will be easier to clean.

To guard against curdling sauces, keep a bowl of iced water at hand when cooking. At first sign of trouble remove pan from heat and immerse in iced water to prevent further cooking.

If mayonnaise curdles don't despair. Beat in another egg yolk.

To flavour salad dressing or sauce, combine dry mustard with equal amount of mild prepared mustard and mix together.

Add subtle lemon flavour to sauce by placing a good-size wedge of lemon on a fork. Stir with this instead of a wooden spoon.

Do not freeze mayonnaise or custard sauce.

When storing sauce cover the surface with a piece of wet greaseproof paper to prevent skin forming.

Quick onion sauce. Add 2 chopped boiled onions to ½ pint of white sauce.

When using defrosted sauces, remember they must be well beaten on being heated to ensure an even texture.

To enrich a sauce, add cream after it has finished cooking.

 Sauces ~

BARBECUE SAUCE 1
Valerie Green

4 tablespoons oil
4 ozs. grated onion
1 tablespoon flour
2 tablespoons tomato purée

2 teaspoons dried tarragon
1 teaspoon salt
½ teaspoon tabasco
3 tablespoons lemon juice

Fry onions in oil until mixture starts to bloom, turn down heat. Add flour and allow to cook, add tomato purée, tarragon, salt, tabasco and lemon juice. Simmer and serve hot. Will freeze well.

BARBECUE SAUCE 2
Gloria Brown

½ cup oil
¾ cup chopped onion
¾ cup tomato juice
¾ cup COLD water
2 teaspoons salt

½ teaspoon black pepper
⅓ cup of lemon juice
3 tablespoons Worcestershire sauce
3 tablespoons sugar
3 tablespoons prepared mustard

Fry onions lightly in oil before mixing in all ingredients and simmer gently for 15 – 20 minutes. Liquidize and store in freezer until needed. Perfect with roasted chicken or beef-burgers.

SAUCE BÉARNAISE
Helpful '8' Wellwisher

2 sprigs tarragon
3 sprigs chervil
1 tablespoon chopped shallots
2 crushed peppercorns
2 tablespoons tarragon vinegar

¼ pint dry white wine
3 egg yolks
½ lb. soft butter
Salt and cayenne pepper
1 tablespoon water

Chop leaves and stems of tarragon and chervil coarsely and mix with shallots, peppercorns, vinegar and white wine in saucepan. Cook over hot flame until liquid is reduced to two-thirds original quantity. Put egg yolks, wine mixture, herbs and water in the top of a double boiler and stir briskly with a whisk until fluffy. Do not let water in saucepan boil. Gradually add the butter to mixture, mixing quickly all the time. Continue adding butter and mixing until sauce thickens. Season to taste, and strain through fine sieve.

BÉCHAMEL SAUCE
Lesley Bennett

2 tablespoons butter
½ finely chopped onion
1 stalk finely chopped celery
2 tablespoons flour
1 pint hot milk

1 small sprig thyme
½ bay leaf
White peppercorns
Nutmeg

Melt butter in thick or double saucepan. Cook finely chopped onion and celery over low heat until onion is soft but not brown. Remove from heat and stir in flour. Return to heat and cook gently for 3 – 5 minutes, stirring until flour is cooked through. Add quarter of the boiling milk and cook over water, stirring continuously. As sauce thickens add the remaining milk stirring with a wooden spoon until the sauce bubbles. Add thyme, bayleaf, pepper and nutmeg to taste. Simmer for 15 minutes. Strain through fine sieve and dot with butter.

CREAM SAUCE:

To one pint béchamel sauce add 4 tablespoons double cream, bring to boiling point and add a few drop of lemon juice. Ideal for fish, eggs or vegetables.

BRANDY SAUCE
Penny Marks

3 eggs
1 cup castor sugar
Pinch of salt

Grated rind of 1 lemon
½ glass brandy

Beat egg yolks, add ½ cup sugar, salt and lemon rind. Fold in stiffly whipped egg whites, remaining sugar and ½ glass brandy. Serve immediately. Delicious with fruit puddings.

BREAD SAUCE
Helpful '8' Wellwisher

3 ozs. bread
1 oz. butter
½ pint milk

1 small onion
2 cloves
Salt and pepper

Heat the onion, cloves and milk in saucepan until boiling and then set aside in a warm place for about 30 minutes. Remove onion. Pour the milk into the liquidizer and add bread. Blend for about 10 seconds on full speed. Pour back into saucepan. Season to taste and reheat to serve.

CHEESE SAUCE
Gillian Burr

½ pint white sauce
2 tablespoons grated cheese

A little made-up mustard

Mix the cheese and mustard with the white sauce. Do not reboil. N.B. If this sauce is to be used for an au gratin dish, add only two thirds of the cheese to the sauce, using the remainder to sprinkle on top of the dish.

CRANBERRY SAUCE
Beatta Polansky

1 lb. cranberries (washed and picked over)
2 cups sugar (American cup = 8 ozs.)
½ cup water

2 teaspoons grated orange rind
½ cup orange juice

Combine all ingredients in a saucepan. Bring to boil. Cook gently until cranberries pop open, about 10 – 15 minutes. Skim foam from surface all the time. Allow to cool. Pour into jars. Serve with turkey, chicken or lamb dishes.

CRANBERRY JELLY
A Berry Lover

4 cups cranberries
2 cups boiling water

2 cups sugar

Wash cranberries, put in saucepan with boiling water and boil for 20 minutes. Sieve. Re-cook for 3 minutes. Add 2 cups sugar and cook for further 2 minutes. Turn into mould and chill.

CREAM SAUCE FOR SALMON KEDGEREE   Lesley Bennett

1 tablespoon butter
¼ chopped onion
1 stalk chopped celery
1 tablespoon flour
½ pint hot milk
¼ teaspoon thyme

½ bayleaf
Nutmeg
Salt and pepper
2 – 3 tablespoons double cream
Few drops lemon juice

Melt butter. Cook onion and celery over low heat until onions are soft and transparent. Remove from heat. Stir in flour, return to heat and cook gently for 3 minutes, stirring continuously. Add a little of the milk, stirring vigorously. As sauce thickens gradually add the rest of the milk, stirring constantly. When sauce bubbles add thyme, bayleaf, pepper, salt and nutmeg. Simmer for 15 minutes. Strain through a fine sieve. Add 2–3 tablespoons double cream to sauce and bring to boiling point. Add a few drops lemon juice.

CURRY SAUCE   Glenda Izsak

1 onion
½ clove garlic
1 oz. oil
1 – 2 tablespoons curry powder
1 dessertspoon flour
10 fl. ozs. vegetable or beef stock

Salt
Mustard
Lemon juice
2 ozs. grated coconut (optional)
2 ozs. grated apple

Chop the onion and garlic finely. Heat oil and immediately add onion, garlic and sprinkle finely with curry powder and flour. Cook gently, do not allow to brown. Add stock, stir until smooth and simmer for approximately 20 minutes. Add grated apple, coconut, salt, mustard, and lemon juice. Add a little more curry powder to taste. This is a good sauce for fondue bourguignonne.

EGG AND LEMON SAUCE FOR HALIBUT   Renee Conway

3 eggs
Juice of 1½ – 2 lemons

1 – 2 tablespoons sugar
2/3 cup fish stock

Beat eggs and add juice of first lemon. Add 1 tablespoon sugar. Check flavour for sweet/sour taste. Add warm fish stock to egg mixture stirring continuously. Transfer to saucepan over medium light, and stir until sufficiently thickened and simmering – DO NOT BOIL.

GARLIC SAUCE   Glenda Izsak

Crush 2 – 3 cloves of garlic until smooth. Add 3 tablespoons of mayonnaise, seasoning to taste and mix well.

HOLLANDAISE SAUCE

A Dutch Friend

6 ozs. butter
3 egg yolks
1 tablespoon lemon juice

½ oz. chilled butter
Salt and pepper

Melt 6 ozs. butter gently in a small thick pan. Put aside and keep warm. In a 3 pint enamel or stainless steel saucepan beat egg yolks with wire whisk for 1 minute until thick. Beat in lemon juice. Place saucepan over very low heat and stir in ½ oz. chilled butter with whisk, stirring constantly, lifting saucepan off heat to prevent overheating, until butter has been absorbed, and mixture thickens enough to coat wires of the whisk lightly. Take off the heat, add droplets of warm melted butter stirring constantly with whisk. The sauce will thicken into a heavy cream. Season to taste with salt and white pepper. A little extra lemon juice may be added if required. This recipe is foolproof.

INDIA RELISH

Gloria Brown
U.S.A. cups

8 lbs. very small green tomatoes
8 cups brown or maple sugar
3 sticks cinnamon
2 tablespoons ginger
2 cups water

3 thinly sliced lemons
2 cups shredded citron
3 cups seedless raisins
Peel of 1 small orange

Wash tomatoes and cut into quarters. Bring sugar and water to the boil stirring until sugar dissolves, and simmer for 2 – 3 minutes. Add tomatoes and all remaining ingredients. Simmer, stirring occasionally for 3 hours or until fruit is clear. Pour into containers and seal. Serve with cold meat. *Yields 8 – 10 pints.*

HOME MADE MAYONNAISE

Pamela Kaye

2 egg yolks
2 tablespoons vinegar

Salt and black pepper
½ pint oil

In blender or with hand mixer beat egg yolks, vinegar and seasoning until well blended. Gradually add oil until thick.

MINT SAUCE

Valerie Ross

1 good handful mint leaves
¼ pint brown vinegar

1 teaspoon sugar
Little warm water

Remove stalks, wash mint leaves and chop finely. Dissolve sugar in warm water, add to vinegar and pour over mint.

ONION SAUCE

1 lb. onions
1 tablespoon flour
Salt and pepper

½ pint stock
2 ozs. margarine
Nutmeg

Finely slice onions and soften gently in margarine. Sprinkle on the flour and stir. Add liquid slowly and continue stirring until mixture thickens. Add salt, pepper. and a little nutmeg. For a smoother sauce this can be put through the blender. For a creamier sauce for fish, milk may be used instead of stock.

SWEET AND SOUR SAUCE

Hannah Mintz

6 eggs
1½ lemons
1½ tablespoons flour

4 tablespoons fish stock
2 teaspoons sugar
Salt and pepper to taste

Beat egg whites until stiff. Set aside. Mix stock with enough flour to make a paste (add more than 4 tablespoons if required). Heat for a few seconds only. Add flour mix to yolks, fold mixture into egg whites and place in saucepan. Put on low heat stirring all the time, until the first bubble comes, then remove immediately. Continue mixing away from heat, for a few minutes, so as not to curdle. Serve at room temperature with salmon or steamed fish.

TARTARE SAUCE

Pauline Israel

Yolk of hard boiled egg
3 small gherkins
1 sprig parsley

6 – 8 capers
4 tablespoons mayonnaise

Chop all ingredients finely and blend well with the mayonnaise.

SAUCE VÉRONIQUE

Veronica Grape

¼ lb. washed and seeded halved grapes
2 ozs. grated cheese

Basic white sauce

Make a basic white sauce. Add ¼ lb. washed and halved grapes, then the 2 ozs. cheese. This is a lovely sauce for fish, especially sole or plaice, starter for a dinner party.

BASIC WHITE SAUCE
Gina Marks

1 oz. flour
1¼ ozs. butter or margarine

¾ pint milk
Salt and pepper

Melt butter and remove from heat. Stir in flour until smooth. Add milk, a little at a time, stirring briskly all the time. Return to heat and continue stirring until thick. This method can also be used for cheese sauce by adding 3 ozs. finely grated cheese and a little made mustard for extra flavour.

YOGHURT AND CHEESE SAUCE
Dianne Zimmerman

5 ozs. plain yoghurt
1 egg yolk
½ teaspoon prepared mustard

2 teaspoons grated Parmesan cheese
Little nutmeg

Mix all ingredients together until mixture thickens. Serve with fish.

Stuffings ~

AUSTRIAN STUFFING FOR TURKEY
Penny Marks

1 finely chopped Spanish onion
Chicken fat
½ lb. sausage meat
2 tablespoons finely chopped parsley
2 eggs

Juice of ½ lemon
Thyme and marjoram
Salt and freshly ground black pepper
½ lb. chopped poultry livers
2 – 3 ozs. dried breadcrumbs

Sauté finely chopped onions in fat until translucent. Add sausage meat and sauté with onions until golden. Combine thyme, marjoram, finely chopped parsley, eggs, lemon juice and seasoning to taste. Sauté chopped livers in chicken fat. Add breadcrumbs and toss until golden. Combine with other ingredients and stuff bird.

CHESTNUT STUFFING
Sandra Prevezer

2 lbs. chestnuts
2 onions
¾ tablespoon sugar

½ lb. margarine
2 slices bread

Split chestnuts and warm in oven for 15 minutes. Shell while still hot. Put through mincer. Mince bread and onion, sauté in a small amount of margarine and add to mixture. Melt the remainder of the margarine. Add to mixture. Place all in ovenware dish and cover with foil. Cook in oven Gas No. 2 (300°) for 1½ hours. If a crispy top is required remove foil after 1 hour. This dish freezes very well. Serve with roast chicken, meat or turkey.

CORNFLAKE CHICKEN STUFFING
Valerie Cooney

1 cup cornflakes
1 cup porridge
1 cup Matzo meal
1 cup plain flour
¼ lb. corn oil margarine

2 large onions
1 tablespoon chicken fat
1 egg
1 teaspoon paprika
Salt, pepper and garlic to taste

Fry onions in corn oil until lightly browned. Add paprika, garlic, salt and pepper. Add the chicken fat and egg over dry ingredients — if too dry add a little warm water. Mix together with onions, allow to cool before stuffing into chicken.

EVOLVED STUFFING FOR 12 - 14 LB. TURKEY
Bernice Burr

5 sticks diced celery
1 Spanish onion
½ diced green pepper
Chicken fat or oil
2 ozs. sliced mushrooms (optional)
2 cups soft breadcrumbs or 1 cup cooked brown rice.

Salt and black pepper
Mixed herbs
Sage
Fresh parsley (optional)
Chicken stock or cube and water

Fry celery, onion and pepper in fat slowly until soft, then more quickly to brown but not burn. Add salt, 10 grinds of pepper, 1 teaspoon sage, 2 tablespoons mixed herbs. Taste to adjust seasoning to your liking. Add bread or rice. Make mixture moist with stock and residue left in frying pan (about 2 ladles full). Add chopped parsley. Mix very well with fork and leave for 2 – 3 hours before using to stuff bird.

PARSLEY STUFFING
Patricia Miller

2 breakfast cups fresh breadcrumbs
1 small finely chopped onion
2 tablespoons freshly chopped parsley
1 egg

1 tablespoon dripping
Hot water
Salt and pepper

Mix crumbs with seasoning, parsley and onion. Add egg and dripping and enough hot water to bind to stiff dough. This stuffing is suitable for chicken, veal or lamb.

PRUNE AND CHESTNUT STUFFING FOR TURKEY
Lesley Bennett

12 large prunes
¼ pint red wine
1 oz. margarine or oil
1 head chopped celery
12 ozs. chopped onion

1 dessertspoon mixed herbs
Grated rind ½ lemon
½ lb. tinned chestnuts
1 beaten egg
Salt and black pepper

Simmer prunes in wine until wine is reduced and prunes are soft. Cut into quarters. Melt margarine or oil. Sauté onion and celery until transparent and soft. Add prunes, herbs, lemon rind and cut up chestnuts. Stir and season to taste with salt and black pepper. Add juice from prunes. Cool. Add beaten egg. Spoon into turkey.

STUFFING FOR BREAST OF VEAL OR LAMB   Thea Singer

½ lb. fine Matzo meal   1 egg
1 carrot   Salt and pepper
1 onion   Water

Mix meal, grated carrot, grated onion, egg, salt and pepper, plus enough water to make a pliable dough. If sticky add more meal, if crumbly more water. Roll into shape and put into pocket of breast of veal. This stuffing can also be rolled into sausage shapes and baked in greased tin foil on Gas No. 3 (325°) for 2 hours, then cut into slices.

STUFFED NECK   Lilly Mallerman

3 dessertspoons Matzo meal   Garlic powder
3 dessertspoons chicken fat   Salt and pepper
Chopped onion   1 egg

Mix all ingredients together and stuff neck. Boil in soup or roast with chicken.

YORKSHIRE PUDDING   Joan Dyson

4 ozs. plain flour   1 egg
Pinch salt   ½ pint water

Sift flour and salt. Add egg and beat well. Gradually add liquid and beat. Allow to stand for about 1 hour. Melt 1 − 2 ozs. margarine in shallow 8 inches by 12 inch tin. When really hot pour on batter. Place immediately in hottest part of oven at Gas No. 8 (450°) for approximately 30 minutes. *Serves 6 − 8.*

NOTES

Desserts for Meat Meals ~

Parev Whip can be used as a substitute for cream.

Keep sponge fingers upright by either dipping the ends in dissolved jelly or greasing the sides of the mould.

When baking a pie with juicy fruits, add sugar at the last minute, to prevent pastry becoming soggy.

Pancakes can become an exotic dessert if filled with chopped nuts, apples and raisins — chopped bananas and cinnamon — sliced strawberries or plain, rolled and flambéed with liqueur. Delicious.

Pie or tart dough will bake to a golden brown if one spoonful of sugar has been added.

Emergency dessert: sprinkle drained tinned pineapple rings with brown sugar and place under a medium hot grill until caramelized.

Dissolve 1 pint jelly in ¼ pint of water, add sufficient ice cubes to make up the pint. Place in the refrigerator for a few minutes.

Super and quick. Pineapple meringue boats. Cut small pineapples in half lengthwise. Cut out centre with curved knife, fill with strawberries, pineapple chunks etcetera, top with meringue and bake in a hot oven until lightly browned on top.

Quick garnishes: crumbled chocolate flakes, roasted flaked almonds, desiccated coconut or tinned fruit.

Light Desserts

APRICOT DELIGHT

Bernice Burr

1 lb. dried apricots
2 tablespoons orange curacao or
2 tablespoons Grand Marnier
Water

Grated rind of 1 orange
4 egg whites
4 ozs. castor sugar
Icing sugar

Soak apricots in cold water overnight. Cover them with more water if necessary and grated orange rind, stew until soft, approximately 30 minutes. When cooked purée them in the blender or mouli. Beat egg whites and castor sugar together until stiff and then add them to cooled apricot mixture, folding them in carefully. Pour mixture into individual glass dishes and when cold dredge each dish with icing sugar, dribble a little liqueur over the sugar and refrigerate. If available, decorate with thin slices of glacé apricots, kumquats or miniature Israeli oranges. *Serves 6.*

HOT APRICOT SOUFFLÉ

Stella Majoram

½ lb. cooked dried apricots

4 egg whites

Drain apricots and pass through sieve. Fold in stiffly beaten egg whites. Put into a greased, sugared, ovenproof dish and bake on Gas No. 6 (400°) for 15 – 20 minutes. *Serves 4 – 6.*

BLACK CHERRY JELLY

Helen Bloom

1 tin pitted black cherries
2½ ozs. of port or sherry plus cherry brandy
Sugar

½ oz. gelatine
Castor sugar
¼ pint water

Drain juice from cherries and put cherries in large glass bowl. Dissolve gelatine in water, add juice from cherries, liqueur and a little sugar if necessary. When cool pour over cherries and allow to set. Decorate with meringues and toasted flaked almonds. *Serves 6 – 8.*

CHOCOLATE MOUSSE

Myrna Sayers

4 eggs
4 ozs. plain chocolate

4 teaspoons water and brandy, or water
Flaked almonds

Melt chocolate in bowl over hot water, stir in liquid. Remove from heat and stir in egg yolks singly. Mix until smooth. Whisk egg whites stiffly and fold into cooked chocolate mixture. Pour into individual dishes and refrigerate. Just before serving sprinkle with toasted flaked almonds or grated chocolate. *Serves 4.*

CHOCOLATE MOUSSE

Susan Mandell

4 ozs. plain chocolate
3 eggs
1 teaspoon vanilla essence

½ oz. margarine
Pinch of salt
1 tablespoon cooking brandy or
Cointreau

Melt chocolate in a bowl over hot water. Remove from heat and stir in margarine, egg yolks, salt, and vanilla and brandy, until smooth. Beat egg whites until stiff and gently fold into chocolate mixture. Pour into dishes and chill. Decorate with flaked chocolate or coconut. *Serves 6.*

EASY CHOCOLATE MOUSSE   Valerie Ross

8 eggs   ½ lb. plain chocolate

Separate egg yolks from whites. Beat yolks well. Melt the chocolate in a bowl over hot water, as soon as the chocolate is ready, stir into the beaten egg yolks. Beat the egg whites until stiff and fold them into the mixture. Pour into a large bowl and chill. *Serves 8.*

ICE CREAM — COFFEE   Valerie Joels

1 carton Snowcrest parev whip   2 tablespoons coffee essence
1 tablespoon castor sugar   1 egg

Whip cream until stiff, add coffee, egg and sugar. Whisk again and pour into two ice trays or into a plastic sandwich box, place in the deep freeze. *Serves 8.*

ICE CREAM — FRUIT   Helene Littlestone

4 ozs. margarine   16 oz. tin strawberries, raspberries or
4 ozs. castor sugar   blackcurrants, or
2 eggs   13 oz. tin crushed pineapple

Put all ingredients into the liquidizer and allow to mix for about 5 minutes until smooth and creamy. If using raspberries or blackcurrants sieve to remove pips. Pour into a container, cover and freeze.
(For variety make different flavours, then layer, freezing the first flavour before adding the second. Repeat as desired). *Serves 6 – 8.*

LEMON CREAM   Vivienne Seymour

Juice of 3 large lemons   ¼ lb. castor sugar
Grated rind of 2 lemons   3 large eggs
1 lemon jelly   ¼ pint hot water

Dissolve jelly in hot water. Separate eggs, beat yolks until frothy, add sugar and rind and beat until fluffy. Gradually add lemon juice and stir in dissolved jelly. Leave in refrigerator until about to set then fold in the beaten egg whites. Chill. *Serves 8.*

LEMON MOUSSE   Rosita Green

½ oz. gelatine   6 ozs. sugar
4 tablespoons water   Grated rind of 3 lemons
4 separated eggs   6 tablespoons lemon juice

Combine the egg yolks, sugar and grated lemon rind, beat until thick. Place the gelatine and water in a cup and dissolve by putting the cup in a saucepan of boiling water. Add to the egg mixture with lemon juice. Beat again until thick. Beat egg whites until stiff and fold into the mixture. Pour into a souffle dish and chill. *Serves 6 – 8.*

LEMON OR ORANGE MOUSSE   Jill Epstein

5 separated eggs
1 teacup castor cugar
Nuts

4 teaspoons gelatine
Grated rind and juice of 2 - 3 lemons
or 2 oranges

Beat the yolks with ½ cup of sugar and grated rind. Warm the gelatine in the juice and let cool. Whisk the egg whites and fold in remaining sugar with a metal spoon. Pour gelatine onto yolk mixture then fold in the whites. Refrigerate. Before serving garnish with nuts. *Serves 6 – 8.* (This is best made the day before it is needed).

LEMON SOUFFLÉ   Doreen Brown

3 separated large eggs
3 lemons
½ oz. gelatine

¼ lb. castor sugar
½ cup warm water

Dissolve the gelatine in warm water. Beat the sugar and egg yolks, add the finely grated rind of 2 lemons and the juice of 3. Beat again. Whisk the egg whites until stiff, add the other ingredients and whisk briskly. Leave for 15 minutes and then whisk briefly again. Pour into a serving bowl and when firm decorate as desired. *Serves 6.*

COLD LEMON SOUFFLÉ   Lesley Bennett

6 egg yolks
6 ozs. castor sugar
6 egg whites
¼ pint water

Juice of 2 lemons
Grated rind of 1 lemon
½ oz. gelatine

Beat egg yolks with sugar, lemon juice, and lemon rind. Place mixture in top of double boiler and cook over hot water stirring all the time with a whisk until mixture thickens. Remove from heat and cool. Fold in stiffly beaten egg whites Dissolve gelatine in water and fold into mixture. Pour into serving dish or individual bowls and chill. *Serves 4 – 6.*

ORANGE DESSERT   Yaffa Wagner

5 tablespoons cornflour
3 cups orange juice
2 tablespoons lemon juice

Pinch of salt
3 separated eggs
½ oz. sugar

Mix the sugar, cornflour and salt. Heat the orange juice and stir in the dry ingredients. Cook in a double saucepan until the mixture is thick, stirring often. Remove the pan from the heat. Beat the egg yolks and add a little of the hot custard to them, stirring well. Pour egg mixture back into the pan. Cook over hot water for 2 minutes more, stirring all the time. Add the lemon juice. Beat the egg whites until stiff and fold into the mixture. Pour into individual glasses and serve cold. *Serves 6.*

COLD ORANGE SOUFFLÉ
Dianne Zimmerman

1 tin frozen orange juice
3 ozs. castor sugar
Juice and grated rind ½ lemon
4 tablespoons water

5 eggs
1 lemon jelly
2 teaspoons castor sugar
Grated chocolate

Beat 3 whole eggs and 2 yolks until thick, add 3 ozs. sugar and beat until very thick. Add just defrosted orange juice, grated lemon rind and jelly which has been dissolved in the water. Beat 2 egg whites until stiff, beat in 2 teaspoons of castor sugar until firm and add to orange mixture. Pour into a glass bowl and decorate with grated chocolate. Chill. *Serves 8.*

ZABAGLIONE
More Please

4 egg yolks
1 egg white

3 ozs. castor sugar
8 tablespoons sherry

Beat egg yolks with sugar until almost white, then add sherry a spoon at a time. Turn mixture into a double saucepan and stir over gentle heat until it thickens. DO NOT LET IT BOIL. Remove from heat. Beat egg white until stiff and fold into the mixture. Serve hot or cold with sponge fingers. *Serves 4.*

Puddings and Pies

APPLE FLAN
Angela Howard

1 lb. cooking apples
½ oz. margarine
1 tablespoon water (if necessary)
Shortcrust pastry

¼ teaspoon grated lemon rind
2 ozs. granulated sugar
7 — 8 inch sandwich or flan tin
GLAZE:
2 ozs. apricot jam
½ tablespoon water

Line tin with shortcrust pastry. Peel and core half the apples and stew with the margarine, lemon rind, 1 oz. of sugar and water if necessary, until it becomes a thick pulp. Cool and spread in the flan tin so that the mixture comes half way up the tin. Peel and slice the rest of the apples thinly and arrange them on the apple pulp in a spiral design. Sprinkle with sugar and bake in oven on Gas No. 4 (350°) until pastry is firm, ½ — ¾ hour. Heat the jam and water together until runny and as soon as the flan comes out of the oven brush the glaze all over the fruit. Cool the flan and lift out of tin. Serve cold. *Serves 6.*

APPLE FLAN
Bobbie Collins

6 ozs. shortcrust pastry
3 ozs. castor sugar
¼ pint unsweetened apple purée

2 eggs
Grated rind of ½ lemon
8 inch flan tin

Line flan or sandwich tin with the pastry. Prick the base and bake blind in a preheated oven on Gas No. 6 (400°) for 15 minutes. Meanwhile, beat the lightly whisked eggs, sugar and lemon rind into the apple purée. Remove the flan from the oven and lower the heat to Gas No. 4 (350°). Take weights and paper out of the flan and pour the filling into the case. Continue to cook for 30 - 35 minutes until the filling is firm. *Serves 6.*

APPLE, CHERRY AND BAKEWELL TART

Mrs. Shine

Shortcrust pastry
Jam
1 large stewed apple
Tin of pitted black cherries

MIXTURE:
4 ozs. margarine)
3 ozs. sugar   ) creamed
2 beaten eggs
4 ozs. ground almonds
A few drops almond essence

Line tin with pastry. Spread jam over, spread apples and cherries on top, then cover with bakewell mixture. Bake on Gas No. 4 (350°) for 40 – 50 minutes or until set. *Serves 6.*

APPLE ROLL

Sheilah Goodman

2 eggs
Self raising flour

2 small cooking apples
Castor sugar

Stew cooking apples without sugar or water. Break eggs into glass. In another glass put an equal amount of flour and in another glass an equal amount of sugar. Beat eggs and sugar until white then quickly fold flour into the mixture. Pour onto a well greased and lined swiss roll tin. Bake for 5 – 10 minutes in oven Gas No. 7 (425°). Meanwhile, strain apples and colour with one to two drops green colouring. Turn out cake onto sugared greased paper, spread apple on top and roll up quickly – leave to set in a refrigerator. Decorate with icing sugar. (If catering for a large number of guests, three or four of these can be made and joined together in pyramid fashion. This can also be sandwiched with cream for the finale of a fish meal.) *Serves 6.*

APPLE SPONGE MERINGUE

Hetty Preshker

SPONGE:
3 egg yolks
½ cup sugar
¾ cup self raising flour
1 teaspoon baking powder
Grated rind and juice of ½ orange

FILLING:
2 lbs. cooking apples
Desiccated coconut
¾ cup sugar
TOPPING:
3 egg whites
¼ cup sugar

For Sponge: Cream the egg yolks with ½ cup of sugar, add the flour, baking powder, orange rind and juice. Bake in a moderate oven Gas No. 4 (350°) until firm but not too brown.
Filling: Grate the peeled and cored apples and mix with ¾ cup of sugar. Pile on to cake about 2 inches high.
Topping: Beat egg whites until stiff add less than ¼ cup of sugar and put meringue on top of apple, place in oven Gas No. 1 (300°) for ½ hour or until golden brown on top. The meringue may be sprinkled with the coconut before it goes into the oven. *Serves 6.*

BARBECUED OR GRILLED BANANAS

Geoffrey Davis

4 unpeeled bananas
Bacardi rum

Honey

Put the bananas on rack over heat or under grill until the skins turn black, then split the skins wide enough to add a little clear honey and some white Bacardi. (Remember to turn them whilst cooking). Serve in their skins when they are ready. (If serving after a fish meal these are even more delicious if cream is added). *Serves 4.*

110

CASTLE PUDDINGS
Valerie Ross

2 ozs. margarine
2 ozs. castor sugar
3 ozs. self raising flour
8 dariole moulds or
Scooped out halves of tangerines or small
oranges

½ teaspoon vanilla essence
2 eggs
1 jar apricot jam
Pinch of salt

Cream margarine and sugar, then add eggs one at a time, beating well. Sieve flour and salt, stir lightly into mixture with essence until well mixed. Fill greased moulds, or two thirds fill fruit cases. Bake on Gas No. 6(400°) for 25 minutes. Before serving, melt jam over low heat and pour over puddings. *Serves 4.*

CHERRY DESSERT
Sandra Hirsh

1 large flan case
Custard powder

2 tins pitted morello cherries
Sherry

Place drained cherries in flan case. Put juice in saucepan and when it reaches boiling point add enough custard powder to thicken, then add sherry and remove from heat. When cool pour over cherries and allow to set. *Serves 10.*

CHOCOLATE MANDARIN MERINGUE
Barbara Eppel

4 ozs. grated plain chocolate
4 eggs
4 dessertspoons castor sugar
16 sponge fingers

4 dessertspoons water
2 small tins mandarin oranges
A few drops vanilla essence
Sherry

Melt chocolate with half the water in a basin over a pan of hot water. Stir well with a teaspoon until smooth then add remaining water. Separate eggs and whisk chocolate and egg yolks for 5 minutes until thick. Place sponge fingers in a shallow dish, drain fruit and pour the juice over sponge fingers. A dash of sherry may be added if wished. Place fruit on sponge, reserving a little for decoration. Pour on the chocolate mixture. Beat egg whites stiffly with vanilla, beat in half the sugar and pipe on to cover the chocolate. Dust with the remaining sugar. Place under a hot grill until the meringue is coloured and crisp. Decorate and serve. *Serves 6 – 8.*

FRUIT PUDDING
Sally Bloom

2 x 1½ pint basins
4 ozs. seedless raisins
8 ozs. sultanas
4 ozs. large seedless raisins
8 ozs. currants
2½ ozs. mixed peel
3 ozs. self raising flour
5 ozs. breadcrumbs
6 ozs. soft brown sugar
1 saltspoon salt

8 ozs suet or 5 ozs. suet and 3 ozs.
margarine
6 tablespoons stout
2½ tablespoons brandy
1 tablespoon black treacle
3 well beaten eggs
Grated rind of ½ orange
Grated rind of ¼ lemon
¾ teaspoon mixed spice and nutmeg
(together)

Cut large raisins in half and then mix all the fruit together. Sift the flour, salt and spice into a large bowl. Stir in the fruit and add dry ingredients. Add treacle, rind, eggs and stout. Mix well and leave overnight. Mix in brandy thoroughly then put into greased and floured basins to 1 inch from top. Cover with foil, then cloth, and boil for 4½ – 5 hours. Boil again for 2 – 3 hours when ready to use. *Serves 12.*

HAZELNUT TORTE
Vivian Seymour

½ lb. grated hazelnuts
7 separated eggs

1 cup sugar
Grated rind of 1 orange

Beat yolks and sugar well, add rind and nuts, then fold in stiffly beaten egg whites. Bake in a moderate oven on Gas No. 4 (350⁰) in greased cake tin lined with greased greaseproof paper. *Serves 6 – 8.*

FRENCH LEMON FLAN
Gloria Brown

½ lb. rich pastry
8 tablespoons sugar
2 tablespoons melted margarine

2 eggs
Rind and juice of 2 lemons
8 inch flan tin

Beat the eggs well, add the sugar and beat again. Add rind and juice of the lemons, the melted margarine and beat again. Pour into the pastry lined flan case and bake in a pre-heated oven on Gas No. 4 (350⁰) for 30 minutes. *Serves 6.*

LOCKSHEN PUDDING
Freida Stewart

6 large Matzos
1 egg
4 ozs. sugar
2 ozs. raisins
½ lb. fine vermicelli

2 ozs. sultanas
4 ozs. margarine
1 oz. ground almonds
1 oz. whole almonds

Cook vermicelli in boiling salted water. When oooked strain and run under cold tap. Soak matzos in boiling water until soft, strain well and mash into pulp. Add melted margarine, egg, sugar, ground almonds, sultanas, raisins and most of the whole almonds. Mix well together then put into oven dish. Decorate with remainder of almonds and bake in a moderate oven, Gas No. 4 (350⁰) for 1 hour. *Serves 4 – 6.*
FOR A DELICIOUS PASSOVER DESSERT OMIT VERMICELLI.

MARRON GÂTEAU
Beverly Curtis

30 sponge fingers
1 tablespoon rum or Tia Maria
1 oz. margarine
17 oz. tin of sweetened marron purée

1 cup of strong black coffee
2 egg yolks
½ lb. plain chocolate

Melt fat in double saucepan and stir in chocolate until smooth, then beat in egg yolks and marron. Add liqueur to coffee. Divide the biscuits for three layers. Dip the biscuits in the coffee and arrange them side by side. Spread with filling and continue to layer with biscuits. Finish with a layer of chocolate mixture and decorate as desired. Refrigerate to set. *Serves 8.*

MERINGUE CAKE
Elissa Bennett

4 egg whites
8 ozs. castor sugar
4 ozs. margarine
1 egg yolk
10 ozs. icing sugar

2 teaspoons grated rind of orange
2 teaspoons grated rind of lemon
1 tablespoon lemon juice
2 tablespoons orange juice

Beat the egg whites until stiff. Beat in half the castor sugar and fold in the rest. Make 2 circles from oiled greaseproof paper and cover with meringue mixture. Bake on Gas No. 1 (300°) until firm but not brown. Put the fruit juices and rinds into a bowl for 10 minutes before straining. Beat the margarine until creamy, then beat in egg yolk, add half the icing sugar, then the juices and the rest of the icing sugar. Beat until light and creamy. Sandwich the meringue cakes with this mixture and pipe with a few rosettes. *Serves 6.*

ORANGE A MARIA
Bobby Collins

4 large oranges
¾ cup sugar
¾ cup water

1 tablespoon brandy
¼ cup orange juice
1 teaspoon lemon juice

Wash the oranges, pare the rind very thinly from one orange and slice into long thin shreds. Peel oranges and remove all pith. Slice thinly and lay in a dish, sprinkle with brandy. Make a syrup by putting the water, sugar, orange and lemon juice into a saucepan and bringing it to the boil. Drop the shredded peel into the syrup and simmer until translucent. Pour the syrup over the orange slices whilst still boiling. Cover, cool, and place in a refrigerator or cool larder. *Serves 4.* (This dish keeps for several days).

ORANGE BLOSSOM OMELETTE
Evelyn Rose

3 egg yolks
3 egg whites
Grated rind of ½ orange

1 tablespoon castor sugar
3 drops vanilla essence
1 teaspoon flour

FILLING:
Juice of ½ orange
1 tablespoon cointreau

2 tablespoons chunky marmalade

Put marmalade, orange juice and liqueur in a pan and warm. Beat yolks, sugar, grated rind and vanilla together until thick and creamy in colour. Beat whites until they form stiff glossy peaks. Into yolk mixture fold flour and then stiffly beaten egg whites. Melt 2 walnuts of margarine in an 8 inch frying pan. The minute it begins to change colour, put in egg mixture and cook gently. (Slower than for an ordinary omelette). When golden underneath slip under grill for 2 minutes or until the top is set. Slide onto a warm plate and make a cut part of the way through the centre. Spread on filling and fold over. If liked sprinkle with icing sugar. *Serves 4.*

PAVLOVA

Sandra Granditer

3 egg whites
6 ozs. granulated sugar
Tinned or fresh fruit for decoration

1 teaspoon vanilla essence
1 teaspoon vinegar

Beat egg whites until stiff and add half the sugar, the essence and vinegar and then the rest of the sugar and beat again. Wet a sheet of greaseproof paper on to which you should draw an 8 inch circle. Pile meringue mixture on to circle and place on baking tray. Cook in over on Gas No. 1 (300°) until firm, approximately 1 hour. When cooked turn out on to a doyley and when cool fill with parev cream and fruit. *Serves 6.*

PEACH AND STRAWBERRY FLAMBÉ

Maxine Davis

4 peaches
1 lb. strawberries
3 oranges
2 lemons

2½ fl. ozs. kirsch
6 ozs. margarine
4 tablespoons castor sugar
Vanilla essence

Skin and halve peaches, poach them in enough water to cover, with a little sugar and a few drops of vanilla essence, for about 5 minutes. Squeeze oranges and lemons. Melt margarine, add sugar, orange and lemon juice, bring to boil. Remove peaches from liquor and place in flambé pan. Add strawberries and pour juice over all. Place pan on burner and pour over heated kirsch. Flambé. Serve immediately. *Serves 8.* (This dessert is nice after a Fondue when the burner is already available).

HOT STUFFED PEACHES

Gillian Burr

3 tins white peaches
Sherry

4 shortbread type biscuits
Equal amounts to biscuits of:—
desiccated coconut and brown sugar

Drain juice from fruit. Put peaches in fireproof dish with the hole facing upwards. Crush biscuits and mix with coconut and sugar. Stuff the peach holes with mixture and pour over enough sherry to cover bottom of dish. Cook in oven on Gas No. 3 (325°) for 20 minutes *Serves 8.*

PEARS IN RED WINE

Valerie Green

2 lbs. small pears
¼ pint water
Juice of ½ lemon
8 ozs. sugar
½ stick cinnamon or few shakes powder

1 clove
1 strip orange peel
1 strip lemon peel
Red food colouring
½ pint red Burgundy

Peel pears, put in water with lemon juice to stop them turning brown. Put sugar, water, peel and spices in a large saucepan. Bring to boil. Add pears, cover saucepan and simmer for 15 minutes. Add wine and cook over low heat uncovered for 15 minutes or until tender. Arrange pears in serving dish. Reduce liquid to light syrup. Colour syrup with colouring, pour over pears and chill. May be served with Kirsch flavoured whipped cream for a fish meal. *Serves 4 – 5.*

STRAWBERRIES WITH RASPBERRY SAUCE   Faith Duke

1 lb. fresh strawberries   Icing sugar
½ lb. fresh raspberries

Wash and hull strawberries, put in serving dish, add sugar if necessary. Wash and drain raspberries, press through sieve. Sweeten with icing sugar to taste. Serve separately. *Serves 3.*

OLD FASHIONED STRUDEL   Hannah Mintz

DOUGH	FILLING
1½ lbs. plain flour	6 lbs. cooking apples
1 cup corn oil	½ jar any red jam
½ cup water	¼ lb. ground almonds
1 drum cinnamon	½ lb. castor sugar
	6 ozs. sultanas
	Cinnamon

DOUGH: – Sieve flour and cinnamon into a bowl, make a hole in the middle, add half the oil and ¼ cup water and mix together. Add rest of oil and water and knead together – form 3 equal balls. Brush large roasting tin with oil and place one layer of rolled pastry in, then add the filling.
FILLING: – Chop the apples, mix together with the dry ingredients, except the ground almonds. Sprinkle on to first layer of dough, then sprinkle half the ground almonds over and dot with half the jam. Roll out second ball of dough and place over apple mixture and repeat, finishing with third layer of dough. Press down firmly all round edges. Mark out square portions cutting through top layer, brush with oil and sprinkle with cinnamon and sugar mixed together. Bake for approximately 3 hours on Gas No. 4 (350°).

SYLVABELLA   Doreen Gainsford

6 ozs. margarine	2 tablespoons water ·
5 ozs. sugar	4 separated eggs
4 ozs. cooking chocolate	4 lumps sugar
1 packet lady fingers	Water and rum

Beat egg yolks, add margarine and sugar then cream together. Heat chocolate gently in double saucepan with 2 tablespoons of water until it is of a creamy consistency. Add slowly to yolk mixture then fold in beaten egg whites. Set aside. Add lump sugar to watered rum (quantity of rum to taste) dip lady fingers in liquid very quickly, one at a time and place round the tin. Pour the chocolate mixture into the middle and decorate with remaining pieces of fingers. Chill and serve. (This is easier to remove from the tin whilst still very cold). *Serves 6.*

NOTES

Desserts for Milk Meals

Substitute slightly sweetened sour cream for whipped cream for use as a dessert topping—less calories than cream!

Try adding honey to whipped cream in place of sugar, it keeps longer and changes the flavour. A little more unusual.

Smarter ice-cream. Put homemade ice cream into a fluted ring mould and freeze. To remove, place under hot water for a second put on a plate, replace in freezer. When needed surround and fill centre with fresh fruit.

Roll scoops of ice-cream in crushed peanut brittle, peppermint candy, chopped nuts or varying shades of tinted coconut. Freeze until firm then put in plastic bags until required.

Quick sauces for ice-cream. Warm applesauce, sprinkle with nutmeg, crumbled macaroons and crushed peppermint candy. Add to chocolate syrup grated orange rind, or honey blended with crunchy peanut butter, or sliced peaches and a dash of cinnamon blended.

Save the juice from tinned fruits for use in making a tastier jelly, when cool add a carton of sour cream. Very tasty!

Always keep a flan case in freezer for emergencies. Takes ½ an hour to defrost.
To rescue over-whipped cream, slowly stir in by hand a little extra fluid cream until correct consistency is reached.

Light Desserts

APRICOT JELLY MOULD
Beryl Kramer U.S.A.

2 packets apricot or yellow jelly
1 pint of vanilla ice cream
½ pint of sour cream

2 American cups of hot water
1 medium tin of apricots

Dissolve jelly in hot water, let cool in the refrigerator. Drain apricots and purée through sieve and add to jelly. Whip sour cream and ice cream together and stir into jelly mixture. Refrigerate. *Serves 8 – 10.*

POTS DE CRÈME CHOCOLAT
Vera Gale

4 eggs
4 ozs. bitter chocolate
Dash liqueur

½ gill double cream
2 ozs. icing sugar

Separate eggs. Mix melted chocolate, yolks and icing sugar with liqueur and cream. Add the whites and beat for 1 minute. Pour into pots. Serve with poured cream. *Serves 4.*

CHOCOLATE MOUSSE
Maxine Davis

6 ozs. cooking chocolate
5 eggs

1 oz. melted butter
1 teaspoon coffee

Melt chocolate and separate egg yolks, add melted butter to the yolks, mix into chocolate with coffee. Stiffly beat egg whites and fold into chocolate mixture. Pour into bowl and refrigerate. Decorate with whipped cream. *Serves 6.*

COFFEE MOUSSE
Maxine Libson

2 tablespoons castor sugar
1 lb. 2 oz. tin of sweetened marrons
½ oz. gelatine
2 - 3 dessertspoons instant coffee
1 teaspoon lemon juice

½ pint single cream
½ pint double cream
2 tablespoons water
6 eggs

Drain syrup from marrons and pour syrup into double saucepan with egg yolks and sugar. Dissolve gelatine in jug with water, let it stand for a few minutes. Add instant coffee and enough boiling water to make it up to 4 fl. ozs. and stir. Add to egg yolks. Beat with electric beater over heat until thick and frothy. Take off heat and continue beating until mixture is cool – stand it in cold water. Beat the cream and fold into the mixture. Beat egg whites in large basin until stiff, add lemon juice and fold mixture into whites. Put layer in bottom of dish about 1 inch thick then put in freezer for a few minutes. Add layer of small pieces of marron, then layer of mousse. Continue in this way finishing with a layer of mousse. *Serves 8.*

CRÈME BRULÉE

Shirley Byre

4 egg yolks
1 tablespoon castor sugar

1 pint double cream
Vanilla essence

Put cream in double saucepan over boiling water. Bring cream slowly to boiling point. In meantime beat egg yolks and sugar together. When the cream boils pour it over the sugar and egg mixture. Stir gently and add a few drops of vanilla essence. Return to steam and stir constantly over very low heat until mixture thickens — about ¼ hour. Strain into a shallow dish. Leave to cool and then put in refrigerator for at least 4 hours. When set sprinkle generously with brown sugar all over the top. Warm the grill and place the dish under until the sugar melts and forms toffee. Leave to cool and then put back in refrigerator until the caramel has set hard. *Serves 4 – 6.*

CRÈME ST VALENTINE

Faith Duke

4 ozs. cream cheese
3 large eggs
1-2 level teaspoons instant coffee

2 ozs. castor sugar
2¾ fl. ozs. double cream

Whisk together cheese, egg yolks, cream until thick. Stir in coffee. Whisk egg whites gradually adding sugar until the mixture is in peaks. Pour coffee cream over egg whites and fold in. Serve in individual glasses and garnish with coffee beans. *Serves 4.*

COLD GINGER SOUFFLÉ

Marian Gold

3 large eggs
2 tablespoons ginger syrup   ) from jar of
2 tablespoons chopped ginger) stem ginger

8 ozs. castor sugar
½ oz. gelatine
¼ pint double cream

Beat egg yolks with sugar until thick and fluffy, add ginger syrup and leave to cool. Dissolve gelatine in boiling water and add to mixture, add chopped ginger and leave until almost set. Add whipped cream and egg whites. Just before serving decorate with whipped cream and slices of ginger. (This soufflé freezes well but do not decorate until defrosted). *Serves 8.*

JELLY WITH SOUR CREAM

Beryl Kramer U.S.A.

1 packet strawberry jelly
1 oz. chopped nuts
1 packet frozen strawberries

8 ozs. sour cream
1 small tin crushed pineapple

Dissolve the jelly in a cup of boiling water, add frozen strawberries and crushed pineapple. Beat sour cream with a fork and mix with nuts, jelly and fruit. Allow to set in glass bowl. *Serves 4.*

LEMON MOUSSE

Adrienne Layton

3 eggs separated
1 tablespoon cold water
6 ozs. castor sugar
5 tablespoons lemon juice

2 teaspoons powdered gelatine
2 tablespoons hot water
Grated rind of 1 lemon

Soak the gelatine in cold water for 10 minutes. Beat the egg yolks with the lemon rind and sugar till creamy, then add the lemon juice. Pour the hot water over the gelatine, stir until dissolved and add to the yolk mixture. Mix well. Whip the egg whites until stiff then fold into the yolk mixture until completely mixed. Turn into a mould or glass dish and chill. Serve with sweetened cream if desired. *Serves 4.*

LIQUEUR DESSERT

Sandra Blackman

3 ozs. caster sugar
Wine glass sherry
Wine glass brandy
Boudoir biscuits

Juice of 1 lemon
Grated rind of ½ lemon
½ pint double cream

Put the sugar, lemon juice and grated rind in a bowl and stir until the sugar is dissolved. Add the sherry, brandy and cream and whisk until the mixture holds its shape. Cut the Boudoir biscuits and put 3 − 4 pieces in the bottom of 5 − 6 glasses: spoon the mixture over and refrigerate. *Serves 4 − 6.*

CRÈME MARRONS

Faith Duke

2 egg whites
½ pint double cream
4 level tablespoons sweetened chestnut purée

1 tablespoon Coffee Liqueur
Marrons glacés

Whisk egg whites until stiff. Whisk cream until it holds its shape. Mix together the chestnut purée, liqueur and 1 − 2 ozs. chopped marrons glacés. Fold into cream with egg whites. Pile into individual dishes. Garnish with stars of piped cream and put ½ a marron in centre of each dish. (If you wish to use after a meat meal substitute Snowcrest cream for fresh cream and use a little more liqueur). *Serves 4 − 6.*

PINEAPPLE SOUFFLÉ

Sheila Rosen

1 large tin pineapple
2 tablespoons lemon juice
3½ ozs. sugar
2 eggs separated

3 teaspoons gelatine
2 tablespoons cold water
½ pint double cream

Cut up the pineapple. Beat the egg yolks with ½ the sugar, stir in the fruit juice, pineapple and lemon juice. Put the gelatine and water in a pan and dissolve over a small heat, add to the egg mixture and chill until just starting to set. Beat the cream and fold into mixture. Beat the egg whites and remaining sugar until very stiff and fold in. Stir in the pineapple and chill for 3 hours in a glass bowl. *Serves 8.*

PRUNE SOUFFLÉ

Penny Marks

16 large dried prunes
½ teaspoon cream of tartar
5 ozs. sugar

5 egg whites
½ pint double cream
Water

Cover prunes with water and cook. Sieve or liquidize. Whisk egg whites, add sugar, cream of tartar and whisk until very stiff. Fold in prunes. Butter soufflé dish, press mixture into dish eliminating the air holes. Stand in tin of boiling water and put in oven Gas No. 5 (375°) for 45 minutes. Allow to cool and cover with whipped cream if desired. *Serves 6 − 8.*

RHUBARB FOOL

Ellissa Bennett

3 ozs. unsalted butter
1 lb. forced rhubarb
5 ozs. double cream

3 ozs. granulated sugar
2 egg yolks

Place butter in saucepan and put over very low heat and when the butter has melted add the rhubarb which has been cut in 1 inch long pieces. Cook gently until tender. While the rhubarb is cooking mix together the egg yolks and cream. When the rhubarb is tender add the sugar to it and stir until the sugar is completely dissolved, allow to bubble. Remove pan from heat and fold in egg and cream mixture. Pour into dish and allow to set in cold place. Serve cold. *Serves 4.* (This dessert can be made the day before needed).

RICE PUDDING

Penny Marks

1 cup of rice
4 tablespoons sugar
1 oz. butter
3 egg yolks

2 pints of milk
Grated rind of ½ lemon
Pinch of salt
Nutmeg or cinnamon

Wash rice and boil gently in 1 pint of milk for 20 minutes, then add another pint of milk and bring to the boil. Add sugar and then boil for 10 minutes, stirring all the time. Remove from heat. Add butter and salt, yolks of eggs and lemon rind. Place on serving dish and sprinkle cinnamon or nutmeg on top. Serve cold. *Serves 4 − 6.*

FRESH STRAWBERRY ICE CREAM

Valerie Ross

1 lb. strawberries
3 tablespoons castor sugar

½ pint double cream

Wash and hull strawberries. Put all ingredients in liquidizer for approximately 5 minutes. Put in freezer tray in freezer until set. This mixture makes an equally nice mousse if not put in freezer. *Serves 8.*

STRAWBERRY MOUSSE

Margaret Lewis

1½ packets strawberry jelly
1½ blocks strawberry ice cream or
strawberry ripple

1 small tin strawberries
½ pint boiling water

Melt jellies in boiling water and when dissolved add the juice of the tin of strawberries. Leave for 15 minutes to cool and then add ice cream and strawberries. After a further 20 minutes whisk a little and then turn into a glass bowl and leave to set. When firm decorate with whipped cream and a few strawberries. You can of course change the flavour, by substituting pineapple, raspberries or tangerines, if doing this, use vanilla ice cream. *Serves 6 – 8.*
(You can pour the mixture into a spring form tin and when set remove the mousse and decorate with sponge fingers).

ZABAGLIONI

Claire Jacobs

¼ pint double cream
1 oz. sugar
2 tablespoons sherry

2 egg yolks
1 egg white

Whisk yolks and sugar until pale in colour. Whisk cream and egg until fairly stiff. Fold in sherry and egg yolk mixture. Chill. *Serves 3.*

Puddings and Pies

SOUR CREAM APPLE PIE

Claire Jacobs

PASTRY
¼ lb. margarine
1 egg
4 teaspoons sugar
1 cup flour
1 teaspoon baking powder

FILLING
2 eggs
8 tablespoons sour cream
½ cup sugar
5 cooking apples

PASTRY:— Cream margarine and sugar, add egg, then flour and baking powder to make soft dough. Pat into deep pie dish.
FILLING:— Mix eggs with cream and sugar. Pour onto pie crust. Peel and thinly slice apples and place in filling in concentric circles. Bake for 40 minutes on Gas No. 4 (350°) until firm. *Serves 6.*

BLUEBERRY NOODLE PUDDING

Pauline Israel

8 ozs. noodles, cooked and drained
2 separated eggs
3 tablespoons sugar

½ cup sour cream (American cup)
3 tablespoons melted butter
1 tin blueberry pie filling or cherry filling

Beat egg whites until stiff. Beat yolks, sugar, butter and sour cream, mix into noodles. Butter large square casserole dish. Place half the noodle mixture in dish, then fruit mixture then rest of noodles. Top with butter. Bake at Gas No. 3 (325°) for 45 minutes. *Serves 6.*

BREAD AND BUTTER PUDDING

Judith Solomons

3 eggs
1 pint milk
2 - 3 slices buttered bread

Handful sultanas
Pinch of nutmeg
1 envelope vanilla sugar

Beat eggs with sugar and whisk into milk. Cut crusts off bread and place slices in buttered pie dish. Sprinkle with handful of sultanas. Pour over egg mixture and sprinkle with nutmeg. Bake in a bain-marie in a cool oven until set, about 45 minutes. Keep an eye on it to see it does not get too brown. *Serves 3 – 4.*

CHEESE BLINTZES

Rebecca Hermer

PANCAKES
½ lb. plain flour
1 pinch of salt
2 eggs
1 pint milk
Oil for frying

FILLING
½ lb. cooking or curd cheese
1 egg
Castor sugar to taste
½ teaspoon cinnamon

Beat all the pancake ingredients together in the mixer and refrigerate in a jug for 1 – 2 hours. Stir before using.

FILLING:— Mix all the ingredients together, until smooth. Put a little oil into an omelette pan and heat. Pour in a little of the batter, just sufficient to cover the bottom thinly. Fry on one side only then lay separately on kitchen paper until cold. Take one pancake at a time and fill with a little of the cheese mixture, fold into a neat parcel then fry in a lightly oiled pan, on all sides, until golden brown. Serve with fresh or sour cream. *Serves 4 – 6.*

BOMBE AU CHOCOLAT

Jacky Leigh

MOUSSE FILLING
8 ozs. plain chocolate
1 dessertspoon water
5 eggs separated
1 tablespoon brandy

BOMBE
1 sponge cake
Brandy
Whipped cream
Chocolate curls

MOUSSE:— Melt the chocolate in water, beat in the egg yolks, one at a time, stir in the brandy. Beat the egg whites stiff and fold into the chocolate mixture.

BOMBE:— Line a 1½ pint basin with sponge cake cut into strips, and spoon over a little brandy, to moisten. (Do not make it too soggy). Pour in the mousse mixture. Cover with a plate, place a weight on top and put into the refrigerator overnight. Turn out on a serving plate, decorate with thick whipped cream, and pipe rosettes and sprinkle with chocolate curls. *Serves 6.*

COFFEE BOUDOIR DESSERT
Caroline Sotnick

1 packet sponge fingers
4 ozs. whipped cream
2 tablespoons instant coffee
Hundreds and thousands
Silver balls to decorate

1½ cups water
½ cup brandy or rum
Grated chocolate or coffee powder

Mix the coffee with the water and brandy or rum and soak the sponge fingers in the mixture until moist. Lay 4 biscuits on a plate and cover with cream. Lay another 4 biscuits in the opposite direction, cover with cream, repeat first layer, and cover the whole thing with cream and decorate with powder chocolate or coffee and silver balls or hundreds and thousands. Refrigerate until a quarter of an hour before serving. *Serves 4.*

CRISPY CRUNCHY SURPRISE
Jennifer Finegold

2 tins sweet pie filling i.e. strawberry or cherry
2 tins rhubarb
2 ozs. unsalted butter

2 tins gooseberries
½ medium packet Frosties
(or as many as required)

Put the sweet pie fillings in bottom of large ovenproof dish. Strain all juice from gooseberries and rhubarb and place on top of sweet pie fillings. Melt butter and toss in frosties until they are all coated with the butter. Cover fruit completely. Serve hot or cold. *Serves 6 – 8.*

GRAPE DESSERT
Barbara Sandler

1½ lbs. white grapes
1 pint double cream
3 tablespoons demerara sugar

2 tablespoons castor sugar
1 dessertspoon marsala wine (optional)

Halve and deseed the grapes, arrange them skin side up in a serving dish – preferably a heatproof glass or china dish. Whisk the cream together with the castor sugar – add the wine and spoon it over the grapes. Put in refrigerator until cream is firm. Sprinkle the demerara sugar over the top evenly, and then place dish under hot grill until sugar melts. Return to refrigerator and chill for at least 1 hour until sugar is hard. *Serves 6.*

LIME CHIFFON PIE
Hetty Prashker

FILLING:
1 pint vanilla ice cream
1 lime jelly (or alternative flavour)

BASE:
8 digestive biscuits
2 tablespoons brown sugar
2 ozs. melted butter
2 teaspoons cocoa

Finely crush digestive biscuits, mix all base ingredients together and place in greased flan dish. Prepare jelly and leave until partly thickened. Then whisk to light frothy texture. Add ice-cream gradually and beat together. Pile onto flan base. Grate plain chocolate on top. Leave overnight in refrigerator. *Serves 6.*

LOCKSHEN PUDDING

Mrs R. Shine

1 box broad noodles
½ lb. cooking cheese
½ lb. cream cheese
6 ozs. sugar

2 ozs. raisins
2 eggs
3 ozs. butter

Cook noodles in boiling water with ½ teaspoon salt for approximately 15 minutes. Strain, do not **rinse**. When cool mix all ingredients into noodles leaving a little butter for melting in bottom of dish. Stir well and pour into prepared dish. Bake in oven Gas No. 4 (350⁰) for about 30 – 40 minutes. Serve hot or cold. *Serves 6 – 8.*

PANCAKES – BASIC CRÊPES MIXTURE

A Fat Friend

8 ozs. flour
1 tablespoon sugar
3 eggs
2 tablespoons brandy or rum (omit if for savoury pancakes)

¾ pint milk
2 tablespoons melted butter or oil

Sift flour, sugar and salt together. Beat eggs and add to dry ingredients. Gradually add milk, melted butter and brandy, work slowly to avoid lumps. Strain through fine sieve and leave to stand for at least 2 hours. The batter should be as thin as cream. add a little water if it is too thick. For each pancake spoon 2 tablespoons batter into heated pan, shaking well to allow batter to cover entire surface. Brush butter round edge of pan and cook over medium heat until just golden, not brown, (about 1 minute each side). Repeat until all mixture is used. To keep for filling cover with waxed paper or silver foil to stop drying. *20 – 24 crêpes.*

PAVLOVA

Leita Coren

3 standard eggs (whites only)
1 teaspoon cornflour
1 teaspoon vinegar
6 ozs. castor sugar
½ teaspoon vanilla essence

FILLING:
¾ pint double cream
2 tablespoons castor sugar
Fruit to fill case i.e. strawberries, mandarin oranges, raspberries.

Whisk egg whites until stiff. Add all other ingredients. When stiff again put into a greased tin and cook slowly for approximately 1½ hours on No. 1 (300⁰). Pavlova should be crisp on outside and like marshmallow in the centre. When cold whip cream and sugar and put on base. Then put strawberry (or whichever fruit you have chosen) all round and decorate with more cream. *Serves 6.*

PEACH MELBA

Lena Fine

¼ pint raspberries or raspberry purée
3 ozs. sugar
1 tablespoon water

1 tablespoon arrowroot
1 tin whole peaches
1 raspberry ripple ice cream

Melba Sauce: – Sieve raspberries to purée, add sugar and bring to boil. Simmer for 5 minutes. Mix arrowroot with water to smooth paste. Add to raspberry mixture and return to boil. Leave to cool. Chill before serving. Decorate dishes with whole peach and ice cream – then pour melba sauce over ice cream. *Serves 4 – 6.*

PEACH MOULD

Lyn Leader Cramer

1 large tin sliced peaches
¼ packet yellow jellow
1 packet gelatine

¼ pint double cream
Angel cake tin

Arrange some of the peach slices decoratively in bottom of tin. Make up the jelly with some of the peach juice, pour on a little at a time and allow to set. Whip cream until thick. Dissolve gelatine in rest of peach juice. Liquidize remaining peaches and add the cream and gelatine folding in carefully. Pour onto jelly and peaches — allow to set and then turn out. *Serves 4 — 6.*

TWO MINUTE PEACH WONDER

Barbara Froomberg

1 tin sliced peaches
¼ pint double cream

A few chopped roasted nuts
Small quantity brown sugar

Put sliced peaches in bottom of ovenproof dish — sprinkle chopped almonds on top — pour over double cream and refrigerate for ½ hour. Heat grill until hot then place brown sugar on top of cream and grill quickly until sugar has melted. (Watch it carefully!). *Serves 4.*

FROSTED RASPBERRIES

Helen Bloom

8 oz. packet frozen raspberries
¼ pint double cream (with a little single cream)

1 egg white
2 — 3 tablespoons castor sugar
1 carton plain yoghurt

Allow raspberries to thaw, approximately 1 — 1½ hours. Whip cream until stiff. Fold yoghurt into cream and then add beaten egg white into both. Fold in sugar. Divide raspberries into four dishes and top with mixture. Refrigerate until ready. Decorate with a few drained raspberries. *Serves 4.*

RHUBARB AND BLACKCURRANT DESSERT

Bernice Burr

1½ lbs. rhubarb
14 ozs. blackcurrant jam or 14 fl. ozs. of fruit juice
½ lemon (free of pips)

1 kosher crystal jelly
3 egg yolks
¼ pint double cream (optional)
Sugar to taste

Stew rhubarb, blackcurrant jam, sugar, ½ lemon sliced. Dissolve jelly in a little of the liquid and blend with the rest of the mixture in liquidizer. When cooled a little, add well beaten egg yolks and fold in whipped cream. (If serving after a meat meal, instead of folding in cream, fold in 3 stiffly beaten egg whites). *Serves 8.*

TÊTE DE NÈGRE

Mrs. Simon R. Jacobs

8 ozs. butter
4 ozs. castor sugar
2 tablespoons rum

8 ozs. bitter chocolate
5 eggs
Packet of sponge fingers

Dissolve chocolate in rum over hot water. Cream together butter and sugar until free of any lumps. Add chocolate and beat. Add egg yolks and mix well. Fold in stiffly beaten egg whites and when all is well blended pour into buttered pudding basin. Soak biscuits in extra rum and place carefully on top of mixture covering it. Place plate same size as basin on top of it and leave in refrigerator until set. Turn out and completely cover with whipped cream. Decorate with grated chocolate. (This sweet is better made the day before use or in the morning for evening dinner). *Serves 8 – 10.*

TRIFLE

Dianne Taylor

1 sponge cake
1 tin fruit or fresh fruit
Jam
Sherry
Butter

1 pint custard
Cream for decoration
Nuts for decoration
Angelica for decoration
Cherries for decoration

Cut sponge cake into small squares, slice through and spread thickly with jam and arrange at the bottom and sides of serving dish. Pour over some sherry according to taste and leave to soak into sponge. Put a thick layer of fruit including juice if tinned fruit is used. Make 1 pint of custard adding in a little butter when thickened and pour over. Leave to cool. Whip cream until thick and spread over the top. Decorate with nuts, cherries and angelica. *Serves 6.*

NOTES

Snacks and Supper Dishes~

Make a fluffier omelette. Add a dessertspoon of sour cream to beaten egg.

Grate cheese immediately upon removal from refrigerator and see how easily it is done.

To reheat cooked rice, fill saucepan with just enough water to cover bottom. Spoon in rice and steam for about 5 minutes, until water is absorbed and rice is fluffy again. Do not freeze rice as it tends to harden.

Serve kipper with sliced onion rings and vinegar for a tasty snack.

Savoury pies freeze well and make emergency supper. Heat frozen for 45 minutes, covered with tinfoil for the first 30 minutes to prevent burning.

Make rice extra white by adding 2 teaspoons of lemon juice to cooking water.

Add 1 tablespoon oil to water when boiling pasta to prevent water boiling over.

Delicious fried cheese sandwiches. Make cheese sandwich with trimmed white bread, keeping cheese well in the middle, press edges firmly together. Soak thoroughly in seasoned beaten egg for 30 minutes. Heat ½ inch oil in wide frying pan, fry sandwiches until golden brown on both sides. Drain on absorbent paper and serve immediately.

CHEESE FONDUE
Valerie Green

¾ lb. gruyère or ementhal cheese
½ pint dry white wine
Dessertspoon potato flour

2 liqueur glasses kirsch
Paprika
Garlic

Grease bottom and sides of an earthenware pan with butter (and garlic if desired). Dice cheese and put in pan with white wine. Stir over very low heat until all cheese is melted. Mix potato flour, paprika and kirsch to a smooth paste and add to cheese mixture. Stir over heat until mixture thickens. It is customary to cook the fondue over a spirit stove at the table in front of guests. Each guest is provided with a fork with which to dip squares of bread or toast into the fondue. *Serves 6.*

TOAST BRIDGE FOR 'DUNKING'
Valerie Green

Large white loaf

Butter

Remove crust from top and sides. Cut two lines lengthwise (not right through). Cut across forming squares. Curve loaf to form a fan. Butter with melted butter on sides and top and bake in oven for ½ hour each side. When finished stand on two ends forming a bridge. Guests pull off pieces for fondue.

CHEESE FONDUE
Bernice Sion

1 small clove garlic
1 lb cheese, ½ gruyère and ½ ementhal
4 small wine glasses dry white wine
Salt and pepper

1 teaspoon cornflour
1 miniature bottle kirsch
1 French bread (cut
in cubes)

Rub pan with garlic. Grate cheese. Pour wine over, mix and season. Heat gently stirring until cheese has melted. Make paste of cornflour and kirsch and add to pan, stirring well. Serve in fondue bowl or heavy-bottomed pan. Bring to the table and if possible keep simmering over a small spirit stove. Each person takes a cube of bread on his fork and dips into the cheese mixture. *Serves 6.*

FRIED CHEESE PANCAKES
Lesley Bennett

1 recipe French pancakes (see desserts
for milk meals)
4 tablespoons butter
4 tablespoons flour
1 pint milk
9 ozs. diced gruyère cheese

Salt and black pepper
Paprika
3 egg yolks
Oil for greasing and frying
Breadcrumbs
1 beaten egg

Melt butter in the top of a double saucepan. Stir in flour and cook stirring constantly for 5 minutes. Add milk slowly and whisk sauce over boiling water until thick and smooth. Add cheese and continue cooking until cheese has melted. Season to taste with salt, pepper and paprika. Remove from heat and beat in the yolks of 2 eggs. Pour batter into an oiled baking dish and leave to cool. When ready for use cut into rectangles 1 inch by 3 inches. Fold a pancake round each rectangle. Dip pancakes in beaten egg and breadcrumbs and fry in deep fat until golden. Serve hot. *Serves 6.*

SAVOURY CHEESE PANCAKES
Esther Taub

Pancakes using ⅔ French pancake recipe)
¾ pint white sauce
1 bay leaf
1 onion
Pinch nutmeg

¾ lb. of any two
(Parmesan cheese
(Gruyère cheese
(Cheddar cheese
Butter

Make pancakes. Make ¾ pint white sauce using milk which has been infused with bay leaf, onion and nutmeg. Grate ¾ lb. cheese using a mixture of any 2 of the cheeses. Add cheese to the white sauce reserving 1 tablespoon for sprinkling on the top. Put 2 tablespoons of cheese mixture into each pancake and roll up. Put into buttered oven dish and sprinkle with reserved cheese and a few knobs of butter. Cook for 15 minutes on Gas No. 5 (375°). *Serves 4.*

CHEESE AND ONION PIE
Valerie Green

Shortcrust pastry for 8 inch pie dish
4 egg yolks
½ pint single cream
Salt and freshly ground black pepper

Nutmeg
2 tablespoons butter
¼ lb. diced gruyère cheese
1 large sliced onion

Slice and fry onion in butter until golden. Put aside until needed. Bake pastry blind for 15 minutes. Whisk yolks in bowl. Add cream and beat until lemon-coloured. Add salt and freshly ground black pepper. Arrange diced cheese and onion in pie-case, pour over the cream and egg mixture and bake for 30 minutes Gas No. 4-5 (375°). Serve hot. *Serves 4-6.*

CHEESE SOUFFLÉ (1)
Jennifer Finegold

1½ ozs. butter
1 oz. flour
1½ gills milk
4 egg yolks
5 egg whites
1½ ozs. each parmesan and strong cheddar cheese

Salt
Cayenne
Paprika pepper
Little extra parmesan cheese
Browned breadcrumbs

Grease soufflé dish. Melt butter in fair sized saucepan, stir in flour, add the milk and stir until boiling. Cool slightly and beat in yolks, add salt and pepper to taste, then work in cheese. Whip whites stiffly, put tablespoon of whites into cheese mixture and stir gently. Fold in remaining whites. Turn mixture into soufflé dish sprinkle top with a little parmesan and browned crumbs. Cook in moderately hot oven Gas No. 4 (350°) for 25-30 minutes. *Serves 4.*

CHEESE SOUFFLÉ (2)
Doreen Gainsford

3 eggs
1 oz. butter
½ oz. flour

¼ pint milk
3 ozs. grated cheese
Salt and pepper

Separate yolks from whites of eggs. Melt butter slowly. Remove from heat and stir in flour. Mix well. Add milk slowly and mix well again. Return to boil stirring all the time, for about 1 minute. Cool slightly. Add cheese, seasoning and egg yolks (one by one) beating well. Fold in stiffly beaten egg whites and put mixture into prepared soufflé dish. Bake in moderately hot oven Gas No. 5-6 (375°-400°) for about 30 minutes until brown and well risen. Serve at once. (If using for a main supper dish serves 2-3). *Serves 4.*

131

GNOCCHI
Faith Duke

1 pint milk
3 ozs. semolina
2 ozs. grated cheese
2 egg yolks

½ oz. melted butter
Salt and pepper
Nutmeg

Bring seasoned milk to boil. Sprinkle in the semolina, stirring all the time, and cook gently until thick. Remove from the heat and beat in egg yolks. Spread mixture onto a greased baking sheet in a ½ inch layer. When cold stamp into rounds approximately the size of a 50p piece. Arrange in a shallow dish, top with grated cheese and melted butter and brown in a moderate oven. *Serves 4.*

PIZZA
Sally Friend

14 ozs flour
1 egg
¼ pint milk and water
Olive oil
2 teaspoons dried yeast
1 tin tomatoes (drained)
Little hot water

½ lb. cheddar or gruyère cheese
¼ lb. mushrooms
2 ozs. black olives
Oregano
Salt and pepper
Pinch sugar

Prepare yeast by mixing it with a pinch of sugar and a little hot water. Leave for ½ hour. Put flour in large bowl, add warmed milk, water, egg, olive oil, pinch of salt and add prepared yeast. Knead to a dough and leave overnight covered with a damp cloth. Oil a baking tray. Roll out dough and place on tray. Prick all over and sprinkle with a little oil. Place tomatoes, cheese, mushrooms, black olives, oregano on top. Add salt and pepper to taste and leave until needed. Cook for 20 minutes on Gas No. 7 (425°). Serve immediately. *Serves 4.*

QUICHE LORRAINE
Mrs R. Shine

¼ pint cream
2 eggs
6 ozs grated cheese
¼ pint milk
Seasoning
2 packets frozen haddock fillets or
1 large fresh haddock fillet

PASTRY:
4 ozs butter or margarine
6 ozs plain flour
2 tablespoons cold water

Make shortcrust pastry as follows:— Mix butter and flour until it resembles crumbs. Add water and knead into dough. Press into 9 inch pie dish, making sure it is pressed well down at the bottom and sides of the dish.

Beat eggs, add cream, milk, cheese, haddock (which has been boiled, skinned and flaked) and seasoning. Pour this mixture into the pastry case very carefully. Bake in oven on Gas No. 6-7 (400°-425°) for 15 minutes, then lower to No. 4 (350°) and cook until pastry is firm and golden, and the filling is well set. *Serves 4.*

QUICHE LORRAINE
Doreen Gainsford

Shortcrust pastry for two 8 inch pie dishes
4 egg yolks
½ pint single cream
Salt and black pepper
Grated nutmeg

2 tablespoons butter
¼ lb. diced gruyère cheese
2 ozs. diced cheddar cheese
6 ozs. mushrooms
1 large spanish onion

Line pie dishes with pastry, prick bottoms with fork, cover bottom with greaseproof paper and bake blind in moderate oven for 15 minutes. Cool slightly. Whisk egg yolks, add cream and whisk until thick, season with salt, black pepper and nutmeg to taste. Chop onion and sauté in butter. Add chopped mushrooms. Continue cooking until onion is soft. Remove from fat. Arrange cheese, onion and mushrooms in the pie dishes. (If preparing in advance pie can be left like this until ready for use). Pour cream and egg mixture over pies and bake in oven on Gas No. 4 (350°) for 30 minutes. Serve hot. (Ideal supper or lunch dish served with tossed salad). Can be frozen in tin foil pie dish, preferably without cream mixture. *Serves 4-6.*

BAKED SPINACH TURNOVERS
Yaffa Wagner

DOUGH:
8 ozs. margarine
1 teaspoon salt
12 ozs. self raising flour
Luke warm water
FILLING:
2 ozs. grated yellow cheese
6-7 ozs. cooked spinach
3 egg yolks

FINISHING:
1 egg yolk
1 teaspoon water
Sesame seeds

Dough: Melt margarine and rub into flour and salt. Add enough water to be able to roll the dough. Roll and cut into small rounds.
Filling: Mix all the ingredients and put a heaped spoonful on each round of dough. Fold dough over and pinch edges together.
To finish: Dilute egg yolk with water and brush each pastry with mixture. Sprinkle on a few sesame seeds. Bake in buttered pan until golden for about 25 minutes Gas No. 6 (400°). *Makes 20 pieces.*

WELSH RAREBIT MIX
Brèr Rabbit

6-8 ozs. strong cheddar cheese
2 eggs
4 tablespoons cream
2 ozs. butter

½ teaspoon mustard
½ teaspoon salt
Pepper

Place all ingredients in the liquidiser and blend for 1 minute. Put in a bowl and chill in the refrigerator. This will keep for several days, and can be used as required. *Serves 4.*

(To freeze spread the mixture ¼ inch thick on a swiss-roll tin, and cover with foil).

COLD ASPARAGUS SOUFFLÉ

Claire Jacobs

3 eggs
1 tablespoon gelatine

¼ pint double cream
12 oz. tin asparagus

Separate eggs, mash asparagus, leaving a few for decoration. Dissolve gelatine in juice from asparagus, heated in a small basin over hot water. Whisk egg yolks in a basin over hot water (do not let the water boil or touch the basin) until thick. Remove from heat and whisk until cold. Add mashed asparagus. Add gelatine in a thin stream, whisking steadily. Lightly whip cream and fold into the mixture using a metal spoon. Whisk egg whites to soft peaks. When mixture is beginning to set, lightly fold in whites. Pour into 1 pint soufflé dish with foil or double grease-proof collar. Leave to set. Remove collar with warm knife. Decorate with remaining asparagus. *Serves 4.*

SCRAMBLED EGGS AND MUSHROOMS

Wendy Frielich

4 ozs mushrooms
1 large Spanish onion
4 eggs

Salt and pepper
Butter or corn oil margarine

Chop onions and mushrooms. Melt butter in frying pan, add onions and cook gently until transparent. Add mushrooms and continue cooking for a further few minutes. Add beaten eggs to the mixture, turn up gas, season to taste, and continue stirring until cooked. Mushrooms and onions can be cooked in advance and kept in the refrigerator for at least one week. Asparagus or tomatoes may be substituted for mushrooms. *Serves 4.*

OEUFS AUX GRATIN

Lauren Brown

Grated cheese
Butter
Eggs

Cream
Salt and black pepper

Put a small pat of butter in a ramekin. Break 1 egg into each ramekin, season with salt and black pepper, sprinkle with grated cheese, add two teaspoons cream and bake in a moderate oven for 10 minutes. Serve 1 ramekin per person.

OEUFS SAUMONÉES EN CROÛTE

Faith Duke

6 round rolls
Melted butter
12 eggs
2 thin slices smoked salmon

4 tablespoons double cream
2 tablespoons finely chopped parsley
4 tablespoons butter
Salt and freshly ground pepper

Slice tops off rolls and pull out interiors of rolls with your fingers. Brush rolls inside and out with melted butter and bake on Gas No. 3 (325º) until they are golden brown. Mix eggs until whites and yolks are well mixed (do not beat them). Cut smoked salmon into thin strips and heat for a moment in 2 tablespoons butter. Add eggs and cook stirring constantly over low heat. As eggs begin to set add remaining butter and cream. Season with salt and pepper to taste. Stuff hot rolls with scrambled egg mixture and sprinkle with finely chopped parsley. Serve immediately. *Serves 6.*

SWISS EGGS

Barbara Froomberg

4 ozs. cheddar cheese
2 ozs. breadcrumbs
Salt and pepper

Butter
4 eggs
Paprika

Grate half the quantity of cheese and mix with breadcrumbs and seasoning. Shred remainder of cheese into 4 ramekins, covering the base of each. Dot with butter and break an egg into each dish. Sprinkle grated cheese and crumbs round each yolk, completely covering white. Sprinkle yolk with paprika. Cook in a moderate oven on Gas No. 4 (350°) for 8-10 minutes. *Serves 4.*

POOR MAN'S SECRET

Mrs H. Lissman

4-6 slices French bread ¼ inch thick
2 eggs
Breakfast cup milk

Granulated sugar
Oil or butter for frying

Beat eggs well, add milk. Dip the bread into the mixture and fry gently in sufficient oil or butter to cover bread, until golden brown on both sides. Drain well on greaseproof paper. Sprinkle bread with sugar on both sides and serve immediately. *Serves 3-4.*

FISH CAKES

Monica Morris

1½ fresh haddock fillets
1 lb. cold mashed potatoes
Parsley

Seasoning
Tabasco

Cook fish for 5 minutes. When cool, cut fish and potatoes together in bowl. Add finely chopped parsley, a little tabasco, salt and pepper. With lightly floured hands shape into small flat cakes and refrigerate. When ready brush with beaten egg and coat with medium matzo meal. Fry in oil until brown on both sides. Serve with a slice of lemon. *Serves 4.*

POISSON MAYONNAISE

Shirley Baum

Skinned and boned haddock
(or any flat fish)
Lemon juice
Mayonnaise

Nutmeg
1 chopped spring onion
1 grated carrot
Salt and pepper

Cut fish into small pieces and marinate covered with lemon juice for 4 hours. Drain lemon juice and toss fish in mayonnaise. Mix in spring onion, carrot, pinch of nutmeg, salt and pepper. Serve on bed of lettuce.

SALMON AND ASPARAGUS PIE   Stella Majoram

7½ oz. tin salmon   ¾ carton potato crisps
1 tin asparagus soup

Drain and flake salmon. Add tinned soup and half carton crushed crisps. Mix thoroughly. Turn into lightly greased dish. Top with remaining whole crisps, dot with very small pieces of butter and place in oven Gas No. 5 (375°) for 25 minutes. *Serves 6.*

COLD SALMON MOUSSE   Karol Solomons

¾ lb. salmon steak   BÉCHAMEL SAUCE:
¾ pint water   ¾ cup milk
Juice of ¼ lemon   ½ bay leaf
½ teaspoon salt   Blade mace
3 peppercorns   6 peppercorns
Sliced cucumber   1 sliced onion
                                      3 ozs. butter
                                      1 oz. flour
                                      Salt
                                      2 tablespoons lightly whipped double cream
                                      1 tablespoon medium sherry

In a large saucepan boil water with lemon juice, salt and peppercorns. Place salmon in saucepan, cover and cook very gently for about 15 minutes. Allow to cool, then drain and remove all skin and bone. DO NOT BOIL.
SAUCE: Heat milk with seasoning, strain when well-flavoured and cool. Melt 1 oz. butter, blend in flour and milk, add salt and stir over gentle heat until boiling. Cook for 2-3 minutes. Turn into dish to cool. Cream remaining butter and mash salmon. Add cold béchamel sauce and butter to salmon and taste for seasoning. Fold in cream and sherry. Turn into soufflé dish, smooth with palette knife and put in cool place for about 10 minutes to set. Decorate with cucumber. *Serves 6.*

SALMON AND MUSHROOM VOL AU VENT   Vivienne Seymour

1 tin condensed mushroom soup   1 small packet petit pois (cooked)
1 tin red salmon (7 ozs.)   6 medium vol au vent cases

Put soup into saucepan undiluted, add flaked (not mashed) salmon and peas. Heat but do not boil. Fill warmed vol au vent cases and serve immediately. *Serves 6.*

SMOKED TROUT ROLLED IN SMOKED SALMON   Faith Duke

Smoked trout   Lettuce
Smoked salmon   Lemon wedges

Fillet the trout into 4 and roll in thin slices of salmon. Arrange on lettuce leaves and garnish with lemon wedges. *Serves 2-4.*

CURRIED TUNA
Barbara Froomberg

2 x 7 oz. cans tuna
2 sliced onions
1 tablespoon flour
1 dessertspoon curry powder
1 tin mushrooms
1 small diced apple

2 cups chicken stock
½ teaspoon salt
¼ teaspoon pepper
1 tablespoon oil
1 dessertspoon chutney
1 dessertspoon sugar

Fry onion and apple until lightly browned. Add curry powder and flour, then sugar, salt and pepper. Cook for a few minutes, add stock, mushrooms, chutney and tuna. Heat well and serve on a bed of rice. *Serves 4-6.*

LIVER AND RICE SNACK
Gillian Berman

1½ cups cooked rice
3 medium sliced onions
1 clove garlic
Few stalks celery
1½ ozs. margarine
½ lb mushrooms

1 diced green pepper
1 large tin tomatoes
2 sliced tinned red pimentos
2 tablespoons chopped mixed herbs
Salt and pepper
¾ lb. calves or chicken livers (cut in squares)

Fry onions and crushed garlic until golden. Lower heat and add celery, mushrooms and pepper. Cook gently for 15 minutes. Add tomatoes, pimentos and seasoning. Fry liver gently and mix with vegetables. Place on rice, adjust seasoning and stir gently together. Serve hot. *Serves 6.*

CHICKEN LIVER RISOTTO
Gillian Fenner

l lb chicken livers
1 x 5 oz. packet frozen corn
3-4 ozs. frozen peas
1 small can red pimentos or
Small chopped green pepper
Corn oil or margarine for frying

3-4 sliced tomatoes
1 large chopped onion
¼ lb thickly sliced mushrooms
4-5 ozs. easy cook rice
Flour
Salt and pepper

Trim and wash livers, then roll in seasoned flour and fry gently with chopped onion, turning frequently until cooked through. Meanwhile cook rice as per instructions on packet. Heat the pimentos, or if using pepper fry gently with the tomatoes and mushrooms in a little margarine. Cook the peas and corn together. Place the cooked rice in an ovenware casserole, place livers on top with all the other cooked ingredients and fold over with a spoon until they are mixed together and look colourful. Place in oven on low heat until ready to serve. *Serves 2-3.*

CHILI CON CARNE
Yaffa Wagner

Corn oil
2 large onions
1½ lbs. raw minced beef
2 tins red kidney beans (not drained)

2 tablespoons chili powder
1 can plum tomatoes (large)
Salt and pepper to taste

Sauté the finely chopped onions in approximately 4 tablespoons of oil. Add the minced beef. After mixing the beef with the onions add the rest of the ingredients and cook slowly for about 45 minutes. Serve in soup dishes together with French bread and red wine. *Serves 6.*

GIBLET PIE

Rose Marks

2-3 sets giblets
(Small chicken quarters can be added
for larger quantity)
Chicken soup with vegetables
(or any meat stock)
½ lb mushrooms

2 large Spanish onions
Flour
Shortcrust pastry
Small tin tomato purée
Seasoning

Boil giblets until soft in a small quantity of chicken soup. When soft, take out and put to one side. Lightly fry chopped onions and mushrooms and add the tomato purée. Add chopped carrots from soup. Make a roux with chicken stock and flour. Add a little seasoning to taste. Add all ingredients to roux and simmer gently until quite thick. Put into ovenproof dish and allow to cool. Top with thickish shortcrust pastry, slit to allow steam to escape. Bake for 25 minutes Gas No. 5 (375°) until golden brown. *Serves 4-5.*

WHOLESOME RICE MEAL (à la CHINESE)

Sybil Hillel

3 lb. packet organically grown Lima
brown rice (cook according to directions)
Fresh bean sprouts
¼ lb. fresh mushrooms

Spring onions
1 large packet frozen peas
1 tablespoon soya bean oil

Sauté chopped mushrooms and sprouts in soya oil. Place 1 tablespoon soya bean oil in large very shallow baking dish and add all ingredients except peas. Bake in oven Gas No. 4 (350°) for approximately 30 minutes, add steamed peas and serve. Goes well with vegetable casseroles, pilaffs, or is lovely on its own. *Serves 8.*

RICE PILAFF

Gloria Brown

¼ cup corn oil margarine
1½ cups uncooked rice
2 chicken cubes
¾ teaspoon salt

¼ teaspoon pepper
1 cup chopped mushroom stalks
3½ cups boiling water
Chopped parsley

Preheat oven on Gas No. 4 (350°). Melt margarine in flameproof casserole. Add rice and sauté, stir until lightly browned (about 10 minutes). Add chicken cubes, salt, pepper, mushrooms and boiling water. Mix well. Bake covered for about 40 minutes or until rice is tender and liquid absorbed. Before serving fluff with fork and decorate with chopped parsley. *Serves 6.*

TASTY PASTA SUPPER DISH

Gillian Burr

Pasta (preferably shells)
Lightly fried tomatoes
Lightly fried mushrooms
Grated cheese or sliced viennas

Salt and pepper
1 egg per person
Butter or margarine

Cook required quantity of pasta in boiling salted water for 6 minutes. Add layer of tomatoes and mushrooms, then another layer of pasta, seasoning each layer with salt and pepper. Finally break eggs on top, and either slice viennas around them or grate cheese on top. Dot with margarine or butter. Bake in oven on Gas No. 5 (375°) until eggs are cooked — approximately 12 minutes.

TOAD IN THE HOLE

Lena Fine

¾ lb. frying sausages or sausage meat
4 ozs. plain flour
½ pint water

2 eggs
Meat extract cube
2 ozs. margarine

If using sausages remove skin. Roll sausage meat into very small sausages and dip into flour. **BATTER**: Make a well in the flour, add a pinch of salt. Mix gradually adding ½ amount of water and meat cube until smooth. Add remaining water and beat briskly. Stand for at least ½ hour. Heat margarine in fireproof dish. Pour in batter and drop in sausages. Cook for 40 minutes on Gas No. 5 (375°). *Serves 6-8.*

TOASTED EGG RAMEKINS

Faith Duke

1 tin asparagus pieces or
1 tin corn
¼ pint cream

4 ozs. grated Cheddar cheese
4 eggs
Salt and pepper

Grease ramekins and put in bottom a layer of asparagus pieces or corn. Sprinkle with cheese, salt and pepper, then put tablespoon of cream on top. Break eggs in, season and add another layer of cheese. Pour rest of cream over. Place on baking tray and put in oven on Gas No. 5 (375°) for 10 minutes. *Serves 2 hungry people.*

NOTES

Biscuits, Breads & Petits Fours

Keep biscuits crisp by putting a lump of sugar in the tin, to absorb moisture. Change cube monthly. If they do soften, restore crispness by placing in oven on Gas No. 1-2 (300^0) for 5 minutes.

If possible make biscuit dough 24 hours before use and refrigerate. This improves the mixture.

Unbaked biscuit dough may be stored in the freezer for up to 9 months.

Melt chocolate by placing on a piece of wax paper in the top of a double boiler.

Cut up dates with wet scissors, dipping scissors in water frequently.

Use a variety of biscuit cutters for eye appeal.

To prevent overbrowning of bottom of biscuits, use 2 pans the same size, place one on top of the other.

Heat raisins in oven before adding to cakes or bread. They will be more evenly distributed. Just wash them and spread out on a flat pan, cover and heat in moderate oven until they plump up.

Store all petits fours in a dry place, with the exception of truffles which must be kept in the refrigerator.

Slice all breads before freezing and package in small quantities.

Biscuits ~

ALMOND BISCUITS
Jewels Leader-Cramer

8 ozs. self raising flour
2½ ozs. ground almonds
2 ozs. blanched almonds

3 ozs. sugar
4 ozs. butter
1 egg

Mix together by hand the flour, sugar, ground almonds and butter, then add the egg. Turn out of the bowl and knead a few times. Roll out the dough and cut biscuits with a small cutter, then put on a well greased large baking tray. Soak the blanched almonds in a little water until tacky, then add ½ an almond to the top of each biscuit. Bake in a pre-heated oven on Gas No. 9 (475°) on the second shelf from the top for 10-15 minutes until light brown.

BRANDY SNAP CONES
Faith Duke

2 ozs. butter
2 ozs. sugar
2 tablespoons golden syrup
2 ozs plain flour .
½ teaspoon grated lemon rind

1 teaspoon brandy
Glacé cherries
½ pint whipped cream
½ teaspoon ground ginger

Melt the butter, sugar and syrup in a pan, remove from the heat and add all the ingredients except the cherries and cream, mix well. Drop in teaspoonsful on a greased baking tray, 2 inches apart, and bake for 7-10 minutes on Gas No. 4 (350°) until golden brown. Meanwhile grease 3-4 cream horn tins, and have a wire rack ready. Remove the tray from the oven and stand on the top to prevent the biscuits cooling too quickly. Using a palette knife remove each biscuit from the tray and roll around a cream horn tin to form a cone. When cold remove tin carefully. Store in an airtight tin until needed, then fill with whipped cream and garnish with a glacé cherry. *Makes 10-12.*

BUTTERSCOTCH COOKIES
Dianne Zimmerman

6 ozs. self raising flour
½ teaspoon vanilla essence
½ teaspoon bicarbonate of soda

6 ozs. golden syrup
2 ozs. margarine

Melt the margarine and syrup, stir in vanilla essence and bicarbonate of soda, then pour on the flour and mix thoroughly. Leave till cold then roll out *very thinly.* Cut into shapes and bake on a greased tin for about 5 minutes on Gas No. 5 (375°). Remove from tin when cold, and store in airtight tin.

CHILDREN'S ICED CHOCOLATE BISCUITS
Dianne Zimmerman

4 ozs. self raising flour
1 oz. sweetened chocolate powder
Pinch of salt

4 ozs. castor sugar
4 ozs. butter

Soften the butter in a bowl then work the sugar well in. Sift the flour, chocolate and a pinch of salt, and stir into the mixture. Roll into walnut sized balls, place well apart on a greased tin and flatten with a wet fork. Cook for about 8 minutes on Gas No. 5 (375°). When cold ice with a glacé icing in as many colours as you have, and decorate with grated chocolate.

CHOCOLATE COFFEE CREAM BISCUITS
Jacky Leigh

4 ozs. butter
2 ozs. castor sugar
4 ozs. self raising flour
1 oz. sweetened chocolate powder
Pinch of salt

FILLING:
2 ozs. sweetened chocolate powder
3 tablespoons black coffee
2 ozs butter

Cream butter then add sugar and beat until white. Stir in flour sifted with a pinch of salt, and chocolate powder. Roll into walnut sized balls, place on a greased baking tray and flatten with a wet fork. Bake in moderate oven on Gas No. 4 (350°) for 7-8 minutes. **FILLING**: Mix the chocolate powder to a smooth paste with the black coffee in a small saucepan and cook gently to a thick cream. Allow to cool slightly and beat in the butter a little at a time. Fill with cream when required or the biscuits will go soft. (Do not overcook these biscuits).

CHOCOLATE CORNFLAKE BISCUITS
Adrienne Layton

2 tablespoons syrup
2 ozs butter
5 tablespoons ½ cream baby food

3 ozs cornflakes
4 teaspoons cocoa

Melt the syrup and butter in a pan, add the dry ingredients and stir for a few minutes over a low heat. Remove from heat and add cornflakes. Mix well and just put into paper cases to set.

CRUNCH BISCUITS
Barbara Green

4 ozs. wholemeal biscuits
4 ozs. butter or margarine
Coloured chocolate buttons

2 ozs icing sugar
5 ozs plain chocolate

Crumble the biscuits into a bowl and mix in the sifted icing sugar. Break the chocolate into small pieces and put with the butter into a small bowl in a pan of hot water and stir over a low heat until the chocolate and butter are well blended. Pour the mixture over the biscuit crumbs mixing thoroughly with a wooden spoon. Press into a well greased shallow square tin and leave to set in the refrigerator for approximately 1 hour. Turn out of the tin, mark in squares with a knife, and decorate each square with a chocolate button

DATE AND WALNUT BISCUITS
Elsie Klyne

3 ozs. flour
3 ozs. butter or margarine
5 ozs. sugar

4 ozs. chopped walnuts
10 ozs. chopped dates
2 eggs

Cream the butter and sugar, add the eggs, flour, nuts and dates and beat well. Spread on a greased swiss roll tin and bake in oven on Gas No. 6 (400°) for 20 minutes. Cool and cut into squares.

HAMANTASCHEN

Evelyn Rose

DOUGH:

10-12 ozs. flour (half plain and half self raising
5 ozs. granulated sugar
4 fl. ozs. oil

2 eggs
1 teaspoon vanilla essence
Rind of ½ orange

Whisk eggs with a rotary beater until they are thick, then whisk in the sugar, oil, vanilla and orange rind. Finally stir in enough of the measured flour to make a rollable dough. To shape dough:– Roll out the chilled dough to an eighth inch thickness, and cut into circles 3 inches in diameter, using a floured pastry board. Put a spoonful of the selected filling onto the dough, then draw up the corners to make a Hamantasch shape. Brush with remaining egg mixture. Cook in oven on Gas No. 4 (350°) for 30 minutes or until golden brown.

FILLINGS:

WINE AND WALNUT FILLING

4 ozs walnuts
4 ozs stoned dates
8 ozs. packet of mixed dried fruits
1 tablespoon Kiddish wine

2 tablespoons warmed golden syrup
Juice and grated rind of ½ lemon
1 level teaspoon cinnamon

Chop walnuts and dates, and mix with all the remaining ingredients. (Leftover mixture can be stored in a screw-top jar in the refrigerator for several weeks).

POPPY SEED FILLING

1 breakfastcup of poppy seeds
½ a cup of milk
2 heaped tablespoons honey

4 level tablespoons raisins
1 level teaspoon grated lemon rind

Pour boiling water over the seeds and leave until cool, then drain well. Either pound in a mortar, or with the end of a rolling pin, or put through a food mill. Put in a pan with the milk and honey, and cook until thick but still juicy, stirring well. Stir in the fruit and rind. Taste and add a little sugar if necessary. Use when cool.

ICE BOX COOKIES

Audrey Stone

2 cups self raising flour
¾ cup dark brown sugar
½ teaspoon vanilla essence

½ lb. unsalted butter
A pinch of salt
2 ozs. crushed walnuts

Mix all ingredients except nuts in the mixer, stir nuts in by hand. When the dough is pliable divide and roll into two long 'sausages.' Wrap in foil and leave in the refrigerator for ½ an hour. Slice pastry sausage into small rounds and place on a baking tray for 12 minutes in Gas No. 5 (375°).

JAM CRESCENTS

Mrs R. Shine

5 ozs. self raising flour
4 ozs. unsalted butter (softened)

4 ozs best cream cheese
Jam

Put all ingredients in mixer and beat until formed into a rich short pastry. Well flour board and roll pastry into oblong shape then cut into triangles. Place a small teaspoonful of jam on broad end of triangle and roll into crescent, pinching ends to stop jam running out. Grease a large flat tin with butter and bake on Gas No. 4 (350°) for 20-25 minutes. Dust with icing sugar when cold.

MANDEL BREAD
Beryl Kramer—U.S.A.

1 cup sugar
4 eggs
Pinch of salt
Vanilla and almond essence

1 cup oil
3½ cups plain flour
1 cup chopped nuts

Beat eggs and sugar, add flavouring, oil and chopped nuts. Fold in flour and salt. Put a handful of flour on a baking sheet and scatter all over. Take about 4 tablespoons of the dough and shape into a long strip, approximately 10 inches by 1½ inches, until it forms a roll. Bake on Gas No. 3 (325°) for 25 minutes, remove from oven and cut diagonally into 1 inch slices. Flip over on side, put back into the oven and brown for about 7 minutes, flip them again and brown the other side. Repeat this with the rest of the mixture. Cool and store in tins or jars. (Will keep for months).

PALMIERS
Gillian Burr

1 packet vegetarian puff pastry

Sugar

Roll the pastry into an oblong on a sugared board until it is very thin. Fold the two long sides in to meet each other in the middle of the bottom layer, then fold in half lengthways. Cut into thin slices, and lay them on their sides well apart on damp baking trays. Sprinkle with a little more sugar and bake on Gas No. 7 (425°) until light brown. Turn over, sprinkle the second side with sugar and bake this side until it is light brown.

PEANUT BISCUITS
Helene Littlestone

8 ozs. chopped peanuts
¾ cup demerara sugar

1 white of egg

Whisk egg white, then add the nuts and sugar and mix well. Place in small piles on a greased tin, then bake for 10 minutes on Gas No. 6 (400°).

PEANUT BUTTER KRISPIES
Barbara Green

2 tablespoons butter
2 tablespoons peanut butter
8 ozs. marshmallows

5 cups rice krispies
½ teaspoon vanilla essence

Cook the butter, peanut butter and marshmallows over a pan of boiling water until syrupy, stirring frequently. Add the vanilla and beat thoroughly. Put the rice krispies into a large greased bowl, and pour the marshmallow mixture over them stirring briskly. Press the mixture into a shallow greased pan. When cold cut into rectangles. *Makes 36.*

ROGALOFF

Pauline Israel

8 ozs. butter
8 ozs. cream cheese
2½ cups plain flour

FILLING:
4 ozs. sultanas
4 ozs. chopped nuts
2 tablespoons cinnamon
4 ozs. sugar

Blend the butter and cheese in the mixer then slowly add the flour. Separate into six balls, wrap in foil and refrigerate for 4 hours. Mix all the filling ingredients together. Roll out one ball of dough and keep in a flat circle. Cut into wedges, like slicing a cake, Each ball should make 16-18 wedges. Sprinkle each wedge with the filling and roll from the outside of the circle towards the centre, i.e., from wide to narrow. Brush with egg and sprinkle with sugar. Bake for 15-20 minutes on Gas No. 4 (350°). *Makes 100.*

RICH SHORTCAKE BISCUITS

Pat Thompson
Doreen Gainsford

6 ozs. plain flour
Pinch of salt

2 ozs. castor sugar
6 ozs. soft but not melted butter

Sift flour and salt into a large bowl, add the fat and sugar and mix well on No. 3 speed. Bind together and form into round or square cakes. Slightly sprinkle with flour and flatten to about ¼ inch thick. Cut into shape required with a sharp knife. Put on a baking tray, prick all over, flute the edges with a fork, and mark portions with a sharp knife. Bake on Gas No. 5 (375°) for 15-25 minutes until beige to golden colour. On removing from the oven, repeat actions with fork and knife, and leave on baking sheet until cold. For less rich flavour reduce the amount of butter.
This is most effective if made to the size of the plate on which it is to be served. Extra can be made into balls, and then wrapped and frozen. When defrosting do not shape until soft.

STRUDEL BISCUITS

Hilda Blaine

2 lbs. self raising flour
8 ozs. margarine
8 ozs. white fat
12 ozs. castor sugar
8 ozs. mixed dried fruit

4 tablespoons cocoa
3 eggs
2 tablespoons water
8 tablespoons any jam

Rub fat, flour and sugar together into very fine crumbs. Beat the eggs with water and add to the flour mixture. Form into a round ball and cut into 4 pieces. Roll out each piece and spread with 2 tablespoons of jam. Sprinkle over 2 tablespoons of the mixed fruit and then 1 tablespoon cocoa. Roll up as for strudel, place on a greased baking tray, and cut lengthways about ½ inch wide. Bake for 20 minutes on Gas No. 6 (400°), repeat with the rest of the dough. *Makes 48.*

Breads ~

CINNAMON TOAST
Barbara Davison

White bread
Butter

Castor sugar
Cinnamon

Toast the bread lightly on both sides, and butter the toast. Mix the sugar with cinnamon to taste, and then when sugar is well mixed and coloured by the cinnamon sprinkle lavishly on the buttered toast. Return toast to grill, sugared side up, and toast until sugar is well caramelised. Remove from the grill, cut off singed edges. Serve hot.
(Good for children's teas or adults T.V. snacks).

DATE BREAD
Shirley Byre

1 packet dried dates
2 ozs. raisins
1 teaspoon butter
½ cup castor sugar
1 teaspoon bicarbonate of soda

3 cups self raising flour
3 cups boiling water
Vanilla essence
1 egg

Put the sugar and butter in a bowl to blend, then add the egg. Cut the dates into small pieces, and put in another bowl with the raisins. Pour the bicarbonate of soda and water on the fruit, then add to the sugar mixture alternately with the flour, and blend, now add a few drops of vanilla essence. The mixture should be quite runny. Turn into a foil lined loaf tin and bake for about 1 hour on Gas No. 3 (325°).

DATE AND SULTANA LOAF
Gillian Burr

1 cup sultanas
1 packet chopped stoned dates
1 cup sugar
3 cups self raising flour

1 cup milk
½ cup mixed golden syrup
and black treacle

Mix all dry ingredients except flour, add the wet ingredients then the flour and mix for 1 minute only. Put mixture into two small loaf tins, and bake for 1 hour on Gas No. 2 (300°).
These loaves should be wrapped in foil when cold, and kept for at least 3 days before using, sliced thinly and buttered. They will keep for 3 weeks. (Walnuts may be substituted for sultanas if required).

FRUIT LOAF
Hetty Collier

2 cups mixed dried fruit
1 cup brown sugar
1 egg

1 cup tea
2 cups self raising flour

Put the fruit, sugar and tea in a bowl and leave overnight. Next morning stir in the egg and sifted flour. Bake for 50 minutes on Gas No. 3 (325°).

GINGERBREAD

Myra Round

8 ozs. plain flour
3-4 level teaspoons ground ginger
4 ozs. butter or margarine
4 ozs. brown sugar
8 ozs. black treacle

8 ozs. golden syrup
¼ pint milk
1 egg
1 level teaspoon bicarbonate of soda

Sieve the flour and ginger together. Melt the butter with the sugar, treacle, syrup and milk over a low heat, stirring constantly. Remove from heat, stir in the bicarbonate of soda quickly. Add this mixture and the beaten egg to the sieved ingredients. Beat for 5 minutes. Pour into a 7 inch tin lined with oiled or buttered greaseproof paper. Spread the mixture evenly. Bake for at least 1½ hours on the middle shelf of oven on Gas No. 2 (300°). When cake is cool, wrap in greaseproof or foil and store for a few days to become sticky before cutting.

CELERY ROLLS IN A LOAF

Valerie Green

1 small unsliced white loaf
½ cup softened butter or margarine
1 teaspoon celery seed

¼ teaspoon salt
¼ teaspoon paprika
Dash of cayenne

Trim crusts from top, sides and end of loaf. Cut down through the centre of the loaf lengthways, almost to bottom crust. Cut at 1 inch intervals crossways, almost to the bottom crust. Mix together the softened butter or margarine, celery seed, salt, paprika and cayenne. Spread butter mixture over the entire cut surfaces. Place on a baking sheet, cover with waxed paper and refrigerate. Bake for 15-18 minutes on Gas No. 6 (400°) or until golden. *Serves 6.*

GARLIC BREAD

Diana Marks

1 large French stick
Garlic powder

4 ozs. butter

Mix the softened butter with garlic powder to taste. Cut the French stick into thick slices, place on a large sheet of foil, and butter thickly on each side. Wrap the foil round the bread and place in the oven for 25-30 minutes on Gas No. 4 (350°). *Serves 4-6.*

HOT HERB LOAF

Karol Solomons

1 French loaf
4 ozs butter
1 tablespoon mixed dried herbs

Juice of ¼ lemon
Black pepper
A little crushed garlic

Cream the butter with the herbs, lemon juice and seasoning. Cut the loaf in even slanting slices about ½ inch thick. Spread each slice generously with the butter mixture and reshape the loaf. Spread the remaining butter over the top and sides. Wrap in foil. Bake for 10 minutes in a hot oven on Gas No. 7 (425°), then reduce to No. 6 (400°) and open the foil so that the bread is crisp. This should take a further 5-8 minutes.

Pastry

CHOUX PASTRY
Valerie Ross

1½ ozs. butter or margarine
¼ pint water

2½ ozs. flour
2 eggs

Put fat and water into a small saucepan and bring to the boil. Remove pan from heat and add the sieved flour. Stir well, return pan to the heat and cook gently, stirring for about a minute, or until a smooth ball is formed. Break the eggs into a basin and beat them lightly. Allow mixture to cool slightly, and add eggs a little at a time. Use enough egg to give a stiff paste that will pipe easily and retain its shape. Beat the mixture very thoroughly, until it is quite smooth.

SHORT CRUST PASTRY
Betty Feltz

1 lb. self raising flour
1 egg
Pinch of salt

2 tablespoons sugar
½ cup water
8 ozs. margarine

Rub the flour and fat together. Make a well in the flour and add the salt, sugar, egg and enough water to make a pliable dough. Use at once or freeze until needed.

RICH SHORT CRUST PASTRY
Valerie Ross

1 lb self raising flour
8 ozs. butter or margarine
2 eggs

2 teaspoons baking powder
10 ozs. castor sugar

Cream the sugar and fat together. Mix in the eggs one at a time. Add the baking powder and sifted flour. Leave in a basin for a few hours before using. (This is made without using the hands).

VERY RICH SHORT CRUST PASTRY
Dianne Zimmerman

8 ozs. margarine
12 ozs. plain flour
Pinch of salt

1 dessertspoon sugar
1 beaten egg

Put flour, fat, salt and sugar into the mixer for about 7 minutes, then add enough egg to bind. Roll out and use as desired. May be made in advance and frozen until needed.

Petits Fours

TUILES D'AMANDES
Faith Duke

½ teaspoon vanilla essence
1 oz. shredded blanched almonds
2 ozs. butter

4 ozs. castor sugar
2 whites of egg
2 ozs. flour

Beat the sugar into the egg whites with a fork, then add the flour, vanilla essence, almonds and cooled melted butter. Put teaspoonfuls of the mixture well apart on a well greased baking sheet. Bake in a moderate oven on Gas No. 4 (350°) until golden brown. Lift off carefully and lay over a rolling pin to cool. Store immediately in an airtight tin.

BALTHAZARS
Renata Knobil

8 ozs. chopped walnuts
8 ozs. grated dark chocolate
2 eggs

½ cup icing sugar
2 tablespoons rum

Mix all the ingredients together and form into a ball. Flatten and shape into a 1 inch wide log. Wrap in a well greased paper and refrigerate for three days. Cut as required. *Serves 10.*

CHOCOLATE LEAVES
Faith Duke

Rose leaves from the garden

8 ozs. chocolate

Melt the chocolate in a small bowl over a pan of hot water, then beat with a wooden spoon until perfectly smooth. Wash and dry the unblemished leaves very carefully. Pull the upper side of the leaf across the top of the melted chocolate, so that it is completely covered. Lay the leaves chocolate side up, on a cold surface for 5-10 minutes until set. Peel the leaf away from the chocolate, then store in an airtight tin in a cool place. (These make a lovely garnish for cakes and desserts.

CHOCOLATE ORANGE TWIGS
Faith Duke

½ cup of water
8 ozs. sugar

Rind of 4 oranges
Chocolate

Cut the rind of the oranges in four quarters lengthways. Turn over and very carefully remove all the white pith. Cut into long strips about ¼ inch wide. Place in a pan and cover with cold water, bring to the boil, strain away the now bitter water and repeat the process twice more. Put the sugar and ½ cup of water into a clean pan, stir until the sugar has dissolved, then bring to the boil. Add the peel and simmer for about 10 minutes, or until the syrup begins to thicken. Drain and cool, then dip each piece into a deep bowl of melted chocolate, and leave on waxed paper until set.

CHOCOLATE TIPPED STRAWBERRIES
Faith Duke

Fresh strawberries

Dark chocolate

Wash and dry the strawberries very well, but *do not hull.* Melt the chocolate then beat with a wooden spoon until smooth. Take each berry by the stalk and half dip in the chocolate. Leave to set on non-stick paper. Keep in a cool place until required. (These also make a very good garnish).

DATES STUFFED WITH ALMONDS
Gillian Burr

Sugar   Blanched almonds
Dates

Split the top of each date and remove the stone. Roll the blanched almonds in sugar and put one into each date. Serve in paper sweet cases.

FLORENTINES
June Gelberg

1 oz. chopped glacé cherries
1 oz. chopped walnuts
2 ozs. blanched almonds
1 oz. shredded blanched almonds
2 ozs. candied peel

3-4 ozs. superfine chocolate
1 oz. sultanas
4 ozs. butter
4 ozs. castor sugar
1 egg

Gently heat the butter and sugar until dissolved. Stir in the cherries, walnuts, sultanas and whole almonds, then add the well beaten egg. Put small teaspoonsful of the mixture on to well greased baking tins, allowing space for the biscuits to spread. Bake above centre of a moderate oven Gas No. 4 (350°). After the first 5 minutes remove the biscuits and sprinkle with the shredded almonds, return to the oven and bake until crisp and golden brown. When cooked, cool and remove from the trays. Melt the chocolate and coat bottom of each biscuit.

GLACÉ GRAPES
Gillian Burr

Black or white grapes
¼ pint water

1 lb granulated sugar

Wash and dry the grapes and cut them singly. Boil the water and sugar together, until the point when it snaps like glass when a drop is put into cold water. After 5 minutes start testing. When ready stand the sugar pan inside another one of hot water. Take the grapes, one at a time, by the stalks, and dip into the syrup. Place on non-stick paper to cool and set.

TRUFFLES (KIRSCH)
Pauline Israel

14 ozs. chocolate
11 ozs. butter
3-4 tablespoons cream
Miniature bottle of kirsch
13 ozs. icing sugar
2 yolks of eggs

Hundred and thousands or
desiccated coconut or
ground almonds or
chocolate bits

Beat egg yolks lightly, cream butter, icing sugar and egg yolks together, add melted chocolate, cream and kirsch. Mix well together and put in the refrigerator overnight. When required roll into small balls and dip into any of the above coatings. (This mixture keeps for weeks if the family allows).

NOTES

Cakes ~

Economical castor sugar. Put granulated sugar in the liquidizer on maximum speed for 30 seconds.

The secret of creamy cheese cake is not to overbake! If the centre doesn't seem quite set, remember it solidifies as the cake cools.

Avoid damaging decorated cakes. Place the cake inside the lid of the tin, and use the bottom as the cover.

When weighing golden syrup dredge scales thickly with flour and the syrup will slide off without sticking. If using spoon measures dip them first into boiling water.

Prevent dried fruit falling to the bottom of a fruit cake by coating it in flour before adding to the cake mixture.

Rejuvenate dry fruit cake by piercing the top all over with a trussing needle and pouring over a little brandy or rum. Wrap in tin foil for a few hours.

When creaming method is required in cake making, first rinse the mixing bowl in hot water, then cream the butter well before beating in the sugar.

Economical vanilla sugar: Put 2 lbs. of castor sugar into an airtight jar, cut a vanilla pod into 3-4 pieces and push into the sugar. Close the jar tightly and leave for 2-3 days for the sugar to absorb the flavour. This is good for all cakes and desserts.

Camouflage your occasional flops. Turn cake upside down and ice.

Quick decoration for a plain cake. Place a doyley on top of the cake, sprinkle with sifted icing sugar and carefully remove the doyley.

SMALL CAKES

MUNCHY BROWNIES

Vivienne Seymour
U.S.A. Cups

⅔ cup sifted self raising flour
1 scant cup castor sugar
2 beaten eggs
1 teaspoon vanilla essence

½ cup butter
2 ozs. melted chocolate
4 teaspoons cocoa
¾ cup chopped walnuts

Beat butter and sugar together, add eggs and vanilla, then sift in the dry ingredients. Add the walnuts and pour into a greased and wax-lined 8 inch tin. Bake for 25-30 minutes on Gas No. 4 (350°). When cool turn onto a cake rack and cool for 5 minutes. Sprinkle with icing sugar and cut into squares.

DATE AND WALNUT LOAF

Fay Lasky

3 ozs. margarine
5 ozs. castor sugar
3 ozs. self raising flour
Vanilla essence

2 eggs
5 ozs. chopped walnuts
8 ozs. chopped dates

Cream fat and sugar, add eggs and flour. Stir in the nuts, dates and a little vanilla essence. Pour into a well greased tin approximately 1½ inches deep by 8 inches long. Bake for 30 minutes on Gas No. 4 (350°). When cold cut into squares.

GINGER CUPS

Faith Duke

2 ozs. butter
2 ozs. castor sugar
2 level tablespoons golden syrup
2 ozs. plain flour
½ teaspoon ground ginger

1 teaspoon grated lemon rind
1 teaspoon brandy
FILLING:
½ pint double cream
Stem ginger to garnish

Melt butter with sugar and golden syrup. Remove from heat and beat in flour, ginger, brandy and lemon rind. Cool for about 2 minutes. Place a few teaspoons of the mixture well apart on a baking sheet lined with non-stick parchment. Bake near the top of the oven on Gas No. 4 (350°) for 7-10 minutes until golden brown. Remove from oven. As mixture begins to firm lift each biscuit with a palette knife and drape over the buttered base of a 1 lb. jam jar. When set remove and store in an airtight tin. To serve, whip cream and fold in chopped ginger. Divide between cases and garnish each with a slice of stem ginger. (Fill just before serving). *Makes 12.*

MADELEINES

Gillian Burr

4 ozs. margarine
1¾ cups self raising flour
3 eggs
Vanilla essence
Desiccated coconut

1 cup castor sugar
2 teaspoons baking powder
½ teaspoon salt
½ cup milk
Jam

Cream the margarine and sugar, add eggs and beat until light and fluffy. Sift flour, salt and baking powder three times, and add to the mixture alternately with the milk and vanilla. ¼ fill well greased madeleine tins, and bake on Gas No. 6 (400°) for 15-20 minutes. Remove from tins, allow to cool, dip in heated red jam and roll in coconut. *Makes 24.*

154

MERINGUES
Charlotte Davis

3 egg whites
6 ozs. castor sugar

FILLING:
Small carton double cream

Beat egg whites until very stiff, slowly fold in sugar then beat fast for 2 seconds. Spoon onto a lightly oiled baking tray. Bake on the lowest shelf for 1¾ hours on Gas No. ¼ (250°). Turn the meringues over and cook for a further ½ hour. (Do not overbake or they will become too sugary). *Makes 20.*

NUT TARTLETS
Gloria Brown
U.S.A. Cups

TARTS:
6 oz. packet cream cheese
8 ozs. butter
2 cups plain flour
4 teaspoons castor sugar

FILLING:
1½ cups brown sugar
1½ cups chopped nuts
2 teaspoons melted butter
2 beaten eggs
Vanilla essence

Mix all tart ingredients to form a dough and refrigerate overnight. Take a small teaspoon of dough, press into ungreased tartlet tins or paper frills and mould with fingers. Replace in refrigerator. **FILLING**: Mix together melted butter and sugar, add nuts, vanilla and eggs. Take cases from refrigerator, half fill them with the mixture and bake on Gas No. 3 (325°) for 25 minutes. (Do not remove tarts from the tins until cool). *Makes 36.*

RUM AND CREAM PASTRIES
Anonymous

Manderin oranges or cherries
1 packet chocolate chip cookies
1 tablespoon rum

1 carton double cream
2-3 tablespoons fruit juice

Mix juice and rum in a shallow dish. Dip in half the biscuits and drain. Leave singly on a plate. Put a little whipped cream on each one, then sandwich with a second dipped biscuit. Put a little whipped cream on top and decorate with mandarin oranges or cherries etc.

LARGE CAKES

ALMOND CAKE
Doris Landsman

8 ozs. butter
8 ozs. castor sugar
6 ozs. self raising flour

4 ozs. ground almonds
4 eggs
½ teaspoon baking powder

Cream fat and sugar, add eggs one at a time. Mix flour with almonds and fold into creamed mixture. Add baking powder and bake in a well greased tin on Gas No. 5 (375°) for 45 minutes.

ALMOND CAKE
Thea Singer

6 ozs. self raising flour
6 ozs. margarine
6 ozs. castor sugar

4 ozs. ground almonds
3 eggs
2 drops almond essence

Cream fat and sugar, add almonds, beat in eggs, sifted flour and essence. Turn into a greased and floured 9 inch tin and bake for 1½ hours on Gas No. 3 (325°).

APPLE CAKE
Jane Manuel

3 eggs
6 ozs. margarine
6 ozs. castor sugar
6 ozs. self raising flour

1 cup orange squash
2 tablespoons apricot jam
3 large cooking apples

Grease an 8 inch loose-bottomed tin. Cream the margarine and sugar, add the eggs one at a time then fold in the flour. Spread in the tin. Peel, core and slice the apples and arrange on top of the mixture. Bake for 1 hour on Gas No. 5 (375°). Melt jam in orange squash and bring to the boil, when foaming pour onto cake. Return to the oven for a further hour. Leave in tin until cool.

APPLE CAKE
Mrs S.B. Courman

6 ozs. margarine
6 ozs. castor sugar
6 ozs. self raising flour
3 eggs

Lemon juice to taste
2 tablespoons warm water
4 large cooking apples

Cream margarine and sugar until light and fluffy. Fold in 1 oz. of flour with 1 egg and beat. Repeat twice more then fold in the remaining flour with water and lemon juice and beat. Grease an 8 inch square baking tin and pour in half the mixture. Cut, peel and slice the apples (not too thin), arrange the slices evenly over the mixture, sprinkle with sufficient sugar to sweeten then cover with remaining mixture. Smooth over then bake for approximately 1 hour on Gas No. 4 (350°).

LAYERED APPLE CAKE
Renata Knobil

4 ozs. butter
8 large cooking apples
1 large cup breadcrumbs

1 large cup brown sugar
2 teaspoons cinnamon
1 tablespoon liqueur

Grate apples, mix crumbs with cinnamon and sugar and melt butter. Line cake tin with foil, place a thick layer of apples on the bottom of the tin then a layer of crumbs and a layer of melted butter. Repeat finishing with a layer of crumbs. Pour liqueur over and bake for approximately 45 minutes on Gas No. 6 (400°) until apples are cooked. Leave in the tin until required. It is best made the day before it is needed.

SWISS APPLE ROLL
Hilda Jacobs

8 ozs. margarine
12 ozs. self raising flour
1 egg
4 ozs sugar

2 dessertspoons ground almonds
1 tin apple purée
or 2 lbs cooking apples
(cooked and puréed)

Cream margarine and sugar lightly, add flour and egg alternately. Mix in ground almonds then portion the dough into three pieces. Roll the first piece ¼ inch thick and place in the bottom of a 10 inch spring form tin, sprinkle with a little more ground almonds then place half the apple purée on top. Repeat once more then place the third piece of pastry on top. Bake for approximately 1 hour on Gas No. 4 (350°) until golden.

156

FLAT ALMOND CAKE
Margaret Silver

6 ozs. ground almonds
6 ozs. butter
6 ozs. castor sugar

1½ ozs. cornflour
3 eggs

Cream butter and sugar, add lightly beaten eggs and ground almonds mixed with cornflour. Bake in a greased 9 inch cake tin on Gas No. 3-4 (325°-350°) for 1 hour.

NORWEGIAN CARAMEL CONFECT ALMOND CAKE
Hetty Prashker

CAKE:
2 eggs
4½ ozs. sugar
4 ozs. butter or margarine
3 ozs. plain flour scant

TOPPING:
3 ozs. chopped blanched almonds
3 ozs. margarine
3 ozs. sugar
1 dessertspoon milk

Melt butter. Beat eggs and sugar together, add cooled melted butter and flour. Bake in a well greased tin, put into a **COLD** oven, turn onto Gas No. 3 (325°) and bake until cake is light brown. **TOPPING:** Cook all ingredients over a low heat, whilst mixture is still hot spread over the hot cake, replace in oven until top of cake is a caramel colour. Serve cold.

APPLE CAKE
Judith Solomons

2 eggs
7 ozs. self raising flour
1 teaspoon baking powder
5 tablespoons milk or water
5 ozs. castor sugar

4 large cooking apples
2 ozs. blanched almonds
½ teaspoon cinnamon
Raisins

Peel, core and slice the apples, mix with nuts, cinnamon and a few raisins. Beat eggs and sugar, fold in flour and baking powder then the milk or water. Grease a tin, pour in half the sponge mixture, cover with the apples then add the rest of the sponge mixture. Bake for 1 hour on Gas No. 3½-4 (338°-350°).

APPLE CAKE
Karol Solomons

½ pint whipped cream
2 cups crushed cornflakes
2 cups castor sugar

Grated chocolate (optional)
2 teaspoons cinnamon
5 lbs cooking apples

Line a 7½ inch by 3¼ inch loose-bottomed cake tin with silver foil. Grate the apples into a bowl, press a plate on top and drain away most of the liquid. Mix the crushed cornflakes, sugar and cinnamon together. Put half the apples into the tin and spread evenly, cover with half the dry ingredients and spread evenly. Repeat with the second half of the mixtures then dot the top with small pieces of butter or margarine. (This forms a toffee-like crunch). Bake for 45 minutes on Gas No. 4 (350°). When cold refrigerate for 24 hours. Turn over onto a serving plate, cover with whipped cream and grated chocolate if desired.

APRICOT CAKE

Hilda Blaine

8 ozs. self raising flour
8 ozs. butter or margarine
2 large tablespoons apricot jam

4 eggs
¾ pint double cream

Cream margarine and sugar well, add eggs and flour, mix well. Bake for about 45 minutes on Gas No. 4 (350°). When cold, sandwich together with jam and whipped cream. Decorate with remaining cream.

BOUDOIR LAYER CAKE

Dianna Marks

2 boxes boudoir biscuits
1 cup hot strong black coffee
3 tablespoons castor sugar

3 tablespoons cognac
¾ pint double cream
1 tin pitted black cherries

Make 1 cup of strong black coffee with the sugar then place in a mixing bowl. Allow to cool then add the cognac. Gently soak biscuits one at a time then place on a plate in a row of 8, cover with whipped cream. Repeat three times more. Cover the top and sides with cream, decorate the top with straight rows of black cherries then pipe the remainder of the cream around the edges. Refrigerate on a plate without a doyley.

FROSTED CARROT CAKE

A Secret Nibbler
U.S.A. Cups

8 fl. ozs. corn oil
8 ozs. castor sugar
3 large eggs
6 ozs. plain flour
1½ level teaspoons baking powder
1½ level teaspoons bicarbonate of soda
¾ level teaspoon salt
1½ level teaspoons ground cinnamon

4 ozs. chopped walnuts
8 ozs. grated raw carrot
1 teaspoon vanilla essence
CREAM CHEESE FROSTING:
2 x 3 oz. packets cream cheese
1 oz. butter or margarine
½-1 teaspoon almond essence
8 ozs. sifted icing sugar

Grease an 8 inch round deep cake tin then line with greased greaseproof paper. Place corn oil and sugar in a bowl and beat well together, add eggs one at a time, beating well after each addition. Sift flour, baking powder, bicarbonate of soda, salt and cinnamon together and stir into oil mixture. Beat well, add chopped walnuts, carrots and vanilla. Turn into prepared tin and bake on Gas No. 4 (350°) for 1 hour until cooked through. Allow to cool in the tin. **FROSTING:** Beat cream cheese and butter together until blended, gradually beat in almond essence to taste and sifted icing sugar. Remove cake from tin and cover top and sides with the frosting. Chill until required.

CHEESE CAKE (1)

Avril Courman

1½ lbs. cooking cheese
1 cup castor sugar
3 eggs
¼ pint double cream

2 tablespoons flour
1 teaspoon lemon juice
Pinch of salt
Digestive biscuit crumbs
or shortcrust pastry thinly rolled
or sponge cake thinly sliced

Grease baking tin and line with shortcrust pastry, sponge cake or biscuit crumbs. Place eggs and sugar in a large bowl and beat until very thick and creamy. In another bowl thoroughly beat the cheese, flour, salt, lemon juice and cream. Combine the contents of the two bowls and beat together. Pour mixture into prepared tin and bake on Gas No. 4 (350°). The cake will rise like a soufflé. Turn off heat and let cake remain in oven for 20 minutes with the oven door slightly open.

(The secret of a successful and delicious cheese cake is long beating).

CHEESE CAKE (2)

B.B. Green

8 ozs. castor sugar
2 lbs. cooking cheese
6 eggs
2 heaped tablespoons cornflour
or arrowroot
4 digestive biscuits or sponge cake

2 cartons sour cream
or 1 large carton single cream
Lemon juice
or vanilla essence to taste
Pinch of salt

Mix cheese with cornflour and beat thoroughly. Mix sugar with eggs, adding 2 eggs at a time and beat thoroughly, add salt and lemon juice or vanilla. Add egg mixture to cheese and beat well, lastly add the cream, and beat again. **BASE**: Grease a loose bottomed 8 inch tin and use a thin layer of sponge cake or crushed digestive biscuits. Pour in the mixture and bake for 1 hour on Gas No. 4 (350°). About 10 minutes before finishing lower heat gradually.

CHEESE CAKE (3)

Marion Gold

¾ lb. cooking cheese
¼ pint double cream
1 carton sour cream
1 cup castor sugar

3 eggs
1 tablespoon lemon juice
1 tablespoon self raising flour
2 sponge cakes

Line a loose bottomed 8 inch tin with foil. Slice sponge cakes thinly and lay on the bottom of the tin. Separate eggs. Mix all ingredients with the egg yolks, beat egg whites until stiff and fold into cheese mixture. Bake for 45 minutes on Gas No. 3 (325°). Turn oven off and leave for 1 hour. Place in refrigerator until needed, preferably until next day then decorate. *Serves 10.*

CHEESE CAKE (4)

Faith Duke

6-8 digestive biscuits
1 lb. cooking cheese
3 eggs
½ packet red jelly

6 ozs. castor sugar
2 tablespoons lemon juice
1 tin loganberries

Crush biscuits and lay crumbs on base of a buttered spring form tin. Beat the cheese until smooth, add the eggs one at a time, then the sugar and lemon juice, beat again. Pour on to crumbs. Bake for 15-20 minutes on Gas No. 4 (350°) until set. When cold top with strained loganberries and pour over ½ pint of semi set jelly made with the fruit juice. Place in the refrigerator until set firm.

CHEESE CAKE (5)

Karol Solomons

1 lb. cooking cheese
4 eggs
6 ozs. castor sugar
For decoration: ½ carton sour cream or
1 carton double cream and fruit

½ packet digestive biscuits
1 teaspoon cinnamon
Little melted butter

Melt butter and crush biscuits. Mix together with cinnamon and line a loose bottomed tin. Beat together sugar, cheese and eggs. Pour on to base and cook for 15 minutes only on Gas No. 4 (350°). Put in the refrigerator overnight and decorate with either sour cream or lightly whipped cream and fruit.

CHEESE CAKE (6)

Thea Singer

1¼ lbs cooking cheese
3 eggs separated
4 tablespoons sugar
1 oz. butter

1 heaped tablespoon cornflour
8 crushed digestive biscuits
1 tin pineapple chunks
1 carton double cream

Mix cheese, butter, sugar, cornflour and egg yolks. Beat whites until stiff and fold in to mixture. Press biscuit crumbs in to a well greased 9 inch tin. Cover with half the pineapple chunks and then the cheese mixture. Bake for 25-30 minutes on Gas No. 4 (350°) until the cake stands away from the tin. When cold top with remaining pineapple and cover with whipped cream. Refrigerate overnight.

CHEESE CAKE TORTE

Pearl Barnett
U.S.A. Cups

BASE:
2 cups Zwieback
4 tablespoons icing sugar
¼ lb. melted butter
TOPPING:
2 cups sour cream
1 teaspoon vanilla essence
4 tablespoons sugar

FILLING:
4 eggs
1 cup sugar
2 lbs. cream cheese
1 tablespoon lemon juice

Blend all the base ingredients reserving ¼ cup. Press remainder in to base of a 9 inch spring form tin and chill. Preheat oven to Gas No. 4 (350°). Beat eggs, sugar and lemon juice until light, add cheese and beat well. Pour filling in to crust and bake for 20 minutes. Remove torte from oven and increase heat to Gas No. 5 (375°). Whilst torte is still hot top with sour cream mixed with sugar and vanilla. Sprinkle with the remaining crumbs and bake for 10 minutes longer. When cool refrigerate and leave for a day before using.

CHOCOLATE CHEESE CAKE

Gloria Brown
U.S.A. Cups

BASE:
8½ ozs. chocolate wafers
1/3rd cup melted butter
2 tablespoons granulated sugar
¼ teaspoon nutmeg
TOPPING:
1 cup double cream
2 tablespoons icing sugar

FILLING:
3 eggs
1 cup granulated sugar
1½ lbs. cream cheese
12 ozs. chocolate pieces
1 teaspoon vanilla
1/8th teaspoon salt
1 cup sour cream

Crush wafers with a rolling pin or in an electric blender. Mix all base ingredients together, press onto the base and sides of a 9 inch spring form tin and refrigerate. Beat eggs with sugar in a large mixer bowl, at high speed until light. Beat in cheese until mixture is smooth. Add melted chocolate, vanilla, salt and sour cream, beat until smooth. Turn into crumb crust and bake for 1 hour on Gas No. 4 (350°) or until cake is just firm when the tin is shaken gently. Cool cake in tin on a wire rack then refrigerate, covered, overnight. Before serving beat double cream with icing sugar until stiff, remove cake from tin and decorate. (This looks nicer if piped on). *Serves 16.*

MOCK CHEESE CAKE

Renata Knobil

1 tin condensed milk
6 eggs
2 large lemons

1 packet digestive biscuits
¼ lb butter
1 teaspoon cinnamon

Crush biscuits, add melted butter and cinnamon. Put in the base of an 8 inch baking tin. Separate eggs, beat together milk and yolks, add grated lemon rind and juice. Beat egg whites until stiff then add to mixture. Bake for approximately 30 minutes on Gas No. 3 (350°).

REFRIGERATED CHEESE CAKE

Another Way to a Man's Heart

1 level teaspoon gelatine
3 ozs. castor sugar
Pinch of salt
¼ pint milk
Grated rind of ½ lemon
10 ozs. sieved cottage cheese
1 egg white
4 tablespoons double cream
1 egg yolk

TOPPING:
2 ozs digestive biscuits
2 level teaspoons castor sugar
1 oz. melted butter
DECORATION:
Pineapple rings
Glacé cherries

Blend gelatine, 2½ ozs. sugar and salt in a saucepan. Beat together egg yolk and milk, stirring with gelatine mixture and beat. Take off heat, add rind and lemon juice. Cool until beginning to set, stir in cheese. Whisk egg white, add ½ oz. sugar and whisk again. Fold quickly into cheese mixture followed by whipped cream. Turn mixture into a 6 inch greased spring form tin (fitted with a fluted tubular base) or a 6 inch ring tin. Crush biscuits and stir in melted butter and sugar. Use to cover cheese cake mixture and press lightly. Chill until firm. Decorate with pineapple rings and glacé cherries.

RUSSIAN CHEESE CAKE

Lola Monk
U.S.A. Cups

½ lb. ginger biscuits
1½ lbs. cooking cheese
Small cup castor sugar
1 teaspoon vanilla essence

¾ pint sour cream
2-3 ozs. butter
4 separated eggs
2 dessertspoons sugar

Crush ginger biscuits and mix with melted butter. Line a deep 9 inch cake tin with foil and press the biscuit mixture on to the bottom and sides. Put cheese in a bowl and add egg yolks, cup of sugar and vanilla. Beat egg whites until stiff and fold into cheese mixture. Pour into tin and bake for 30 minutes on Gas No. 5 (375°). Mix sour cream with remaining sugar, beat until it doubles in quantity. Pour over cheese cake and return to the oven for a further 10 minutes. When cool refrigerate in the tin, leave overnight.

UNCOOKED LEMON CHEESE CAKE

Betty Redstone

CRUST:
8 crushed digestive biscuits
1 oz. demerara sugar
2 ozs. melted butter
FILLING:
12 oz. packet cream cheese
3 tablespoons castor sugar

1 teaspoon vanilla essence
Juice and rind of ½ lemon
2 beaten egg yolks
½ oz. gelatine
3 egg whites
½ pint whipped double cream

Mix first three ingredients together to form a pastry crust, put into 8 inch greased spring form tin and press down. Mix cheese, sugar and vanilla add lemon juice, rind and egg yolks and whisk. Add gelatine which has been dissolved in 2 tablespoons of warm water. Beat egg whites until stiff and fold gently into mixture, then fold in whipped cream and pour over crust. Refrigerate overnight.

CHERRY CAKE

Barbara Green

2 eggs
Juice of a medium orange
½ cup oil
2 cups plain flour

2 teaspoons baking powder
Pinch of salt
1 cup sugar
2 tins pitted cherries

Mix all ingredients together, adding flour last. Pour batter into an 8 inch by 12 inch baking tin or pyrex dish. Reserve 4 tablespoons of batter. Drain the cherries well, place on top of the mixture in the tin. To the remaining batter add sufficient flour to thicken enough to roll out for long thin strips. Put strips crosswise over cherries about 1 inch apart. Bake for 45-60 minutes on Gas No. 4 (350°). *Serves 6-8.*

CHOCOLATE CAKE

Dianne Zimmerman

4 ozs. castor sugar
4 ozs. butter or margarine
2 ozs. ground almonds
2 ozs. self raising flour
4 ozs. drinking chocolate
½ teaspoon baking powder

3 eggs

ICING:
3 ozs butter
4 ozs. icing sugar
2 ozs. cocoa

Cream fat and sugar. Sieve together ground almonds, flour, chocolate and baking powder. Add to mixture in three parts with eggs and mix well. Bake in well greased ring tin for 40 minutes on Gas No. 3-4 (325°-350°). When cold ice with butter icing made with the above ingredients.

REFRIGERATED CHOCOLATE BISCUIT CAKE

Marion Cohen

8 ozs. melted plain chocolate
8 ozs. butter or margarine
2 eggs
2 level dessertspoons sugar

Chopped walnuts
Glacé cherries
8 ozs. digestive biscuits
2 dessertspoons brandy or rum

Butter a 6 inch-7 inch loose bottomed cake tin. Melt chocolate in a basin over a pan of boiling water. While chocolate is softening, melt 8 ozs. butter in another pan. Beat the eggs and add the sugar in a large bowl. Pour melted butter on to the eggs, in a steady stream stirring constantly. Add melted chocolate and beat. Break digestive biscuits into approximately 12 pieces per biscuit and fold into mixture. Add 1-2 ozs. chopped walnuts and chopped glacé cherries. Add the brandy or rum and mix well with a wooden spoon. Put mixture into cake tin, decorate with cherries and walnuts then refrigerate.

CHOCOLATE CREAM CAKE

Betty Feltz

3 eggs
3 ozs. castor sugar
1 oz. cocoa
2 ozs. self raising flour

2 drops vanilla essence
½ pint double cream
Chopped walnuts

Beat eggs and sugar until white, add vanilla. Sieve flour and cocoa and fold into egg mixture. Grease and flour two sandwich tins and divide mixture. Bake for 20-25 minutes on Gas No. 4 (350°). When cold split **BOTH** cakes and fill with whipped cream. Restack, cover cake with cream and sprinkle with chopped nuts or chocolate.

CHOCOLATE LAYER CAKE
Diana Marks

CAKE:
5 ozs. self raising flour
1 oz. cocoa powder
6 ozs. butter
6 ozs. soft brown sugar
1 teaspoon vanilla essence
4 ozs. plain chocolate
3 tablespoons boiling water
4 eggs

TOPPING:
6 ozs. icing sugar
2 ozs. cocoa powder
2½ ozs. butter
4 tablespoons water
4 ozs. castor sugar
½ teaspoon vanilla essence

Sift flour and cocoa on to plate. Cream butter, sugar and vanilla essence in machine until soft, break chocolate into basin and add 3 tablespoons of boiling water and stir until melted. Beat chocolate into butter and sugar mixture, separate eggs, beat yolks in one at a time. Beat egg whites until stiff. Fold sieved flour, cocoa and beaten egg whites into chocolate mixture. Spoon into greased 8 inch sandwich tins and smooth. Place in pre-heated oven on Gas No. 4 (350°) for 25-30 minutes. **TOPPING:** Sift icing sugar and cocoa into a basin, measure butter, water, sugar and vanilla essence into a saucepan, set over low heat and slowly bring to the boil. Pour on to dry ingredients and beat with a wooden spoon. When cool, spread on to bottom layer of sponge and coat top layer. Decorate with grated chocolate.

CHOCOLATE MARBLE CAKE
Kitty Massey

4 ozs. sugar
4 ozs. butter
4 ozs. self raising flour
1 teaspoon baking powder
2 eggs

1 teaspoon vanilla essence
2 tablespoons milk
4 ozs. melted cooking chocolate
Icing sugar

Cream butter and sugar, add 1 egg and ½ the quantity of flour. Beat, then add 1 more egg and rest of flour. Add vanilla. Put milk into melted chocolate and add by spoonfuls to the mixture, smoothing with a fork so that it looks streaky and not too well mixed. Pour into a greased round marble tin and bake on Gas No. 5 (375°) for 35-40 minutes. When cool, sprinkle with icing sugar.

CHOME TORTE
Faith Duke
U.S.A. Cups

THIS MAKES 2 TORTES

6 egg whites
½ teaspoon baking powder
1/8th teaspoon salt
2 teaspoons vanilla essence

2 teaspoons brown vinegar
2 teaspoons water
2 cups castor sugar
Whipped cream
Fresh or tinned fruit

Combine all ingredients except sugar. Beat at high speed until stiff. Add sifted sugar, 1 teaspoon at a time and continue beating. Bake in two 10 inch spring form tins which have been well greased and lightly floured, for 1½ hours on Gas No. ¾ (288°). When required fill with cream and fruit. Tortes may be made in advance and kept in an airtight tin.

CHOICE FRUIT CAKE

Betty Feltz

THIS QUANTITY MAKES 2 CAKES

1 lb. flour
¼ teaspoon salt
1 teaspoon mixed spice
1 lb. currants
1 lb. sultanas
½ lb mixed peel
½ lb. raisins
½ lb. glacé cherries
½ lb. shelled almonds

Grated rind of 1 lemon
Rind and juice of 1 orange
6-8 eggs
12 ozs. butter
12 ozs. castor sugar
A little milk
1 teaspoon coffee essence
1 tablespoon gravy browning
Brandy to taste

Mix together flour, salt and spice. Prepare fruit, chop raisins, peel and cherries, blanche and chop nuts, grate orange and lemon rind. Mix fruit, nuts and rind with flour. Blend butter and sugar until white, beat eggs in one at a time. Stir in flour and fruit mixture, then orange juice with a little milk if necessary to give a soft dropping consistency. Colour mixture a good brown with coffee and browning. Put in prepared tins and shake down well. Bake in oven on Gas No. 2 (300°) for 1-1½ hours, then reduce to Gas No. 1½ (290°) and bake for a further 1-1½ hours. Finish baking on Gas No. ¼ (250°) allowing 5-5½ hours cooking time. Cool on rack. Next day pierce the top of the cakes and pour brandy over. Wrap in greaseproof paper and put in a tin. (This will keep for weeks).

CINNAMON CONTINENTAL

Valerie Halpern

CAKE:
8 ozs. self raising flour
1 teaspoon baking powder
3 ozs. castor sugar
3 ozs. butter or margarine
1 egg
¼ pint milk

TOPPING:
1½ ozs. butter or margarine
2 ozs. castor sugar
1 oz. flour
1 teaspoon cinnamon

Sift together flour and baking powder. Combine with sugar and rub in butter until mixture resembles breadcrumbs. Mix egg with milk and stir into mixture until a thick batter is obtained. Pour into a 6 inch tin. Cover with topping. Rub butter into flour, sugar and cinnamon, sprinkle on top of cake batter. Bake for 35 minutes on Gas No. 6 (400°).

COFFEE CAKE

Lesley Bennett

8 ozs. butter
8 ozs. castor sugar
4 eggs
1 tablespoon instant coffee
2 tablespoons hot water
3 teaspoons baking powder
8 ozs. plain flour

ICING:
¾ lb. icing sugar
1 tablespoon instant coffee
1 tablespoon hot water
6 ozs. butter

Cream butter and sugar until pale lemon coloured. Separate eggs and beat yolks one at a time into mixture. Dissolve instant coffee with boiled water and beat into mixture. Sift flour and baking powder and fold in until well blended. Beat egg whites until stiff and fold gently into batter. Spoon into a greased 8 inch deep tin and bake for 45-50 minutes on Gas No. 4 (350°) until firm to the touch. Turn on to cake rack and cool. **ICING:** Cream softened butter, blend in icing sugar, dissolve coffee with water and beat into icing. Cut cake through centre and sandwich together with filling, spreading the remainder thickly over top and sides.

COFFEE LOG

Gillian Burr

2 packets boudoir biscuits
1 packet cat's tongues biscuits
¾ pint double cream
¼ pint single cream

1 tumbler of milk
3 tablespoons brandy
Chocolate bits
3 tablespoons coffee extract

Mix together coffee and milk. Dip boudoir biscuits in, one at a time and place 12 biscuits side by side on a long plate. Dribble brandy over them and cover with creams that have been mixed together and whipped. Repeat and finish by covering top and sides with cream. Decorate by placing cat's tongues standing upright around the sides of the cake. Sprinkle with chocolate bits.

CRANBERRY CREAM CAKE

Gloria Brown
U.S.A. Cups

1½ cups digestive biscuits
6 tablespoons melted butter
8 oz. packet cream cheese
1 cup double cream

¼ cup castor sugar
½ teaspoon vanilla
1 lb. tin whole cranberry sauce

Crush biscuits and mix with melted butter. Cover base of a 9 inch loose bottomed cake tin with mixture. Beat cream cheese until fluffy, combine double cream, sugar and vanilla. Whip until thickened but not stiff. Gradually add to cream cheese, beating until smooth and creamy. Set aside a few whole cranberries from the sauce for garnish. Fold remaining sauce into mixture and freeze. Remove from freezer 10 mins. before serving and top with a little whipped cream.

FRUIT CAKE

Lola Monk

8 ozs. margarine
8 ozs. castor sugar
4 eggs
8 ozs. sultanas
8 ozs. currants
¼ teaspoon salt

4 ozs. mixed peel
4 ozs. glacé cherries
2 ozs. almonds
1 lemon
10 ozs. plain flour
½ teaspoon baking powder

Cream fat and sugar and beat in eggs. Blanche almonds and chop half of them, reserve remainder for decoration. Mix fruit and chopped cherries with nuts and fold into the creamed mixture, together with juice and grated lemon rind, add sifted flour and baking powder. Put into greased and lined 8 inch cake tin, arrange remaining nuts around the top of the cake and bake for 3-3½ hours on Gas No. 2 (300°).

GINGER SPONGE CAKE

Sheila Rosen

⅓ cup oil
½ cup demerara sugar
½ cup golden syrup
½ cup boiling water
1 egg

8 ozs. plain flour
1 teaspoon cinnamon
1 teaspoon bicarbonate of soda
¼ teaspoon ginger or to taste
Pinch of salt

Line an 8 inch cake tin with foil. Mix sugar and oil, add beaten egg, measure golden syrup and fill cup with boiling water, add this to oil and sugar mixture. Sift all dry ingredients together and add to liquid mixture. Pour into lined tin and bake for 1-1¼ hours, middle shelf, on Gas No.4 (325°). *Serves 20.*

166

HAZELNUT CAKE
Lesley Bennett

4 ozs. butter
½ cup milk
6 ozs. sugar
4 ozs. ground hazelnuts

2 eggs
6 ozs. self raising flour
1 level teaspoon baking powder

Cream butter and sugar, add beaten eggs, and mix well. Add nuts, flour and baking powder and lastly milk. Cook in an 8 inch tin for 1 hour on Gas No. 4 (350°). Serve covered with whipped cream or a dusting of icing sugar.

HONEY CAKE
Mrs E. Silver

6 ozs. castor sugar
2 eggs
½ cup oil
½ lb honey
2 tablespoons golden syrup
6 ozs. plain flour
6 ozs. self raising flour

1 teaspoon baking powder
½ teaspoon bicarbonate of soda
1 teaspoon cinnamon
1 teaspoon mixed spice
1 teaspoon ground ginger
1 cup warm water

Mix first five ingredients in the mixer. Sieve together all the other ingredients with 1 cup of warm water to form a runny mixture, add this to the sugar and oil mixture and pour into a large oiled and lined tin. Bake for 1 hour on Gas No. 3-4 (325°-350°).

HONEY CAKE
Marylin Ford

16 tablespoons self raising flour
1 cup sugar
1 cup oil
1 cup water
3 eggs

1 cup golden syrup
1 teaspoon cinnamon
1 heaped teaspoon bicarbonate of soda
Pinch of ginger

Mix all dry ingredients together then add the remainder. Beat well and pour into a well greased 8 inch tin. Bake for 1-1½ hours on Gas No. 4 (350°).

HONEY SPICE CAKE
Pearl Barnett
U.S.A. Cups

1½ cups sugar
1 cup warm honey
1 cup warm water
2 teaspoons baking powder
2½ teaspoons mixed spice

1 teaspoon cinnamon
3 eggs
¾ cup oil
3 cups plain flour
¼ teaspoon bicarbonate of soda

Beat eggs and sugar together, sift dry ingredients and add alternately with oil and water. Pour into greased 8 inch tin and bake for 1 hour on Gas No. 3 (325°).

LEMON CAKE
Sadie Morgan
U.S.A. Cups

1 packet yellow cake mix
1 packet lemon jelly powder
¾ cup orange juice

¾ cup oil
4 eggs
2 lemons
¾ cup icing sugar

Mix all the above ingredients together except for the icing sugar and lemons. Bake for 45-50 minutes in an 8 inch greased tin on Gas No. 5 (375°). Whilst still warm pour a mixture of the icing sugar and juice of 2 lemons over cake. Allow to cool before slicing.

LEMON CAKE

Jane Manuel

4 ozs. soft butter
6 ozs. self raising flour
6 ozs. castor sugar
2 large eggs

4 tablespoons milk
Pinch of salt
grated rind of 1 lemon
ICING:
3 tablespoons icing sugar
3 tablespoons lemon juice

Well oil a 2 lb loaf tin and line the bottom with greaseproof paper. Place all ingredients in a bowl and mix until smooth. Bake for 45 minutes on Gas No. 4 (350°). Remove from oven and leave in tin. **ICING**: Heat the icing sugar with the lemon juice until syrupy. Prick cake all over with a fork and pour on syrup. Leave cake until cool before turning out of tin.

LINZER TORTE

Ann Brown

6 ozs. ground almonds
6 ozs. butter
1 egg
4 ozs. sugar

6 ozs. plain flour
Grated rind and juice of 2 lemons
Raspberry jam

Mix all ingredients except jam to a smooth pastry. Roll out and spread on a flan tin with loose sides. Put extra piece all round edge so that it is raised. Spread surface with jam and rest of pastry like a lattice work top. Brush with beaten egg. Bake for 25 minutes on Gas No. 3-4 (325°-350°).

LINZER TORTE

Renata Knobil

4 ozs. margarine
4 ozs. sugar
4 ozs. hazelnuts
5 ozs. plain flour

1 egg yolk
Cinnamon
Cocoa
Grated lemon rind
Cranberry jelly or jam

Cream together sugar and fat, beat in egg yolk. Add lemon, cinnamon and cocoa to taste and finally fold in sifted flour and nuts. Roll out this crumbly pastry, patting it into place in a greased loose bottomed flan tin. Spread cranberry jelly or jam over it and decorate with pastry strips. Bake for approximately 1 hour on Gas No. 4-5 (350°-375°).

MADEIRA CAKE

Vivienne Seymour

6 ozs. self raising flour
6 ozs. scant castor sugar
Rind of ½ lemon

6 ozs. butter
3 eggs
4 ozs. sultanas and currants

Cream butter and sugar until light and fluffy. Add lemon rind and egg yolks. Fold in **BY HAND** sifted flour. Add sultanas and currants. Beat egg whites until stiff and fold in. Bake in a greased and floured fluted Angel cake tin for 50-60 minutes on Gas No. 4-5 (350°-375°).

MARMALADE CAKE
Jennifer Finegold

6 ozs. self raising flour
6 ozs. margarine
3 eggs
6 ozs. sugar

½ teaspoon salt
½ teaspoon baking powder
3 tablespoons marmalade

Grease and flour a 9 inch cake tin. Cream sugar and margarine until white. Add eggs and beat until creamy. Fold in sifted flour and remaining ingredients adding marmalade last. Bake for 1-1¼ hours on Gas No. 4 (350°).

MARRON CAKE
Gillian Burr

3 ozs. plain flour
Pinch of salt
1 tin sweetened marron purée
Icing sugar

3 separated eggs
3 ozs. castor sugar
½ pint double cream
Vanilla essence to taste

Beat egg whites and salt until stiff. Beat egg yolks in, one at a time. Add sugar and beat for 5 minutes until white. Fold in flour with a little vanilla essence. Put mixture in a large greased and floured flan case, or two 7 inch sandwich tins. Bake for 25 minutes on Gas No. 5 (375°). When cool fill inside of flan case with the whipped cream and pipe on the sweetened marron purée mixed with a knob of butter and a little cream and vanilla. Shake icing sugar over side of cake.

MERINGUE CAKE
Karol Solomons

4 egg whites
4 ozs. granulated sugar
Fruit—strawberries or bananas

4 ozs. castor sugar
Whipped cream
Nuts

Add a pinch of salt to egg whites, beat until stiff, add granulated sugar and fold in castor sugar. Divide mixture into three rounds on oiled paper, dredge with sugar, bake in oven on Gas No. ½ (275°). Sandwich with fruit and cream.

MOCHA GÂTEAU
Beryl Kramer
U.S.A. Cups

CAKE:
7 separated eggs
1 cup plain flour
1¼ cups granulated sugar

FILLING:
12 ozs. butter
1½ cups icing sugar
3 whole eggs or 6 yolks
4-6 ozs. almonds
2 tablespoons instant coffee diluted with
2 tablespoons water

CAKE: Beat egg whites until very stiff, set aside. Beat egg yolks until thick gradually add sugar until light coloured. Add alternately flour and egg whites, beating very slowly. Grease and flour a large Angel cake tin. Bake for 1 hour on Gas No. 3 (325°). Cool well and split into three. **FILLING:** Let butter soften, beat until very light, add sugar gradually, add one egg at a time, then coffee. Use this as a filling and covering. Brown almonds in oven by placing them on a biscuit tray sprinkled with sugar, for 5 minutes. When cool, flip on to cake. Keep in refrigerator until required.

169

NO-NAME CAKE
Toby Green

½ lb. packet digestive biscuits
Handful of raisins
Handful of sultanas
1 teaspoon vanilla essence

Chopped nuts
4 ozs. margarine
1½ tablespoons golden syrup
1½ tablespoons chocolate powder

Moulie digestive biscuits into a bowl, add fruit and nuts. Melt the margarine with golden syrup, add chocolate powder and vanilla. Pour this over the dry ingredients and mix well. Press firmly into a small greased (not floured) loose bottomed cake tin and refrigerate overnight.

POPPYSEED CAKE
Yaffa Wagner

11 ozs. castor sugar
7 ozs. ground poppyseeds
1 tablespoon rum
1 cup milk

6 separated eggs
Butter
2 ozs. plain flour
1 pint whipped cream

Mix together 7½ ozs. sugar, poppyseeds, rum and milk, cook over a low heat stirring often, for about 20 minutes. Cool. Mix egg yolks with 3½ ozs. sugar and cream together well. Gradually add the yolk mixture to the poppyseeds. Beat egg whites until stiff and beat in remaining sugar. Fold the two together, spread butter rather thickly on to a deep pie dish and sprinkle with flour until butter is hidden. Carefully spoon on the cake mixture and bake for approximately 1 hour on Gas No. 4 (350°).
This is even better served with whipped cream.

PRUNE CAKE
Dianne Zimmerman
U.S.A. Cups

1 cup sugar
⅔ cup oil
½ cup cooked chopped prunes
½ cup prune juice
2 eggs
1 teaspoon salt
2 teaspoon vanilla essence

2 teaspoons bicarbonate of soda
2 tablespoons sour milk
1⅔ cup plain flour
2 tablespoons drinking chocolate
1 teaspoon cinnamon
1 teaspoon allspice

Cream sugar and oil together, add prunes and prune juice and beat well. Add unbeaten eggs and beat again. Stir bicarbonate of soda into sour milk and add to mixture. Sift flour, chocolate, spices and add to mixture, add vanilla. Bake in two greased and floured 9 inch sponge tins on Gas No. 4 (350°) for 25 minutes. When cool layer together with whipped cream.

REFRIGERATED RUM CAKE
Renata Knobil

3 packets boudoir biscuits
½ lb. ground hazelnuts
8 tablespoons rum

½ pint milk
½ pint double cream
Flaked chocolate

Place into a dish half the quantity of rum and half the milk. (More rum may be added for a stronger flavour). Choose a square tin or dish which will act as a mould for the cake. Dip the biscuits into liquid to moisten well, then cover the bottom of the mould with one layer. Mix the ground nuts with the same liquid to form a paste, spread this on the layer of biscuits. Then repeat process. Refrigerate overnight. To serve turn on to platter and cover with whipped cream and decorate with flaked chocolate.

SAVARIN AUX FRAISES

Gillian Burr

SAVARIN MIXTURE:
4½ ozs. flour
Pinch of salt
½ oz. sugar
½ oz. fresh yeast
½ gill warm milk
1¾ ozs. butter
2 eggs

SYRUP:
6 ozs. loaf sugar
1½ gills water
½ split vanilla pod
FILLING:
6 ozs. strawberries
A little kirsch
Sugar

SAVARIN: Sift flour and salt into a warm bowl. Cream yeast and sugar together and pour in the milk. Mix well and add to the flour with the beaten eggs. Beat thoroughly by hand for 5 minutes. Cover bowl with greaseproof paper and leave in a warm place until it has doubled its bulk (approximately 45 minutes). Cream butter until soft and beat into dough for 5 minutes. Grease well a savarin tin, pour in mixture and leave for 10-15 minutes in a warm place until it rises to top of tin. Then bake on Gas No. 5-6 (370°–400°) until golden brown — approximately 30 minutes. Turn out carefully and whilst still hot pour over syrup.

SYRUP: Dissolve sugar slowly in the water. Add the vanilla and boil rapidly without stirring for approximately 5 minutes. Remove vanilla and use syrup while hot. If too thick, dilute with a little water.

When cool, fill centre of savarin with strawberries, which have been soaked in a little kirsch and sugar.

SOUR CREAM CAKE

Karol Solomons

1 packet digestive biscuits
2 ozs. melted butter
½ teaspoon cinnamon

4 cartons sour cream
1 large tin loganberries
1 cup castor sugar

Make base with first three ingredients, and press into the bottom of a 7 inch spring form tin. Drain the loganberries and mix well with the rest of the ingredients. Pour into tin. Bake in oven on Gas No. 4 (350°) for 20 minutes. (This is equally delicious decorated with whipped cream.)

STRAWBERRY GÂTEAU

Gillian Burr

2½ packets boudoir biscuits
2 cartons double cream
1 carton single cream
Little sherry

2 tablespoons sugar
1 tin strawberries
or ¾ lb. fresh strawberries

Grease an 8 inch sandwich tin, cut biscuits ⅔ long. Whip cream and sugar until fairly stiff. If using tinned strawberries drain, reserving the juice. Dip biscuits in sherry or strawberry juice. Place side by side round tin standing the biscuits upright. Use the end pieces to fill the base completely. Fill case with ½ amount of cream, cover with strawberries and cover with remaining cream. Put in freezer for a few hours, then place in refrigerator until ready to serve. **REMOVE CAKE FROM TIN WHILST STILL FROZEN**. Decorate with flaked chocolate.

STRAWBERRY AND REDCURRANT FLAN

A Fresh Fruit Lover

8 inch flan case
Redcurrant jelly
Sweetened whipped cream
Maraschino
½ lb. fresh strawberries

GARNISH:
Small bunch of redcurrants
White of egg
Castor sugar

Bake flan case blind, and spread bottom with broken-up redcurrant jelly. Spread with a layer of sweetened whipped cream, to which a little maraschino has been added.
Decorate with strawberries, pour over a little cool melted redcurrant jelly and garnish with a small bunch of red currants, which have been brushed with slightly whipped egg white, then dipped in castor sugar and dried.

TREACLE SCONES

A Good Mixer

2 ozs. margarine
8 ozs. plain flour
½ teaspoon cream of tartar
½ teaspoon bicarbonate of soda

Milk to mix
Pinch of salt
1 oz. golden syrup

Sieve all dry ingredients into a bowl, add margarine and beat. Gently heat syrup and add to dry ingredients with a little milk to make a soft dough. Roll out until ¾ inch thick and cut into rounds. Cook on Gas No. 5 (375°) for approximately 15 minutes. Serve with butter. *Makes 10-12 scones.*

WALNUT CAKE

Marlene Rodin

8 ozs. plain flour
8 ozs. sugar
4 eggs
8 ozs. margarine

Almond essence
½ teaspoon baking powder
4 ozs. chopped walnuts

Cream sugar and margarine, add eggs one at a time alternately with a spoon of flour. Beat in electric mixer at low speed. Add essence and walnuts. Preheat oven to Gas No. 3-4 (325°-350°). Bake in an oiled tin for 45 minutes on the middle shelf.

WALNUT AND COFFEE CAKE

Gillian Burr

6 ozs. margarine
6 ozs. castor sugar
3 eggs
2 tablespoons milk
8 ozs. plain flour
1½ level teaspoons baking powder
3 ozs. chopped walnuts.

ICING:
3 ozs. margarine
3 dessertspoons milk
3 dessertspoons coffee essence
12 ozs. sifted icing sugar

Sieve flour and baking powder together. Cream margarine and beat in eggs one at a time with a little flour, then fold in rest of flour and milk and walnuts. Put in a 7 inch lined cake tin, and bake on Gas No. 3 (325°) for 1½-2 hours.
TO MAKE ICING: Stir margarine, milk and coffee essence in saucepan over low heat until margarine has melted. Cool a little, then pour over icing sugar and beat until smooth. When cold stir and use.

YEAST CAKE

A Danish Friend

1 teacup warm milk
3 eggs
1 oz. fresh yeast
2 tablespoons warm milk
1 teaspoon sugar

4 ozs. margarine
2 ozs. sugar
2 ozs. sultanas
1 lb. flour
1 tablespoon flour

Cream margarine with 2 ozs. sugar and eggs. Cream yeast with 2 tablespoons warm milk, then add 1 teaspoon sugar and 1 tablespoon flour, and leave to sponge in warm place for 5 minutes. Add yeast mixture to egg mixture and add 1 teacup of warm milk; then add sultanas and 1 lb. flour, and beat well until mixture leaves the sides of the bowl clean. Put dough in a well greased and floured high tin or pudding basin. Leave in a warm place for approximately 1 hour. Bake slowly in oven on Gas No. 4 (350°), covered with greased paper, until cake is set—approximately 1 hour. Test by sticking in a knife, which should come out clean. Dust with sugar. This cake is especially good with coffee.

NOTES

Jewish Home

HINTS FOR THE JEWISH HOME

NEW HOME
—for good luck in a new home one should have a box containing a candle (light), coal (heat), sugar (sweet life), bread (sustenance) and salt (an offering).

SHABAT (SABBATH)
A Friday night table should be laid with a white tablecloth. On the table there should be two candles (to be lit by the wife), two covered Chollas (bread), salt to dip the cholla in, and a cup of Kosher wine over which the husband makes the Kiddush (blessing).

YOMTOVIM
All Yomtov (festival) tables, except for Yom Kippur, should be set in the same manner as Shabat, but with occasional variations as stated below:—

ROSH HASHANA
NEW YEAR
marks the start of the 10 days of penitence. Round chollas are used to symbolize life without end. A piece of apple dipped in honey is eaten for a sweet year. Honey cake (p. 167) and Tsimmes (p. 80) are traditionally served.

YOM KIPPUR
DAY OF ATONEMENT
This is the last of the 10 Penetential days. It is the only yomtov when a memorial candle is lit before going to Synagogue. Two yom-tov candles are also lit. The fast lasts 25 hours.

SUCCOTH FEAST OF TABERNACLES	This is a harvest festival and commemorates the time when the Israelites wandered in the wilderness and lived in temporary shelters or succahs—many orthodox Jews eat in a succah during this feast. The cholla is dipped in sugar or honey instead of salt. Stuffed cabbage (p. 71) is often eaten. Lulavim (palm branches) and Esrogim (citron) are taken to the synagogue.
SIMCHAT TORAH	—is the 9th day of Succoth and marks the completion of the reading of the Torah (law). It is a time of rejoicing and children should have flags topped with apples and candles to take to synagogue.
CHANUKACH FEAST OF LIGHTS	The lighting of the Menorah symbolizes the miracle of the oil burning in the Temple for 8 days. Gifts are usually given to the children and latkes (p. 77) are eaten at this festival.
PURIM FEAST OF LOTS	Commemorates the survival of the Persian Jews from the massacre planned by Haman. Small cakes with poppy seed called Hamantaschen (Haman's ears p. 144) are traditionally eaten at this time.
PESACH PASSOVER	The liberation of the Israelites from bondage in Egypt is commemorated with two Seder nights. A seder plate containing the following:—

> A ROASTED EGG—Festival sacrifice
> A ROASTED NECK—Pascal offering
> BITTER HERBS—Bitterness of life
> CHAROSETH—To sweeten the bitterness of life
> PARSLEY—So children should not go hungry
> SALT WATER—Sorrow

should be placed in front of the Head of the house together with three covered matzos—afikomen (the three tribes of Israel), sufficient wine for four full cups per person and a cup of wine for the prophet Elijah. A jug of water and towels for the men to wash their hands should be near the table. A cushion is given to the head of the house on which to lean. Prior to the meal, hard boiled eggs in a dish of salt water should be served. Unleavened food only is eaten during this festival.

SHAVUOTH FESTIVAL OF WEEKS	This commemorates the revelation of the 10 Commandments to Moses at Mount Sinai. It is a dairy festival and cheese cake (p. 158) and cheese blintzes (p. 123) are the most popular dishes made.

Passover Recipes ~

CHAROSETH
Walter Jacobs

2 grated apples
2 ozs. blanched chopped almonds
1 oz. chopped raisins
Sugar to taste

1 oz. chopped walnuts
3 chopped dates
Cinnamon to taste
Wine to moisten

Combine all the ingredients and place on the Seder plate in a small bowl.

EGG LOCKSHEN
Faith Duke

6 beaten eggs
Margarine for frying

Salt
Pepper

Melt the fat in a non-stick omelette pan. Season the beaten eggs, and pour just sufficient into the frying pan to make a thin pancake. Cook until nicely set, then lay on kitchen paper to cool. Repeat the process until all the egg has been used, then roll up the pancakes and cut across, forming thin noodles. Keep covered until required so that they do not go dry. *Serves 6.*

KNEIDLECH
Penny Marks

2 eggs
Melted chicken fat
Pepper
1 tablespoon ground almonds

¼ glass lukewarm water
1 pinch salt
Cinnamon
Fine matzo meal to bind

Mix all the ingredients to a smooth consistency, and leave to stand for ½ hour in the refrigerator. Make into small balls and boil them for 20 minutes.

MATZO BREI
Matzo Muncher

2 matzos
Salt and pepper

4 lightly beaten eggs
2 ozs. butter

Break the matzos into small pieces, put into a colander and pour over some boiling water. Drain well, but leave moist. Mix the matzos with the beaten eggs, salt and pepper and fry gently in butter over a low light. *Serves 2-3.* (Good for breakfast).

MATZO KUGEL
Kugel Kook

3-4 matzos
1 diced and friend onion
Left over chopped meat, chicken or chopped liver

4 eggs
Salt and pepper
Chicken fat

Crumble the matzos and soak in water. Squeeze out the excess water, then add the onion, chicken, fat and eggs. Mix well, then place half the mixture on a well greased square baking tin. Cover with meat or chicken, then the remaining half of the batter. Brush with chicken fat and bake for about 45 minutes Gas No. 4 (350°). Cut into squares. *Serves 3.* (Good as a side dish with meat or chicken).

BISCUITS

ALMOND MACAROONS
Lesley Bennett

2 large egg whites
8 ozs. ground almonds
Split almonds

½ lb. castor sugar
½ lemon (grated rind only)

Beat the egg whites until stiff. Beat in half the sugar, a spoonful at a time. Fold in the lemon rind, remaining sugar and ground almonds. Wet hands in cold water and roll small amounts of the mixture into 1 inch balls. Place on greased trays with a split almond in the centre of each. Bake at Gas No. 3 (325°) for about 25 minutes until pale golden.

CHOCOLATE BROWNIES
A. Brownie

½ lb. bitter sweet chocolate
2 eggs
⅔ cup sugar
1 teaspoon instant coffee (optional)

½ cup oil or margarine
1 pinch salt
½ cup cake meal
½ cup chopped nuts

Melt the chocolate and oil or margarine in a double saucepan. Meanwhile beat the eggs and salt, add the dry ingredients and beat well. Add the chocolate to the egg mixture. Bake in a greased and floured square pan at Gas No. 4 (350°) for 25-30 minutes. Cut into squares.

CINNAMON BALLS
Lesley Bennett
by courtesy of Evelyn Rose

Icing sugar
2 egg whites
8 ozs. ground almonds

4 ozs. castor sugar
1 level tablespoon cinnamon

Beat the egg whites until stiff. Fold in all the other ingredients. Form into balls with wetted hands. Bake on well greased trays at Gas No. 3 (325°) for 25 minutes until just firm to the touch. Roll in icing sugar while warm and again when cold.

CINNAMON BALLS
Mrs E. Silver

6 ozs. ground almonds
2 dessertspoons cinnamon
Icing sugar

½ lb castor sugar
2 egg whites

Mix all the ingredients together without beating the egg whites. With wet hands roll the mixture into round balls the size of a walnut, and put on oiled trays in the oven on Gas No. 3 (325°) for 15 minutes approximately, until they appear dry but not hard. Roll in icing sugar while still warm.

COCONUT BISCUITS

Lesley Bennett
by courtesey of Evelyn Rose

4 ozs. plain chocolate
4 ozs. desiccated coconut
2 ozs. chopped toasted almonds

2 ozs. butter
3 ozs. castor sugar
1 egg

Line an 8 inch biscuit tin with greaseproof paper. Melt the chocolate in a bowl over a pan of hot water, then pour the melted chocolate into the lined tin and spread evenly. Leave to set. In a small pan, melt the butter. Stir in the sugar, coconut and toasted nuts. Add the beaten egg and stir well. Spread over the chocolate which will have set. Bake for 25 minutes Gas No. 4 (325°-350°) until golden brown. Allow to get cold before cutting into fingers or squares.

COCONUT PYRAMIDS

Betty Feltz

1 lb. coconut
¾ lb. castor sugar

6 egg whites

Mix the coconut and sugar together, then add the beaten egg whites. Grease a baking sheet with oil, shape the mixture into small pyramids and bake on Gas No. 6 (400°) for approximately 10 minutes until pale biscuit colour.

ICE BOX COOKIES

Katy Kook
U.S.A. Cups

¼ lb butter
2 eggs
1 cup cake meal
1 pinch of salt

1 cup sugar
½ cup chopped nuts
Lemon juice to taste

Cream the butter and sugar, add all the remaining ingredients. Mix well and form into one or two long rolls. Wrap in waxed paper and chill overnight. Cut into slices and bake on Gas No. 4 (350°) for 20-25 minutes.

NUT COOKIES

A Nutty Cook
U.S.A. Cups

2 eggs
2 tablespoons potato flour
1 cup cake meal
Crushed nuts

½ cup oil
¾ cup castor sugar
½ cup chopped nuts

Beat together the eggs and sugar, add the oil and chopped nuts, then the sifted meal and potato flour. Leave in a cool place for 1½ hours. Form into small balls and roll in crushed nuts. Bake for 20 minutes on Gas No. 4 (350°).

SPONGE BISCUITS

Faith Duke

3 ozs. castor sugar
1½ ozs. fine matzo meal
1 pinch of salt

1 oz. potato flour
2 separated eggs

Beat the egg yolks and sugar until frothy, stir in the sieved matzo meal, and potato flour and salt. Beat the egg whites until stiff then fold into the meal mixture. Cover baking trays with non-stick paper and put on teaspoonfuls of the mixture, well apart to allow for spreading. Bake on Gas No. 5 (375°) until set and lightly browned. Cool on a cake rack and dredge with castor sugar. Keep in an airtight tin.

BREADS

PASSOVER BAGELS

Beryl Kramer
U.S.A. Cups

1½ cups water
¾ cup oil
¼ teaspoon salt

2½ cups matzo meal
4 tablespoons sugar
6 separated eggs

Boil together the water and oil, add the matzo meal, sugar and salt. Mix well. Add the egg yolks, then the well beaten egg whites. Roll into balls and place on a well greased baking tray. Make a hole in the centre of each, and bake for 1 hour on Gas No. 6 (400°) until golden brown.

PASSOVER ROLLS

American Friend
U.S.A. Cups

½ cup shortening
2 cups matzo meal
1 teaspoon salt

1 cup boiling water
1 teaspoon sugar
4 eggs

Add the fat to the boiling water in a saucepan and heat until shortening has melted. Add the dry ingredients all at once and beat rapidly over low heat until mixture leaves the sides of the pan and forms a ball. Remove from the heat and beat in the eggs one at a time. Beat hard after adding each egg, until the batter is thick and smooth. Shape into 8 balls and place on a well greased baking sheet. Using the tip of a paring knife cut roll design on top of each dough round. Bake for approximately 1 hour on Gas No. 4 (350°).

CAKES

CHOCOLATE MATZO SQUARES

Mrs Kaufman

3 matzos
½ lb. margarine
Sugar to taste
1 tablespoon strong black coffee
1 teaspoon lemon juice

2 eggs
Cinnamon to taste
Cocoa to taste
Chocolate powder to taste

Blend the margarine with the sugar and beat well. Add all the ingredients except the matzos and mix until smooth and creamy. Spread the mixture on to one side of each matzo and stack, finishing with a plain matzo. Leave for 2-3 hours, then cut into squares. (Good for children's teas).

CHOCOLATE NUT CAKE

Lesley Bennett

8 ozs. margarine
8 ozs. icing sugar
4 eggs
½ teaspoon cinnamon
3 ozs. grated chocolate
8 ozs. ground almonds

ICING:
3 ozs. plain chocolate
4 ozs. icing sugar
1½ teaspoons nut oil

Cream the margarine and sugar. Beat in the eggs alternately with the chocolate and almonds. Bake in a 10 inch spring form tin for 45 minutes on Gas No. 4 (325°). Leave to cool in the tin. ICING: Melt the chocolate in a saucepan and stir in the sugar, oil and enough water to obtain the correct consistency. Spread over the cake. Leave for 48 hours before cutting. (This cake also makes a delicious dessert).

HAZELNUT PLAVA

Lesley Bennett

8 separated eggs
Juice and grated rind of 1 lemon
1 oz. medium matzo meal

½ lb. castor sugar
½ lb. ground hazelnuts

Cream yolks and sugar until thick and creamy. Add the grated rind and juice of the lemon, nuts and meal. Beat the whites until stiff, fold into the mixture. Bake for 1 hour on Gas No. 4 (325°). Do not open the oven before time. Cover with a plate until cool and then turn out.

PLAVA

Rebecca Hermer

9 eggs
¾ lb. castor sugar
Juice and grated rind of 1 lemon
3 ozs. potato flour
3 ozs cake meal

TOPPING:
4 teaspoons potato flour
4 teaspoons castor sugar

Beat the eggs and sugar well in the mixer. Fold in the sifted meal, potato flour, lemon juice and rind. For a crisp topping mix together the potato flour and castor sugar and sieve over the top of the cakes. Bake for 1½ hours on Gas No. 2 (300°). *Makes 2 cakes.*

DESSERTS

APPLE ALMOND SURPRISE

Gillian Burr

½ lb. ground almonds
½ oz. packet vanilla sugar
2 ozs. butter
1 lb. cooking apples

6½ ozs. castor sugar
2 eggs
1 tablespoon medium matzo meal
Icing sugar

Stew apples with vanilla sugar and purée. Cream the butter and sugar, add the eggs and beat well. Add the ground almonds and matzo meal. Place half the mixture in a well greased loose bottomed cake tin, spread over all the apple purée, and cover with the remaining mixture. Dredge with icing sugar and bake for 40 minutes Gas No. 4 (350°).

APPLE FRITTERS

Pat Fauer

U.S.A. Cups

2 eggs
1 tablespoon honey
2 large cooking apples

1 cup sifted medium matzo meal
½ cup shortening
Castor sugar

Beat the eggs with the honey. Pare and core the apples and cut into 1/8th inch slices across the width of the apples. Coat the apple slices with matzo meal then dip into egg mixture. Meanwhile heat fat in a deep frying pan for 2 minutes and fry the apple slices in the hot fat for 3 minutes over a medium heat, turn over and fry for a further 2 minutes. Drain on absorbent paper, and sprinkle with castor sugar. *Serves 4.* (Serve hot and enjoy).

APPLE PUDDING

Lesley Bennett

4 ozs. sugar
1 lemon
3 tablespoons fine matzo meal
½ teaspoon cinnamon

3 separated eggs
1 lb. cooking apples
1 tablespoon ground almonds

Peel core and grate the apples. Beat the egg yolks lightly with sugar, add the grated apples, meal, almonds, cinnamon and the grated rind and juice of the lemon. Mix thoroughly and fold in the stiffly beaten egg whites. Turn into a greased oven dish and bake on Gas No. 4 (350°) for about 1 hour.

CHREMSEL

Faith Duke

3 ozs. fine matzo meal
2 eggs
⅛-½ pint water
Lemon juice optional

1½ tablespoons castor sugar
1 pinch of salt
Oil for frying

Mix the meal, sugar and salt. Beat the egg yolks lightly with the water and pour on to the meal, mixing very well. Whisk the egg whites until stiff but not dry, and fold into the meal mixture. Pour ½ inch of oil into a heavy frying pan, and when hot put small spoonful of the mixture into the pan, allowing plenty of room for spreading. When one side is nicely brown, turn over and brown the other side. Serve immediately sprinkled with plenty of sugar. Add lemon juice, if desired. *Serves 4-6.* (If necessary these can be kept hot in the oven until needed but they do not stay quite so crisp).

ORANGE CUSTARD

Vivienne Simon

4 large oranges (juice only)
2 lemons (juice only)

5 eggs
3 tablespoons sugar

Squeeze the juice from the oranges and lemons, and strain. Beat the eggs and sugar together then very slowly add the juice. Put the mixture in a greased soufflé dish, place in a pan of water in oven on Gas No. 3 (325°) for approximately 45 minutes or until set. Serve cold. *Serves 6.*

PIE CRUST

Gloria Brown

¼ cup shortening
¼ teaspoon cinnamon

¼ cup sugar
1½ cups sponge cake crumbs

Cream the fat with the sugar and add the cinnamon. Work in the cake crumbs. Press the mixture as evenly as possible, on to the bottom and sides of a 9 inch pie plate. Bake blind for 7 minutes on Gas No. 4 (350°) or until golden brown. Cool and fill with any desired filling.

HOT SPONGE PANCAKES IN WINE

Mrs Kaufman

2 tablespoons potato flour
2 tablespoons matzo meal
4 eggs separated
4 tablespoons castor sugar

Grated rind of ½ lemon
Red wine
Oil for frying

Beat the yolks and sugar together very well, add the lemon rind and sifted potato flour, and mix together. Beat the egg whites until stiff and fold into the yolk mixture. Drop spoonfuls of the mixture into a deep pan of boiling oil, turn and allow to become golden, then drain on greaseproof paper. Use all the mixture in the same way. Heat 2 inches of red wine in a saucepan, add the pancakes and simmer for 10 minutes. Serve immediately. Sprinkle with sugar if desired. *Serves 6.* (The pancakes can be made in the morning for the same evening).

MISCELLANEOUS

EINGEMACHT—BEETROOT JAM

Betty Ashe

4 lbs. boiled beetroots
3 lemons
¼ lb. blanched chopped almonds

3 lbs. sugar
2 teaspoons ginger to taste

Grate the beetroots and place in a pan with the sugar, ginger, lemon juice and grated rind. Cook gently until thick and clear, for about 1 hour. When nearly done add the chopped almonds. Put in jars and use on matzo.

LEMON CURD

Stella Majaran

2 lemons
4 ozs. butter

2 eggs
3 ozs. castor sugar

Melt the butter, add the well beaten eggs, sugar and the grated rind and juice of the lemons. Stir well over a gentle heat until it thickens.

INGBER—CARROT CANDY

Betty Ashe

2 cups grated carrot
2 cups sugar

1 cup water
Ground ginger to taste

Place all the ingredients in a pan and boil till the colour changes. It becomes sugary and leaves the sides of the pan. Place on a wet board and cut into squares.

DRY MEASURE

	1	oz	30 gms
	2	oz	50 gms
	3	oz	80 gms
	3½ oz		100 gms
(¼ lb)	4	oz	100 gms
	5	oz	150 gms
	6	oz	175 gms
	7	oz	200 gms
(½ lb)	8	oz	225 gms
(¼ kilo)	8¾ oz		250 gms
	9	oz	250 gms
	10	oz	275 gms
	11	oz	300 gms
	12	oz	350 gms
	13	oz	375 gms
	14	oz	400 gms
	15	oz	425 gms
(1 lb)	16	oz	450 gms
(½ kilo)	17½ oz		500 gms
	1½ lbs		700 gms

LIQUID MEASURE

1	tablespoon	1 tablespoon
2	tablespoon	2 tablespoon (½ DL)
3	tablespoon	3 tablespoon
4	tablespoon	4 tablespoon
5	tablespoon	1 decilitre
6	tablespoon	1¼ decilitre
8	tablespoon (¼ pint)	1½ decilitre
¼	pint − generous	2 decilitre
½	pint − scant	¼ litre (2½ DL)
½	pint	3 decilitre
¾	pint	½ litre − scant
¾	pint − generous	½ litre
1	pint	½ litre − generous
1¼ pints		¾ litre
1½ pints		1 litre − scant
1¾ pints		1 litre
2	pints	1 litre − generous
2½ pints		1¼ litres
3	pints	1½ litres
3½ pints		2 litres
4	pints	2¼ litres
4¼ pints		2½ litres
5	pints	3 litres

OVEN TEMPERATURE GUIDE

Gas No.	Fahrenheit	Centigrade	Description
¼	250	120	
½	275	140	Very Cool
¾	288	145	
1	300	150	
2	325	160	Cool or Slow
3	350	180	
4	360	185	Moderate
5	375	190	
6	400	200	Moderately Hot
7	425	220	
8	450	230	Hot
9	475	240	Very Hot

2 level tablespoons of flour = 1 oz.
A British pint = 20 fl. ozs.
A British cup = 10 fl. ozs.

1 level tablespoon of sugar = 1 oz.
An American pint = 16 fl. ozs.
An American cup = 8 fl. ozs.

When making American recipes always use American measuring spoons.

All gas temperatures given are prior to conversion to Natural Gas.

Please note that Kosher Gelatine or vegetarian substitute may be used by the Orthodox Jewish housewife. All packet instructions must be carefully followed. This also applies to the following items:− cheese, margarine and biscuits.

184

Index~

DIPS AND STARTERS

SOUPS AND ACCOMPANIMENTS

FISH

MEATS

POULTRY

VEGETABLES

SALADS AND SALAD DRESSINGS

SAUCES, STUFFINGS AND ACCOMPANIMENTS

DESSERTS FOR MEAT MEALS

DESERTS FOR MILK MEALS

SNACKS AND SUPPER DISHES

BISCUITS, BREADS AND PETITS FOURS

CAKES

PASSOVER RECIPES